As Equals
The Oei Women of Java

As Equals
The Oei Women of Java

DARYL YEAP

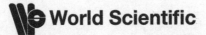
World Scientific

NEW JERSEY · LONDON · SINGAPORE · BEIJING · SHANGHAI · HONG KONG · TAIPEI · CHENNAI · TOKYO

Published by

World Scientific Publishing Co. Pte. Ltd.
5 Toh Tuck Link, Singapore 596224
USA office: 27 Warren Street, Suite 401-402, Hackensack, NJ 07601
UK office: 57 Shelton Street, Covent Garden, London WC2H 9HE

Library of Congress Cataloging-in-Publication Data
Names: Yeap, Daryl, author.
Title: As equals : the Oei women of Java / Daryl Yeap.
Description: Hackensack : World Scientific Publishing Company, [2024] |
   Includes bibliographical references.
Identifiers: LCCN 2023030349 | ISBN 9789811279027 (hardback) |
   ISBN 9789811280238 (paperback) | ISBN 9789811279034 (ebook) |
   ISBN 9789811279041 (ebook)
Subjects: LCSH: Women--China--History--19th century. | Women--China--History--20th century. |
   Women--Indonesia--History--19th century. | Women--Indonesia--History--20th century. |
   Chinese--Foreign countries--History--19th century. |
   Chinese--Foreign countries--History--20th century.
Classification: LCC HQ1767.5.A3 Y437 2024 | DDC 305.420951--dc23/eng/20230712
LC record available at https://lccn.loc.gov/2023030349

British Library Cataloguing-in-Publication Data
A catalogue record for this book is available from the British Library.

Copyright © 2024 by Daryl Yeap

All rights reserved.

For any available supplementary material, please visit
https://www.worldscientific.com/worldscibooks/10.1142/13489#t=suppl

Desk Editors: Claire Lum/Nicole Ong

Cover Illustration: Nicholas Liem
Design and layout: Loo Chuan Ming

To you, who paved the way.

CONTENT

PROLOGUE viii
1. Meteor-Heavenly Orchid 2
2. Rockefeller of the East 8
3. A Privileged Upbringing 15
4. Foreign Orientals 21
5. The Go-To Guy 27
6. "Westernisation" 32
7. Is the East so far Apart from the West? 40
8. Dutch vs. British 45
9. Taboo 49
10. The Yellow Peril 53
11. Birthplace of the Most Recognisable Chinese 58
12. The Great Cabang Atas Tree 66
13. Mesdames Oei Tiong-ham – The Wives 70
14. Lucy 75
15. Dollar Princesses 80
16. An Educated Woman 83
17. A Question of Domicile 88
18. To Congenial Climes 92
19. Singapore 97
20. May Fourth Movement 104
21. Marital Melodrama 108
22. The Career Diplomat 111

23. A Proposal	116
24. Paris Courtship	121
25. China	127
26. Farewell To The Sugar King	140
27. Asia's Largest Estate	146
28. Femme Sole	150
29. Matriarch	155
30. Ida	162
31. An Arranged Marriage	167
32. When Two Poles Apart	174
33. Forbidden Romances	183
34. A Modern Woman	187
35. Accounts Of Hui-Lan's Life	194
36. A Difficile Lady	197
37. Wealth & Style	204
38. Madame Ambassadress	212
POSTFACE	219
ACKNOWLEDGEMENTS	227
ABOUT THE AUTHOR	229
BIBLIOGRAPHY	230

PROLOGUE

Woman

How sad it is to be a woman.
Nothing on earth is held so cheap.
Boys stand leaning at the door
Like gods fallen out of heaven.
Their hearts brave the Four Oceans,
The wind and dust of a thousand miles.
No one is glad when a girl is born:
By her the family sets no store.

Fu Xuan (217-278)

Winter. Somewhere in Shaanxi, China. 21 December 1889.

She stood still, like a startled mouse deer. Her eyes filled with terror, watching Father pin the lamb to the floor with his knee. "Don't be afraid", he said. With one hand, he grabbed its furry head, and with the other, stuck a knife into its belly. She never once blinked, holding her breath, hands clenched together. Only a few minutes ago it had been her friend, a plaything Father brought home from pasture that morning. The stricken animal defends itself against the weight of the farmer, bleating away in its struggle. Its legs frantically scampering in the air, as if trying to run away. Blood, dark cherry red, seeped out exposing its deep coloured organs on the kitchen floor. A peculiar sweet metallic odour began to fill the air. They say that the smell of blood makes you seize with anxiety. It makes your body tense, your heart pound, your sense of alertness heighten. It makes you think of danger, of pain and death. She carried that feeling for a long time, for the rest of her life, of that terrifying Saturday afternoon in winter.

Father was a cotton farmer in a small village in Shaanxi, northwest of China. He worked the land around the village. Mother spun cotton and cooked meals for the family at home. They kept busy all year round with harvest and planting seasons. On that Saturday afternoon, just before her sixth birthday, her parents prepared her for her future.

The more the lamb struggled, the stronger Father was. She stood still. Mother hurried to put the fire on, relying on memory, recalling what was required and what had to be done. The smoke and sound of fire crackling provided a fleeting distraction. Mother reached out to her, sat her on her lap, then removed her shoes. When the time came and the lamb laid listless, barely alive, Mother slowly eased her feet, pushing it into the bloodied stomach, holding them firmly. She wailed, squirmed and tried to pull her legs away but Mother and Father were insistent. They calmed her down, consoling her and reminding her that she would soon have pretty feet – ones that would be cherished by her future husband – ones that would entitle her the opportunity of marrying into a rich family. Finally, like the sacrificial lamb, she yielded. Inside the belly, her tiny feet could feel the ribs and squashy organs of the lamb but most of all, she could feel the warmth of its blood. Occasionally, Father stuck his hand in the cavity to check if the blood had turned cold. Sobbing, she quietened down, watery snot dribbling down her nose. Her gaze solemnly fixed upon the kitchen god above the stove, almost as if pleading for the whole ordeal to end immediately.

When the skin of her feet was crinkled and her little toes pliable, mother brought a bucket of warm water to wash off the blood. Father removed the carcass, by then, dead. It had done its job. The next few moments would be the most agonising and would literally reshape her life forever. With two hands holding her left foot firmly, and with all her might, Mother forced her smallest toe inwards, dislodging it from its socket. "You will never find a husband if you don't have small feet," shouted Mother repeatedly as she screamed in agony at the top of her voice, struggling to free herself from the excruciating pain. All four toes, except the big one, were broken. Mother repeated the process on the right foot. By then, she had lost consciousness. Her pain vanished. And for some surreal reason, an old woman appeared, lifting her off the floor onto a chair. Suddenly, the old woman disappeared. In her place a vision arose. White lights. Extremely bright, and then, the world went quiet. When she opened her eyes, the sharp searing pain came back. Mother had dressed her broken toes with powdered alum to prevent infection. With a binding cloth ten feet long and two inches wide, Mother wrapped the dislodged toes tightly, the edges of the cloth neatly stitched to a corner so that they could not be undone.

That evening, she laid in bed whimpering, the raw burning pain keeping her awake all night long. The following morning, Mother forced her to walk up and down the room with her eyes still swollen and red from shedding tears throughout the night. Using the wall as support, she obediently did as she was told until her own weight finally broke the bones and ligaments on her feet. More pain. More anguish. More tears. Every week, the pus and blood-stained bindings got tighter. Every week, a new pair of shoes was given to her, each pair smaller than the previous one. Some days, she found relief outside, burying her feet into the pure white snow to numb the sharp blistering pain. When spring came, she was forced to walk longer distances to accelerate the arches from both feet to break. When they did, her heels were forced under her feet towards the ball, rupturing the tendons and ligaments. Any excess flesh that had formed around the deformed feet was cut off. By the age of seven, she was put to work. Because she could not walk properly, Father carried her on his back to the fields to pick cotton.

Prologue

They set out every morning when there was half-light and only came home in the evenings when it got dark. By the time she turned nine, her feet were crushed and bound so tightly they had formed a deep cleft on the soles such that they could hold a coin in place. Almost half of the thirty-three joints, a hundred muscles, tendons, and ligaments and twenty-six bones in both feet were twisted and contorted. Most of the pain had subsided and she had learnt to walk on the heels. The shape of her bound foot resembled that of her mother's and of the other women and girls in her village. They all bore a resemblance to that of a lotus flower.

No one knows when and where foot binding originated. Dorothy Ko, a historian in women's study at Columbia University, explains that because of various local traditions and distinct practices, a single chronicle of its origins and practice makes it difficult to pinpoint how it came about. For that reason, there are various accounts as to who the first female to have had her feet bound was. The most recognised woman was a Han Chinese who lived a thousand years ago during the Tang (618–907AD) and Song Dynasties (907–1279 AD). Her name was Yao-niang, a favourite concubine of an Emperor with a sexual fetish for tiny feet. To please the amorous Emperor, as the story was told, Yao-niang performed a dance like ballet called the "toe dance" by binding her feet with strips of white silk. So graceful and delicate were her movements, it apparently inspired other court women to follow. As the practice caught on centuries later, particularly from the lower rungs of society, the upper classes began to tighten their bindings. The smaller the feet, the greater the incapacitation. And so, the three-inch foot, the fabled "golden lotus", became the most sought-after size only meant for girls who led an idle life of which only the extremely rich could afford. Four-inch feet were coined "silver lotus" while those above five-inches were known as "iron lotus".

Most historians today see a sexual dimension connected to foot binding – that the reason why the practice had perpetuated for so long was because it had to do with male sexual satisfaction. As Dorothy Ko pointed out, "it rendered (women as) sex objects to satisfy certain perverted erotic fantasies of men". Others state that the act controlled sexual access to females and ensured female chastity and fidelity. By unnaturally distorting their feet, bound-foot women were forced to walk in such a way where their inner thighs and pelvic muscles became unusually tight. They lightly swayed and tottered and because they were kept hidden, tiny feet, presumably, caused a great deal of arousal. "During love making, men would touch it, caress it, kiss it, suck it and even put the whole foot inside their mouth as part of the erotic foreplay of love." And for that reason, ancient Chinese erotica almost always showed women with bound feet. The red silk shoes that women wore to bed, the peculiar odor when the bindings were undone and the experience of holding the foot in one's palm, heightened love making. For men, the "lotus foot" with its cleft in the sole, resembled a second female genitalia – alluring and erotic to the touch, enhancing sensory stimulations. The main preoccupying challenge for a man was to wait until the girl reached marriageable age, which could be as young as twelve years old. Other reasons cited for why foot binding existed include impairing women's mobility so that they were less likely to have sexual relations with other men, and as a husband's symbol of wealth of her "explicit uselessness and costly maintenance". Still, others argue that it was for economic considerations and to keep young girls on task to produce goods. Sigmund Freud viewed foot binding as a pacifier to men's castration anxieties and that it signified male and female status in a patriarchal world.

The golden age of foot binding was the 19th century, by which point scholars reckon almost half of the women in China had their feet bound of which almost one hundred percent came from the elite classes of society. It was around this time that the quest for the three-inch golden lotus became an obsession, because the lower classes were increasingly getting their feet bound, in so doing damaging the exclusivity of foot

Prologue

binding. Millions were told that if they did not bind their feet, they would never find a husband. They were told that they brought shame to the family if their feet were big. From being a status symbol, foot binding became one of the cruelest forms of oppression for women. Western corsets paled by comparison. Though finally outlawed in 1902 by Dowager Empress T'zu-hsi of the Qing Dynasty (1644–1912 AD), it took at least two generations before the gruesome practice completely ended. Chinese women had its symbolised status so deeply ingrained that many refused to drop the idea even after the dynasty fell.

Wives and Children of Oei Tiong-ham

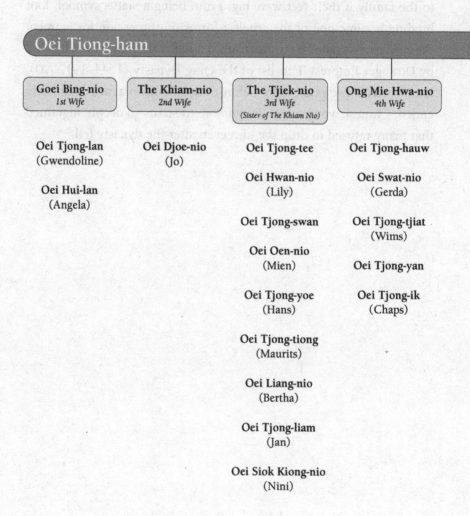

Source: Oei Ing-siang (Eric)

Ong Tjiang Tjoe-nio 5th Wife (Daughter of The Khiam Nio)	Njoo Swat Ting-nio 6th Wife	Hoo Kiem Hwa-nio (Lucy) 7th Wife	Tan Sien-nio 8th Wife
Oei Sioe-nio (Noes)	Oei Siok Ing-nio (Betsy)	Oei Tjong-le (Humphrey/Jack)	Oei Siang-nio (Corry)
Oei Bien-nio (Ida)		Oei Twan-nio (Lovy)	
		Oei Tjong-bo (Hervey)	
		Oei Tjong-hiong (Horry)	
		Oei Tjong-tjay (Benny)	

Fig. 1: Portrait of Hui-lan appearing in The British Tatler, 28 August 1918.
Source: Mary Evans Picture Library
© Illustrated London News Ltd/Mary Evans

Oei Hui-lan

1

Meteor-Heavenly Orchid

On the same day – 21 December 1889 – a Chinese baby was born four and a half thousand kilometres across the South China Seas in Semarang on the island of Java. Semarang was a trading town in the Dutch East Indies, a great archipelago made up of 17,000 islands. As far as anyone can remember, the Chinese have been involved in maritime trade in that region, long before the arrival of the first Europeans. Some settled down as pepper growers, some as traders and artisans, but the bulk were labourers. The largest and most important of the islands was Java, and Semarang was its second largest town after Batavia.

It was an important birth for the mother, Bing-nio, a fifth generation Semarang-born Chinese who was approaching twenty-one. The baby's grandmother was equally anxious, instinctively fussing over her pregnant daughter months beforehand, nourishing her with wholesome diets, pumping her with homemade remedies, reminding her of all the pre-natal rituals and the consequences if broken. Protocol shall rule your every action during pregnancy, Bing-nio was told. No heavy lifting. No jarring movements. Sleep lying on the back. Sit up straight, with weight evenly distributed. Don't eat "cooling" foods that weaken the womb. Don't laugh out loud. Don't let the eyes see bad deeds. Think good thoughts. Steer clear from obscenities. Most of all, don't gossip. Bing-nio had already gone through three pregnancies before. The first, a girl was born. The second and third were boys but both tragically died in infancy. For this pregnancy, she must not fail again. The birth of a son would be her crowning glory.

The baby's father, Oei Tiong-ham was a first-generation Semarang-born Chinese. He was as anxious for a son, as was his father, Oei Tjie-sien. Grandpa Tjie-sien, a cultured man with an auspicious mole on his nose, was the first to migrate from China to Semarang. As a young boy, Tjie-sien received an education and when he was old enough, was involved in politics and eventually got himself into trouble with the Manchu Government. He had been attacking the administration for forming a rice cooperative which presumably left out smaller stakeholders including local farmers. Constantly at loggerheads with the authorities, Tjie-sien fled China for the Dutch East Indies with his brother and nephew at the age of twenty-three but had to leave his wife behind. When they left, emigration out of China was still prohibited. Until after the Treaty of Tientsin of 1858, no one could leave the motherland except traders. Those who left before then were either sojourners who intended to return after seeking their fortune, or dissidents looking for refuge like Tjie-sien.

Amoy in southern China was a free harbour then, opened to foreign ships. The three Oei men – Tjie-sien, his brother and nephew – boarded one of them and ended up in Semarang. In his new home, Tjie-sien married a *peranakan* (local born) woman whose father was a local merchant. Even though she was four years younger than him, she was in her early twenties when they wedded – an age considered quite old for a Chinese bride. She gave Tjie-sien three sons (one died at birth) and five daughters. Of his children, Tiong-ham was the most exceptional. Born on 19 November 1866, he was the oldest of the siblings. At the age of eight, Tiong-ham was sent to a school where he learnt the Malay language and roman alphabets. When he came of age, his father took him under his wing and showed him the family business. As a young man, Tiong-ham was intelligent, gutsy and a risk taker. Above all, he was highly ambitious. By the time he was eighteen, his family had arranged for him to marry Goei Bing-nio, whose father was an established merchant and landowner in Semarang. More notably, his in-laws were from the *cabang atas* echelon, a privileged social class that controlled much of the economic and social life in the Dutch East Indies.

The Oei family house was in Gang Bessen, a street in the Chinese *kamp* of Semarang. When the Dutch Government took possession of Java, they implemented laws to segregate the Chinese in the colony from the rest of the community. Chinese, or Foreign Orientals as they were known, were subjected to movement restrictions and had to obtain passes approved by *priyayi* officials if they wanted to travel around the country. They were also separated and strictly confined to *kamps* (ghettos), forbidden to live outside these compounds. All this meant that the Chinese in the Dutch colony spent most of their lives within the boundaries of the *kamps*. Not surprisingly, the restriction caused a great deal of grievance because officials had discretionary powers to issue out permits, forcing the Chinese to be under the clutches of these men. Accommodating so many of them also meant that the houses were generally narrow, cramped and often laid out on grids characterised by crowded streets that seemed to huddle together with temples in between. Sanitation was poor but the *kamps* were the centre of commerce. Everyone doing business in the colony involved a Chinese. They were the suppliers of life's necessities – furniture makers, tinsmiths, leather tanners, hardware suppliers, builders and repairmen, carpenters, masons, egg sellers, fruits and vegetables hawkers, pig farmers, warehousing and storage services, rice and tapioca millers, traders of pepper, sugar, cotton, coconut, soybean, copra, and cooking oil, to name a few. They were also the first source for loans and credit as moneylenders. The fact that the *kamps* could produce so much economic activity tells us something important about the Chinese – that they were enterprising. Perhaps partly because of the unfriendly conditions in which they lived, they had to be.

Three generations of family members lived in the Oei family house, not because they could not afford housing but because tradition required it. For the Chinese, it was a demonstration of harmony, that the offspring of a common ancestor can live together in the same household for generations. The grandparents were the most senior, followed by the parents, the uncle and unmarried aunts. Once married, the other aunts were regarded as having no more relations with the family. They became daughters-in-law of other families. When they visited the family home, it was usually on a strictly business basis or for special occasions to celebrate Chinese New Year or ancestral worship. Not far from the family house was the family business, Kian Gwan, a trading company that Tjie-sien established a few years after settling down in Semarang. There, he sold teas, herbs, incense and silks from China. The firm also exported Javanese products of rice, sugar, tobacco and gambier to the region. Tjie-sien ran the business quite successfully for over twenty-five years despite having nothing when he came.

After months of living cautiously under the vigilant eyes of her mother, Bing-nio went into labour. The entire household, filled with anxieties, waited patiently. When the midwife finally announced the gender of the baby – a girl – the birth, so enthused by the family a while ago, now seemed so muted. One could tell at a glance how the family felt when the gender of the new-born was revealed. Weak, drained, but most of all, disappointed, Bing-nio held her baby girl in her arms. A smile broke out. A mother's love is always pure regardless of the baby's gender.

Bing-nio was confined in the house for the next few weeks to recuperate and allow time for her womb to heal. A month later, the family held a celebration for friends to meet the baby girl and mother for the first time. They dressed the house in red. Even food was practically covered in red. The idea behind this long-held traditional celebration was to do with high rates of infant mortality. Because infant deaths were so frequent in the past, families tended to celebrate only once a baby had crossed the first month; it meant that they were more likely to survive into adulthood. They dressed Bing-nio's baby girl in a little red outfit, for luck. She had skin like tallow, fine bone structure and eyes, big and bright. Somehow, they knew she was going to grow up beautiful. Around her neck and wrist, her grandmother had strung a red cord with charms to protect her from evil spirits. A barber was called in to shave her head. On that day, she also received her name – Hui-lan, or, Meteor-Heavenly Orchid.

By the time Bing-nio's baby was born in 1889, grandfather Tjie-sien had accumulated sufficient wealth to build a country house of granite and timber in the hills on Simongan. There, he spent much of his time with friends, reading and writing poetry. Locked away in his remote estate, Tjie-sien also took two concubines and forbade the senior wife from visiting. One of his young concubines gave him a son and a daughter. Each year, he returned to his family home in the Chinese *kamp* to celebrate Chinese New Year with the extended family. For the rest of his life, he concentrated on building his tomb and devoted his life to horticultural pursuits, crossbreeding lotuses that grew on the pond below his mausoleum. To his own astonishment, Tjie-sien received an award, the Tiong-gie tay-hoe, from the Manchu Government in 1897 but never displayed it nor acknowledged it. Although he had made good his relationship with his homeland, he refused to have his gravestone engraved with the year of the Qing Dynasty.

On the face of it, it would seem that the Oeis were considered a typical Chinese family. If they had continued on with traditions, it would have hardly been surprising that little Hui-lan's feet would be bound into the shape of a three-inch golden lotus, just like the cotton farmer's daughter and millions of other Chinese girls. It would have also not been altogether unexpected, if Hui-lan was betrothed early on in life to a boy she had never met and to a family she knew nothing of. But then, a number of profound events emerged, beginning on the year she was born.

Meteor-Heavenly Orchid

Fig. 2: Oei family. Standing from left to right: Goei Keh-hoo, Oei Tiong-ham, Oei Tjong-khay (toddler), Oei Tiong-bhing, Liem Ie-ging. Seated in middle from left to right: Oei Tiem-nio (Maud), Mrs. Goei Keh-hoo (Oei Bok-nio), Mrs. Oei Tiong-ham (Goei Bing-nio), Mrs. Oei Tjie-sien (Tan Biet-nio), Oei Tjie-sien, Mrs. Oei Tiong-bhing (Oh Tjien-nio), Mrs. Liem Ie-ging (Oei Khoon-nio), Mrs. Go Boen-kwan (Oei Siok-nio), Gan Khik-djien. Front row from left to right: Liem Djoen-nio, Oei Hui-lan, Oei Tjong-lan, Liem Liat-djwee. Source: Kenneth Bé.

2
Rockefeller of the East

Hui-lan's birth was said to have brought her father luck because it coincided with the year Tiong-ham made his first million. Exactly six months before her birth and shortly after Bing-nio discovered she was pregnant, Tiong-ham made a bold decision. He made a bid for one of the most lucrative opium concessions in the colony – the Semarang Opium Farm. The day was Tuesday, 23 July 1889.

Opium was the single largest money-making venture for the Chinese in the Dutch East Indies. Hand-picked and primed from the *cabang atas* community, opium farmers pulled together resources and organised themselves into partnerships called *kongsi*. The business generated high levels of cash flow and created large pools of capital which allowed them to expand into other ventures like rice, gambier and sugar production. Before the 19th century, capitalism or private enterprise did not exist in this part of the world. There was no real middle-class society, no commercial forms of production, nor were there any financial or legal systems to regulate such enterprises. As Carl Trocki, a Southeast Asian historian put it, the Chinese in this region created capitalist institutions and forms of organisation mainly through opium. Put simply, opium money fuelled the colonial economy.

On auction that Tuesday afternoon was the highly prized concession to distribute and sell opium in territories controlled by Ho Tjiauw-ing, second son of Ho Yam-lo, a well-respected merchant who recently passed on. Carriages carrying officials and wealthy Chinese men in full regalia drove up to the main entrance of the resident of the Dutch Resident. Many of them were descendants from the *cabang atas* families who had profited from the colony's progression into a trading post.

Many were also titled, either a lieutenant or a major. Champagne and *Kirschwässer* were served just before the auction. It was in the interest of the Dutch to loosen up inhibitions of prospective bidders and keep the auctions giddily buoyant. The higher the bids, the bigger the contribution to state coffers. It was also in the interest of the farmers to work together so that they didn't overpay for the concessions. Because revenue farms produced so much wealth and power, competition was ruthless, leading to feuds that lasted generations. For that reason, opium auctions in the colony were regarded as the "battle of the kings".

Tiong-ham had a few allies with him that Tuesday afternoon – namely, his cousin and two of his brothers-in-law. At only 23, Tiong-ham was new to the game and unfamiliar to many of the opium kings from out of town. And unlike most of the rival groups, the Oei partnership at first did not belong to a *cabang atas* lineage. But Tiong-ham's father, Tjie-sien obtained instant pedigrees for his children by marrying them off to notable families. Seeing as the influential Yam-lo was no longer around, others too braved their way from across the seas to use their clout and make their bids.

As soon as the Semarang farm came up for auction, the farmers threw in their offers, equally daring in their bids. When the price escalated, a few dropped out, leaving Tiong-ham to battle it out with another rival. With nerves of a seasoned gambler, Tiong-ham confidently stepped up his offer, and through a combination of burning aggression and determination, out-bid his veteran challenger and took control of Semarang. Tiong-ham paid a staggering 125,300 guilders or USD1.5 million in today's money, far more than what his father had intended.

Rumour has it that the father was infuriated by his son's reckless bidding. But Tiong-ham did something unexpected. Quick as a fox, he put together a dream team for his acquisition. Two previous partners from the Ho partnership jumped camp and joined forces with him, among them the eldest son of Yam-lo who became the new manager of the farm. The other was someone who had worked with other opium kings before. By doing so, Tiong-ham armed himself with men of experience to run the family enterprise. He had proven himself more willing and more astute than the other kings to take risks in pursuit of profit. The Tuesday auction became the most publicised opium auction in the history of the colony thanks to a satirist by the name of Tan Tjien-hwa. Written in creole Malay in the form of a poem, Tjien-hwa presented the characters as animals to describe the political and economic relationships that linked the *cabang atas* families together and the strategies they took to protect their dominance. The work enjoyed considerable success and would remain so for decades.

A year after the hotly contested auction, Tiong-ham's father handed control of Kian Gwan to him – and so began his mighty rule. Within the next four years, the ambitious son boldly acquired four additional opium farms and rose to become one of the greatest revenue farmers in the colony. Over the next fifteen years, Tiong-ham made well over eighteen million guilders from just that business alone – more than USD210 million by today's calculation. As he ascended, the Ho family's fate and fortune went on a downward trajectory.

Miserable and ruined, one of Tjiauw-ing's partner desperately tried to take his own life by first consuming crushed diamond powder and when that didn't work, he tragically ended it with cyanide. Tjiauw-ing's debts caught up to him and everything of value belonging to him went up for sale at public auctions – real estate, landed properties, the sugar, indigo, coffee and rice businesses, jewelry, collectibles – right down to hairpins and buttons. Even his revered title, Captain, was duly stripped away from him before they awarded it to Tiong-ham, who emerged as the new captain of Semarang in 1891.

A few years later, Ho Tjiauw-ing's nephew attempted to break the Oei family opium monopoly by teaming up with another rival group. They managed to raise funds to win back the Semarang farm but their plans were thwarted when Stijhoff, the new Dutch Resident, denied them participation. In the words of historian Peter Post, "Sijthoff who had just arrived in Semarang, knew little of local Chinese power politics and had turned to Baron van Heeckeren, the Oei family's lawyer and business partner, for advice." With no serious contenders, the Semarang farm was again licensed to Tiong-ham for another three years. Nephew Ho was eventually forced to resign from the Chinese Counsel and in 1898, asked to be dismissed as lieutenant. As a result, the relationship between the Ho and Oei families was one of chronic tension. Quite ironically, a surprising bond would eventually develop between them in later years, but more on that in the subsequent chapters.

Meanwhile, what the Dutch had given, the Dutch were about to take away. Holland leaked out plans to set up an opium regie, a government monopoly to take back control of opium production and distribution in the last decade of the 19th century. The intention was to abolish the profitable farms controlled by Chinese farmers. Although they used ethical grounds to justify their decision, the underlying basis was more cynical – Chinese opium farmers were becoming too powerful and potentially a political liability. To rein in their influence, a new system was needed to replace the current one. To achieve this, the Dutch took cues from the French who implemented a similar programme to seize control of the manufacture and sale of opium across Cochin China. As soon as the Dutch abolished the farms, the authorities ramped up their own production which reached its peak in 1914, and encouraged a new segment of the market by opening special opium dens for women.

Hearing the news and sensing his galloping prosperity was about to come to an end, Tiong-ham re-evaluated his strategy. It was this heightened urgency of maintaining his financial dominance that propelled him to diversify away from opium into sugar in late 1890. Although Tiong-ham had been dealing with the commodity for some time, Kian Gwan was a trading house with land holdings. It did not have full control of the entire supply chain, from access to inputs to control on costs, quality, and delivery times.

As Equals: The Oei Women of Java

Recognising the limits of the opium business and convinced sugar had a golden future, Tiong-ham invested his opium profits in sugar. In 1893, just when the regie's first opium factory commenced operations in Batavia, Tiong-ham acquired his first sugar estate and mill called Suikerfabriek Pakkies. His timing was impeccable. The Dutch East Indies was already a major producer in the global sugar trade but lagged behind Cuba historically. When Tiong-ham entered the market, Cuba's sugar industry was badly affected by their war of independence (1895-1898). From just a third in 1850, the Dutch East Indies' production in 1900 ran ahead and outstripped that of Cuba by over two and a half times. At 744,000 tons, the Dutch East Indies commanded 14 percent of world sugar production. The success of Tiong-ham's first mill led him to purchase another estate called Tanggoelangin in 1897. The continued tempo of the global demand for Java sugar saw him purchase three other mills – Redjoagung, Ponen and Krebet. All his factories were acquired from Chinese owners, including one from his brother-in-law. At first, the financing and consignment-contracts of the factories were managed by his company, Kian Gwan. By the 1920s, the operations were merged under one organisational umbrella and renamed the Oei Tiong-ham Concern. Combined, his mills could produce 100,000 tons of sugar per annum.

In the next two decades, Java sugar reached new heights thanks to a series of calamities in other sugar producing nations. Droughts in Australia, hurricanes in Mauritius and a war-ravaged Cuba shifted global demand of sugar to the Dutch East Indies. The growing taste among the new middle classes of early 20th century Asia for white sugar saw a surge in sales for Dutch East Indies factories. Then, for a decade or so from the time of the outbreak of WW1, Dutch East Indies sugar producers had the Asian markets all to itself because European sugar beets were cut off from that market. Sugar soon replaced opium to become Kian Gwan's golden goose. At its peak in 1912, Kian Gwan supplied about 60 percent of the domestic market and exported a similar tonnage. It was this formidable presence in the global sugar trade that earned Oei Tiong-ham the name "Sugar King of Asia".

Outside of the Dutch East Indies, Tiong-ham became known by another name – Rockefeller of Asia. At the peak of his business career in the early 1920s, Tiong-ham's personal wealth was put at something between 150 to 200 million guilders or roughly USD60 to USD80 million. Apart from his businesses in sugar, banking, shipping, and trading, he owned vast tracts of "rice countries", his own "neighbourhoods" of Randoesari and Tjandi with 200 houses which he rented out in Semarang, his country house in Salatiga and properties in Singapore, China, and Europe. The figure undoubtedly ranked him the richest man in Southeast Asia.

Up against the rest of the world, he was not too far off from the top either. Compared with America's impressive roll call of financial magnates and business titans of that era, Tiong-ham's net worth would have easily put him amongst the top twelve richest in America. He would have been at par with the likes of Charles Schwab, who made his wealth from steel, JP Morgan in banking, Vincent Astor in real estate and Daniel Guggenheim in mining. He would also not have been far off from Henry Ford nor William Vanderbilt, heir to the Vanderbilt railway fortune.

No other turn of the 20th century Chinese had ever been this affluent. In less than two decades since Tiong-ham took over the family business, his net worth expanded at a pace that was swift and effortless, multiplying tenfold within that space of time. Sugar formed roughly a third of his total assets. His business genius has been a matter of debate among scholars for over half a century with most agreeing that it was his "modern approach" to doing business that catapulted him to that height.

As for little Hui-lan, the daughter who brought him luck and good fortune in that eventful year of 1889: Tiong-ham lavished her with an expensive gift when she turned three, but one of little value to a child

– an eighty-carat diamond pendant. The precious stone was so large it thumped against her when she ran, causing a bruise on the pit of her neck.

3
A Privileged Upbringing

For the first few years of her early childhood, Hui-lan grew up in a typical Chinese household in the Chinese *kamp*. Tiong-ham's wealth had grown so inexhaustibly great that by the time Hui-lan reached middle childhood, he moved his family away from life in the Chinese neighbourhood, its poky houses and crowded streets to a great estate in the hills of Tjandi. There, the daughters were given a privileged European upbringing and every possible advantage in life.

Considered one of the grandest residences in Semarang, Gergadji, the home they lived in was the ultimate symbol of wealth and of conspicuous consumption. It had sixteen rooms and a very large dining room for entertainment. The floors were laid in Italian marble, a luxury considering wooden floors were the norm in humbler dwellings. Surrounding the residence were deep verandahs where one sat and dined when the evenings were cool and pleasant. Walkways connected the pavilion to two wings. Modern bathrooms with proper plumbing and baths were installed, a rare luxury back then. The house had three separate kitchens running simultaneously: a Chinese kitchen, a European kitchen and a kitchen specialising in delicacies. Behind the main wing was an informal garden and beyond that a landscaped park filled with rockeries, curving paths, wandering ponds and goldfish-filled canals. Exotic plants, trees of all sorts and shrubbery shaped into topiaries added a different texture to the landscape. A small zoo at the end of the park housed a collection of exotic animals – fuzzy bears, deer, cassowaries, peacocks and monkeys. The gardens remained private except on Sundays and public holidays when it was opened to the public.

As Equals: The Oei Women of Java

An army of servants and groundsmen ran the sprawling estate. A Malay *majordomo* (chief steward) held the top position in the household supervising forty household staff. Under him came a Malay butler who was in charge of twelve serving boys. The boys were elegantly dressed in bright sarongs and high collared starched jackets. Running the big kitchens were four head Chinese cooks and a Malay chef who was in charge of French cuisine. Equally important to the household was a private Chinese masseuse who was an opium addict. She was solely devoted to Bing-nio but always not before a puff of opium for "strength" before she began her job. There was also a particular laundress whose only duty was to wash and starch the family's clothes. Ironing and folding were done by others. Tiong-ham leaned heavily on his valet who made sure his master's day went smoothly. The valet's wife tended to Bing-nio's daily needs providing her all the creature comforts. Outside the house, the head gardener held the chain of command for dozens of groundsmen including grooms for the horses and carriages. When Tiong-ham bought his first car, he hired an English chauffeur to drive him around in the automobile because none of the locals knew how to operate the vehicle. During the evening, when the house staff retreated to their quarters in the kampung, four strapping Africans, whom the locals referred to as "Black Dutchmen", guarded the house.

Tiong-ham indulged Hui-lan by giving in to her whims. Her favourite color was pale blue, so he had her bedroom decorated in that colour with matching blue linen sheets on the bed, lace and tulle window curtains with blue stain bows to shade the afternoon sun. Her little Chihuahua, then very rare, had his own tiny four poster bed made for him, with mosquito curtains just like hers. When she wanted to play with dolls, her father instructed his Dutch manager to look for a doll's house in Europe. When it arrived, it came up to her chin, large enough for her to crawl inside. The miniature house came with its own furnishings – matching bath towels in the bathrooms, beds with springs and mattresses, tiny hangers in the cupboards, stoves in the kitchen

A Privileged Upbringing

with its own set of cutleries. Tiong-ham spoiled her outrageously with presents and forbade anyone but himself to punish her, even his wife. In the evenings, little Hui-lan would accompany the driver in her father's stylish landau hauled by two pairs of beautiful French horses, to fetch him from work. Her seat at dinner was often next to his.

As a girl, Hui-lan was lonely. She was never close to her older sister, who was the mother's favourite. When she went on her weekly visits to her maternal family's house, she loathed playing with her cousins. They thought her spoiled and gave her the nickname "Princess", which she absolutely hated. The children from the village were terrified whenever they saw her wandering into their compound for fear they may be punished as the village was out of bounds for little Princess. The only child she would ever call a friend was an Australian girl who belonged to the family of a trick cyclist in a circus performing in town. When the circus left, Hui-lan wept bitterly. Her constant companions were her two terriers and her mother. Because her sister was kept busy with lessons, little Hui-lan became her mother's travelling companion whenever she went out. At home, Hui-lan's temper tantrums and bouts of impudence scared the servants. She terrorised her own nannies into submission by biting them. The only one who seemed able to manage Hui-lan was an old toothless Javanese nanny, but she wasn't capable of educating and refining little Princess. Adamant her young daughter was to cut a figure in the world, Bing-nio insisted on a British governess to do the job. So, the Dutch manager quickly put out a search.

Her name was Ms. Elizabeth Jones and she had come from England with the best references. Her previous charges included the daughters of the Marquis of Bute, Lord Edmund Talbot and the Governor of Trinidad. True to form, the new governess uncannily resembled Mary Poppins – a devout Roman Catholic with mild brown hair, a long thin nose and without a trace of humour. She dressed smartly, was "painfully neat" and, just like Mary Poppins, never left the house without her parasol. The children were already conversant in Malay because their

Javanese maids spoke it. They could speak French, a language introduced to them by their Belgian governess who came and went as quick as a flash. And when they had a series of Dutch governesses, their Dutch became polished and fluent. They were also taught to read and write Chinese classics by "paunchy Chinese men with long queues and voices which droned like tired voices". But none had an impact on Hui-lan as Ms. Jones did. Tiong-ham paid her handsomely, gave her a separate cottage and her own horse and carriage. The little Princess was, at first, suspicious of this new governess. To her, the English woman seemed overtly peculiar whose habits she thought rather odd. But Ms. Jones' stern, no-nonsense approach to managing children immediately put a stop to Hui-lan's shenanigans. One of the first things the new governess did was rid Hui-lan of her dramatic outbursts. She required the girls to behave like how Victorian British upper-class children behaved – obedient and emotionally self-contained.

With the crushing of temper tantrums came lessons and a respect for knowledge. At first, French was the only mutual language Hui-lan and Tjong-lan spoke with Ms. Jones. But it was not long before their new educator introduced them to English. Within a year, they could translate French history to English. From there, they studied Shakespeare, explored, and discussed the old-world civilisations of the Greeks, Egyptians and Romans. Ms. Jones was firm but engaging. Above all, she instilled in them lady-like etiquette and social graces. She also believed in a strict regime, starting them out at five o'clock in the morning for an early riding lesson with correct posture and even more importantly, proper attire. Gone were their days of galloping around the estate like freewheeling youngsters. Occasionally, they drove out in style, Hui-lan in a dainty dress and Ms. Jones with her parasol. Evenings were sometimes spent exploring the streets in their father's handsome carriage, soaking up lessons on European culture. Whenever Hui-lan felt a bit lonely, she often wandered down to the pavilions where the staff lived. Ms. Jones sometimes offered her tea and let her read her old copies of *The Tatler*.

By the time the Oei girls reached their teens, they had a French *kamenier* (lady's maid) who helped them with their wardrobe and accompanied them on walks and outings. The sight of two Chinese girls with their well-dressed English governess and French maid almost always caused much surprise to passers-by, for it was highly unusual to see Western faces at the service of Orientals, particularly young Chinese girls. It wasn't only the fact that they had European retainers but also their impeccable command of the Dutch language, their poise and fashionable Parisian dresses that always turned heads and captured attention. Their European upbringing was decidedly unusual for a Chinese family and certainly an exceptional lifestyle at that age. No doubt Tiong-ham's wealth had much to do with it, but there was another powerful invincible force that compelled them to lead such a life.

Fig. 3: Gergadji, Semarang.
Source: Universiteit Leiden.

4
Foreign Orientals

To the unsuspecting eye, it might have seemed like life for the Chinese in the colony was favourable and trouble-free if men like Tiong-ham could prosper and accumulate so much wealth over a short period of time. That their families could live in great style and comfort would seem consistent with the belief that life was indeed agreeable and kind. But it was not quite so. For the Chinese in the Dutch East Indies, life was saddled with restrictions and prejudices. Many were subjected to the callous coolness with which Europeans received them.

By their very nature, colonies demanded clear separations between subjects and rulers. There were all sorts of laws to control them. Not only were the Chinese subjected to travel constraints but also restrictive laws that kept them from moving into most neighbourhoods. Laws also sought to regulate the dress worn by them, stipulating who was allowed to wear what and for what occasion, even if it made no sense. If they attended official receptions, the Dutch allowed them to dress the same attire as that of the high-ranking mandarins in China, even though the Chinese in the colony were not from the same class. It would be, just as a matter of comparison, as ridiculous as allowing a pre-schooler to wear the full academic regalia of a professor at his own nursery graduation. Any attempt to violate the rules was viewed as a covert assault on the supremacy of the Europeans in the colony. A few tried to assimilate by changing their religion, but the majority had little choice. Even their youth were singled out and often excluded from education; Chinese children were permitted to enter the lower native schools only if there was room for them. Before the establishment of

Tiong Hoa Hwe Koan (THHK) in 1901, there were no institutions where they could be taught their own language.

When it came to the question of citizenship, the Dutch devised half a dozen laws to confound the matter for the Chinese. They were put into a separate category from the natives which created considerable political friction that continues to linger till this day. The Chinese were classified as "Foreign Orientals", a category that lumped them together with the Arabs, Indians, Moors and Bengalis. Since they were not considered natives, their legal status was complicated, often resulting in much confusion. In criminal and civil matters, they were subjected to native laws. In commercial ones, they had to follow laws for Europeans, but Europeans had greater protection when it came to arbitrary actions. For that matter, even the Japanese had better protection than the Chinese. Japan during the Meiji Era (1868-1912) had adopted Western models and values and was regarded a modern nation-state. Since Chinese businesses were mostly kin-based or family owned, the laws tended to overlap, resulting in long and expensive litigations. In the end, Foreign Orientals would have rather settled among themselves.

Foreign Orientals were also subjected to all sorts of taxes, some with glaring distinctions between the different classes of people. Natives, for instance, only paid two percent of business tax when it was introduced in 1839 whereas the Chinese had to pay twice as much at four percent. Europeans were exempted from business tax until forty years later in 1878, and even then, they paid the same rate as the natives. The Chinese and Europeans were also obliged to pay personal property tax at a rate of five percent which the natives were exempted from. It is no wonder that when it came to total tax collected by the state, the Chinese were the biggest contributors. In 1890, they accounted for more than a third of personal taxes, almost a quarter for business tax and an equally large share for a special tax related to leased land. In addition, the Chinese contributed 26 percent of the value of imports and about 12 percent of the value of exports — all these payments from a group that only made up less than one percent of the colony's total population.

There were a couple of reasons for this persistent and systematic discrimination. At first it developed from the attitude of the Chinese Government towards its nationals around the 18th century. At around that time, many who left their motherland were rebels and dissidents, like Tiong-ham's father. In the eyes of the Chinese Government, they were regarded as traitors and rogue nationals and thus, shorn of protection. When thousands of Chinese were slaughtered in a bloody massacre by the Dutch in Batavia in 1740, the VOC (Dutch East India Company) anxiously dispatched an apology to the Chinese Emperor, Kao Tsung Shun. Instead of seeking redress for his subjects, the Emperor apparently declared to the Dutch emissaries that "he was a little solicitous for the fate of unworthy subjects who, in the pursuit of lucre, had quit their country and abandoned the tombs of their ancestors". From then on, the Chinese were left to fend for themselves.

By late 19th century, racial tensions began to increase. Chinese dominance of revenue farms gave them economic power, but also led to anti-Chinese sentiments. It attracted everyone's attention that one percent of the population held almost half of the land bank in the colony. The Chinese also owned over two-thirds of all private estates and about a third of buildings on land which did not belong to them. Almost a quarter of all shipping tonnage and almost a fifth of sugar mills in operation were also owned by them. To the struggling natives, the Chinese were seen as greedy and exploitative. Additionally, the natives keenly felt the grip of having to deal with the Chinese for credit. In a society short of cash, almost every transaction in the colony, including petty trades, were conducted based on short-term credit. Credit terms were generally quite stiff with high interest rates, making life a struggle for the poorer segment of the community. Not surprisingly, images of usury and extortion became part of the collective memory of the natives.

There was a another problem. As the opening of the Suez Canal had set off a trade boom around the globe, the demand for labourers rose. European planters opened new lands to cultivate sugar, tobacco, and coffee. At the same time, China lifted its emigration ban and steamships began to take over the bulk of passenger traffic, making transit easier. So began the first wave of the Chinese diaspora. They left in droves. Most ended up in the British colonies of Singapore and Penang but also elsewhere, the Dutch East Indies included. This new generation of immigrants, or *tokoks* as they were called, were mostly labourers and semi-skilled artisans representing a wide variety of trades. Chinese *kamps* became overcrowded and created internal strains in what had been a relatively harmonious population. Even though they were Chinese, the *tokoks* spoke differently, dressed differently, prayed differently and even ate differently from the culturally bastardised *peranakans*.

The emergence of a full-blown *tokok* community also raised fears among the natives. An overwhelming mass piled into the labouring classes, ousting their predecessors in many trades. They competed with the natives for positions such as contract labourers in plantations and construction work, farmers, peddlers and roles in the tobacco and textile industries. The invasion was naturally met with resentment and as a result, anti-Chinese sentiments emerged, adding fuel to the works of men like M. T. H. Perelaer, a retired military man, and Dr. Isaac Groneman, a physician to the sultan. Their books which touched on Javanese society made a considerable impact across the Western world, indeed, clearly targeting the Chinese as villains.

Meanwhile, socialists and concerned middle classes in Holland began to draw a connection between pauperism in the colonies and the rising wealth of the Dutch Government. It was no secret that the natives in the colonies were still living below subsistence level and in need of assistance. By then, critical commentators – the vociferous Dutch press and members of the Dutch Parliament – took up the cause and campaigned against what they saw as an abuse of colonial powers and the immoral exploits of the Chinese. They firmly called for a change in policy and a more aggressive stance against Foreign Orientals. Sentiments in the Dutch East Indies and Holland also coincided with a powerful wave of Sinophobia spreading across the world. The particular worry was that the Chinese were going to take over the world.

Back in Holland, the works of the concerned men from the Dutch press led to a reform movement which expanded steadily. By the turn of the century, Queen Wilhelmina, on the advice of her Prime Minister, launched an anti-Chinese campaign by formally declaring the "Ethical Policy" (1901-1930). Its purpose was to bring progress and prosperity to the peoples of the Indies. The Dutch took this opportunity to curb the economic power of the Chinese whose business practices were blamed for diminishing the welfare of native people. Monopoly and revenue privileges were abolished, and the Chinese were prohibited from owning native agricultural land. But as a peace offering, the Dutch proposed to assimilate the Chinese into the Dutch regime. They extended Dutch subjectship to local-born Chinese in 1910 and opened Dutch-language education to ethnic Chinese. However, as some historians believe, the measures were not entirely in earnest. They were made months after China decided to recognise all Chinese living abroad and their descendants as Chinese nationals. By then, China had softened her stance towards her own nationals abroad. No longer were they seen as renegades but as useful resources for knowledge and capital in their fight against Western powers. For a while, Holland and China claimed jurisdiction over the Chinese in the Dutch East Indies. But the Ethical Policy had more far-reaching side effects. Scholars argued that it was this policy that contributed to the awakening of pan-Indonesia nationalism by supplying Indonesians the intellectual tools to shape and articulate their indignation to colonial rule.

The Dutch East Indies had become fragmented. No longer close to power and to the old ways of doing things, the Chinese there were left with two choices: to look to China with renewed loyalty for a sense of unity and nationalism, or to look to the West and to the age of modernity for technological creativity.

Tiong-ham chose the latter.

5
The Go-To-Guy

No Chinese in the Dutch East Indies had taken on to the occidental way of doing things more swiftly, more stunningly, than Oei Tiong-ham. If he wanted a slice of the world, he knew he had to move away from conventions, traditions and from the confines of restrictive laws. Over the next decade after Tiong-ham had taken over Kian Gwan, the town people of Semarang watched his bold transformation in awe – from the son of a traditional Chinese merchant to a thoroughly modern merchant prince. And the man who helped facilitate his transformation was C.W. Baron Van Heeckeren.

In March 1888, Tiong-ham's father decided to take a calculated step by relocating Kian Gwan's office in the Chinese *kamp* to Hogendorpstraat, a major commercial street in the European business district part of town. It was this small move that was, in part, the beginning of something big. Kian Gwan took up the vacant office and warehouse which once housed a European general trading company. Next door to them was the Commissioner of the Netherlands India Commercial Bank. The move was exceptionally bold and an important step to cultivate relationships within the European mercantile community. Not only were they in direct access to the town's banks and powerful figures in the emerging corporate economy but also to a pool of talented professionals which was absent in the Chinese *kamp*. Crucial among these professional talents were lawyers, who typical Chinese firms tended to avoid. Lawyers were not only useful in litigations but also experts in providing legal, managerial, and financial advice to businesses. They also served as board directors, as advisors to social and cultural organisations, as lobbyists and sometimes, as executors to trusts and estates. Indeed, Semarang attracted many lawyers from The Netherlands who were drawn to the Indies, chiefly by the alluring pull of money. Among them was C. W. Baron Van Heeckeren.

Van Heeckeren was a striking bespectacled young man with deep penetrating eyes and a highbrow face. When he first arrived in Java in 1879, he took a job as a clerk of the High Court and, finding the pay too low, joined a private law firm of the Government Prosecutor, Caesar Voute, three years later. While working there, he showed an extraordinary flair for business. Van Heeckeren made acquaintance with the business elites in town and ventured into a tangled network of interconnected dealings along with other partners from the law firm. Collectively, these influential men of enterprise owned a seemingly endless string of ventures from plantations to real estate holdings, trading, and manufacturing. Some of the ventures were compassionate in nature – like the time when he persuaded backers to set up a quinine factory in Bandung to compete with the Germans in the world market sometime in the 1890s. The project turned out so successful it became the largest producer of quinine in the world by the turn of the 20th century, surpassing even the Germans. But his other enterprises were not so altruistic in nature, such as his role as President of an organisation which had an active interest in the highly lucrative slave-trade which recruited coolies from East Java, then shipped them off as contract labourers to neighbouring provinces. The painful irony was that Van Heeckeren took over the top post from C. Th. Van Deventer, the same man who became spokesperson of the Ethical Policy. While strongly arguing for the progress and betterment of the natives, Van Deventer had also made himself well-off from dispatching them out as slaves.

When Voute retired in 1890, Van Heeckeren succeeded him as Government Prosecutor of Semarang, a post he held for twenty years and one which gave him immense influence. Historian Peter Post noted that it was during these twenty years that Van Heeckeren became closely involved in Tiong-ham's businesses. Like Van Heeckereen, Tiong-ham and his father were men of enterprise who had become one of a small group of venturesome merchant-financiers in the colony. They extended capital to, and eventually assumed control over, numerous businesses. Almost all their commercial transactions were financed through credit rather than equity, and for good practical reasons. For one thing, collecting reliable business information was not easy back then, which meant that one had to ultimately trust management's account on how much profit the business was making. Secondly, before limited liability became common practice, too many risks were involved in taking on an equity stake because shareholders were potentially liable for all the debts incurred by the company. A safer way to secure returns on investments was to lend money. And to protect their money, they took on a new tack and relied on Van Heeckeren to structure air-tight contracts. The Oei's method was contrary to how other Chinese businessmen operated – by sealing deals within the kinship networks and family ties derived from the concept of *guanxi* (personal trust).

Van Heeckeren also introduced Western legal concepts to Kian Gwan such as the registration of trademarks to protect against intellectual property theft, something which was not a common Chinese business practice. Above all, Van Heeckeren had one immeasurably important advantage as Government Prosecutor – he had the power to indict and make lives miserable for many. Another service which made him indispensable to Kian Gwan and Tiong-ham was his work of dealing with local authorities. Maintaining cordial relations with officers and judicial authorities was key to getting approvals and dealing with issues such as labour unrest. And just like his predecessor Voute, Van Heeckeren had direct access to the Batavian High Court and the General Secretariat which gave him immense power and influence. As business progressed, Tiong-ham and his father increasingly relied on this de-facto partnership. How a Government Prosecutor could act on behalf of and advise private clients, then profit from decisions made in court, was obviously a question that seemed to have escaped official enquiry back then.

In any case, Van Heeckeren did his job well but expensively. At a time when a bookkeeper might earn 150 guilders and a young lawyer could take home 175 guilders a month, Van Heeckeren received a handsome monthly retainer of 1,000 guilders for the services he rendered. In addition to being on Kian Gwan's munificent payroll, Van Heeckeren and a few of his associates also served as board members to Tiong-ham's companies and pocketed a lot of fees for their trouble. Quite remarkably, they could artfully serve on boards of firms they had prosecuted or given legal advice against. A number of these concerns included sugar mills which Tiong-ham attained because of the owners defaulting on loans extended to them. The Oeis were prepared to pay handsomely and treated the expense as a routine cost of doing business in the colony. The partnership benefitted Kian Gwan in other ways too: the opportunity to participate in Van Heeckeren's network of enterprising schemes. By the turn of the 20th century, Semarang became closely tied to the plantation towns around the region. Their demand for cheap and servile labour turned Semarang into a collection point for Java's coolie trade. Thousands of men recruited by Van Heeckeren's brokerage firm were shipped out on Kian Gwan's steamers to regional towns, notorious for its treatment of workers on plantations such as Deli in North Sumatra.

For an expanding business like Kian Gwan, access to a talent pool of professionals was vital to its survival and there was no one more able to consult than Van Heeckeren. His capable network of advisors helped the firm replace unskilled employees with a more professional team. These trained professionals reassembled bankrupt competitors into viable entities by imposing operational standards. They appointed professional managers to run the business in much the same way modern venture capitalists might operate. The team controlled the flow of products from factory to distributors, managed sales agents, audited costs, supervised and deployed the workforce, tracked inventory, handled logistics and warehousing, complied and prepared reports and paid taxes. And below the team swelled the ranks of thousands of native workers. They were the army of workers who swarmed through the fields, cut, and hauled cane to be crushed into syrup that flowed into boiling rooms.

Meanwhile, a wave of technological improvement in sugar production emerged towards the end of the 19th century. Quick to capitalise, the men of Kian Gwan built everything newer and better. They improved the speed and capacity of production, hired machinists with knowledge in metallurgy and engineering, then invested in the best of class equipment. The young Dutch and Chinese employees were sent to factories in Europe to learn how to work, maintain and repair the machines, thus periodically upgrading their skills.

But of all their business manoeuvrings, the most novel perhaps was the decision to incorporate Kian Gwan from a simple partnership into a public limited liability company in 1893. The business was renamed N.V. Handel Maatschappij Kian Gwan with a paid-up capital of 1.4 million guilders. The shareholders included Tiong-ham's father, holding the majority share at 90 percent, Tiong-ham (7 percent) and his brother Tiong Bhing (3 percent). A corporation was contrary to how a Chinese *kongsi* was structured. It differed in two vital respects: legally speaking, a *kongsi* was like a sole proprietorship or a partnership. In the event a *kongsi* crumbled, it lacked a legal and administrative structure to protect its shareholders. In other words, creditors could go after the business, the owner's personal assets and whatever else they had stashed away as nest eggs. There were also other limitations with a Chinese *kongsi*. Foreign companies were wary of them, mainly because there was no such thing as business registration back then. Bankers and brokers had long considered them difficult to deal with and stock exchanges refused to list them. By converting the family business from a *kongsi* into a limited liability company as early as 1893, N.V. Handel Maatschappij Kian Gwan would be among the earliest modern corporations of the world.

6
"Westernisation"

The change in Tiong-ham's business approach was accompanied by a similar determination to transform his lifestyle and ease his way into Dutch society. One of the first things Tiong-ham did was to upgrade his residential address simply because it would have been unthinkable for a man his stature not to have a great house in which to entertain. The choicest area to live was the exclusive district of Tjandi. The hilly residential area was off limits to natives and Foreign Orientals, reserved only for Europeans. The only Chinese family at that time who owned real estate in the neighbourhood was the Ho family. When Tjiauw-ing's properties came up at the public auction, Tiong-ham's father successfully placed a bid for the entire estate, all 200 acres of it. Tiong-ham received Gergadji, the mansion Yam-lo built on the estate while his younger brother took over the hotel. Tiong-ham then engaged Van Heeckeren to apply for permission for him and his family to move out from the Chinese *kamp*.

In order to entice Dutch officials to cooperate, Tiong-ham invited them for sumptuous meals and showered them with expensive gifts. The wives of the Dutch officials and foreign guests always seemed enthralled when the invitations arrived. Tiong-ham also kept the officials well fed for he knew that many of them were underpaid and could not afford all the "table luxuries which their robust Dutch appetites craved". With his limited Dutch vocabulary, he cultivated cordial relations with Dutch officers, wined and dined the European fraternity and threw all-male parties for the mercantile men in town. Over time, Gergadji became the preferred address for Dutch officials to host formal dinners for foreign dignitaries on a grand scale.

"Westernisation"

One of Tiong-ham's most memorable guests was His Majesty King Chulalongkorn, Rama V of Siam, who seemingly had a genuine fondness for Java. During his lifetime, His Majesty visited the Dutch East Indies three times. The first visit was as a young man in 1871 when he went on a study tour to see how the Dutch ruled. Like his father King Mongkut, the young king was confronted with the weighty task of thwarting the rising tide of European aggression around Asia. Siam's neighbours had all surrendered to the British and French, leaving it to stand alone as the only independent state in the region. His father had groomed him to understand the West and to recognise that the way to avert colonial domination was to modernise. The other was through diplomacy, both of which King Rama V excelled far above any Asian ruler.

The monarch made two further trips to Java in 1896 and 1901, again to cultivate social contact with his counterparts through diplomacy. Each royal expedition took over a year to plan as His Majesty hardly ever travelled without his harem and his seemingly endless string of servants. Their visits would last at least two to three months, so it was not altogether surprising that his emissaries had the difficult task of feeding, housing and entertaining all 200 of them. On one of the King's visits, Tiong-ham was sought upon to entertain the royal guests and, in his usual manner, he took the trouble in a big way to please them. He had the verandahs extended and house decorated lavishly. Dinner tables filled the entire house, spilling into corridors overlooking a garden illuminated with thousands of lanterns. Guests mingled, drank and feasted on sumptuous menus. The evening ended with a performance by Siamese and Javanese dancers, followed by a gigantic exhibition of fireworks in his Majesty's honour.

Tiong-ham's next visible change was his dress code. Just before the turn of the 20th century, he had the pluckiness to seek permission from the colonial government to dispose his Chinese *samfoo*, opting for tailored Western suits and Italian linens. It was again Van Heeckeren who wrote to the Governor General in 1898 for that special request. As usual, the men triumphed but not without consequences. Anecdotal accounts of the sensation caused by his choice of dressing appeared in the *Singapore Free Press* roughly a year later. During a state function attended by the Governor General, Tiong-ham turned up in European formal evening wear, to which a Dutch official by the name of General Riesz enquired as to what costume he was wearing. One observer overheard Tiong-ham's angry reply that the General was to "get out" and mind his own business. Another account claimed the General turned Tiong-ham around and on seeing his braided hair on his back, muttered *"Apa kway orang China!"* – What kind of Chinese are you?

Even his children were received with the same coolness by the Dutch as the rest of the Chinese in the colony. Hui-lan's personal experience left her in tears when no one turned up at her extravagant fifteenth birthday in Semarang. Six months before the party, Tiong-ham put forward a plea to the Dutch authorities for Hui-lan and Tjong-lan, to be treated as Europeans in terms of rights, burdens and obligations. As the family found to their unending exasperation later on, the request was snubbed by the entire European fraternity in Semarang. For the occasion, Tiong-ham hired the same musicians who played for the King of Siam, decked Gergadji for a grand party and instructed the chefs to cook up a storm. But when the day came, none of the children from his Dutch business associates turned up. In her own words "socially, we were not on par with the Dutch, and no one knew better than the Dutch *mevrouws* (woman). They took the batik sarongs from Papa as gifts, they accepted the other presents of food, but they would not let their children come to my party." In his customary style of not backing down, Tiong-ham got his lawyers to change the surname of both daughters from Oei to Oeitiongham the following month. It would seem that the sudden name change was to serve as a guarded reminder of who these girls were. On hindsight, Hui-lan musingly admitted, they should have handled it differently.

"Westernisation"

But it was a year after his father's passing that Tiong-ham made his most liberating move. In December 1901, after a year of mourning and shortly after the launch of the Ethical Policy, Tiong-ham became the centre of the most stunning news when the colony came to know of his trip to Holland to meet the Queen. According to the *Soerabaijasch Handelsblad*, the purpose of his travel was to seek permission for Dutch citizenship and for him to be treated and compete in business with the Europeans on equal terms. Accompanied by his entourage, included his lawyers, real estate agent and servants, the men travelled on board his liner, the *SS Simongan*, to Singapore and Hong Kong before heading to Japan. Japan was the first country in Asia to embrace Western ideologies. After centuries of isolation and seclusion, its leaders, like Siam, were faced with the daunting task of circumventing Western imperialism. Through industrialisation and "Westernisation", and by shedding off centuries of feudal rule and archaic customs, Japan prospered and emerged as a global power on its own right. Why and how it was able to adopt Western ideas, then regain complete control of its foreign trade and legal system in a little more than a generation created great interest for many people. Encouraged by Japan's success story, Tiong-ham made several trips to that part of the world for business and to see what he could learn from them.

On a journey there, at precisely noon on Christmas Day, Tiong-ham sent out a message to the rest of the world that he had cut off his queue, better known as the pigtail in the West. The men celebrated on board with champagne and got deliriously drunk. Since there was no further need to braid his hair nor shave his head, he shipped his personal barber, who had been travelling with them on board, back to Semarang. The hairstyle was a visual signifier for the Chinese but often a source of foreign ridicule and insult. It was introduced by the Qing government on the Han Chinese four centuries earlier as a sign of submission and loyalty towards the new sovereign. Non-compliance meant grave punishment which often amounted to death. The symbolic hairstyle was finally banned in 1911. By cutting it off ten years ahead of time, Tiong-ham would have appeared defiant in the eyes of the Chinese but through Europeans eyes, the move would have personified him as a modern gentleman – or so he had hoped.

With his shaved head, the men travelled across the Pacific from Japan to San Francisco for a tour of North America before sailing from New York to London. By the time they finally reached Holland after months of voyage, Tiong-ham's hair had grown which he wore in a modish style when he appeared before the Queen. With the help of his lawyer, Van Deventer, and other prominent Dutchmen, they presented a strong case to the monarch and her advisors, glowingly praising Tiong-ham's outstanding contributions to the colony. They put forth their reasoning that there would be common good and great benefit to all if the Chinese were put on equal footing with the Europeans in the colony. The Dutch monarch and her advisers were impressed but rejected them all anyway. Although feeling despondent, Tiong-ham was not about to give up. On their journey back to the East, he decided to stop over in Japan and stay on for a while. There, the Japanese welcomed him with open arms and apparently awarded him citizenship, a move that would immediately liberate him from the shackles of a Foreign Oriental. More importantly, his new nationality afforded him similar privileges as the rest of the Europeans in his own country. So, in the end, Tiong-ham achieved his goal through other means.

For a man who had gone through so much trouble to change his appearance, there was only one other thing to do – show it off. He made a trip to Europe in the spring the following year in 1902 and created a sensation when he took part in a floral parade in Bois de Boulogne, Paris' largest and most fashionable park. A popular social event where the stylish and well-to-do strolled along promenades, floral parades were the *Belle Epoque*'s version of a fashion show. This colourful affair was held in honour of the self-made French millionaire, Alfred Chauchard, owner of the city's fashionable departmental store, Les

Magasins du Louvre. To everyone's astonishment, Tiong-ham appeared looking magnificently dapper with half a dozen youthful Javanese girls on his side. They rode an elegant four-horse carriage swathed by festoons of orchids, lilacs, azaleas, roses and blue hydrangeas. Its decorator, Paris' most established florist, assured his rich client that despite the handsome price tag, his creation was certain to win a prize. And indeed, he was right. Parisian society was charmed by the lavishly decorated carriage and equally impressed by the exotic copper-toned oriental beauties. The carriage won a beaming Tiong-ham second prize. More importantly, it brought attention to many Parisians, evidently for the first time, a view of a debonair Chinese gentleman.

To modern eyes, the thought of an elaborately decorated carriage full of Javanese girls and a Chinese gentleman might not seem overly peculiar, but in 1902, it was an extraordinary sight and somewhat rebellious for that matter. For context, five years after Tiong-ham's exceptionally bold showmanship, a large exhibition emerged fifteen kilometers away on the eastern edge of Paris in the Vincennes inside the Jardin d'Agronomie Tropical – Exposition Tropicale. Over a million visitors came to gawk at bare breasted men, women and children from far-flung colonies. Shipped in by agents then rented out to zoological and tropical gardens, thousands of Africans, Asians and indigenous people were put on show alongside exotic animals. They were made to wear mock traditional costumes, put in makeshift habitats and sometimes displayed in cages under the misleading label of science. Of course, Paris was not the only city to stage such large-scale exhibitions, known as human zoos. Amsterdam, New York, Cincinnati, London, Berlin, Brussels, Hamburg, Geneva, Lausanne, Madrid, Barcelona, Moscow, St Petersburg and more, participated in such derogatory displays – all for the sake of endorsing racial hierarchy and generating enthusiasm for their colonial efforts.

In all these ways, Tiong-ham distinguished himself from the rest of the Chinese community. To the casual observer, he had made significant headway in embracing a European way of life. It is apparent that these transformations were his determination to stay ahead of economic competition but, more crucially, a manifestation of the discontent of being labelled a Foreign Oriental. In other ways, Tiong-ham remained Chinese at heart. A gauge of how stubbornly ingrained he was to keep his "Chineseness" was his refusal to learn Dutch properly, preferring to communicate in Malay or Chinese and on rare occasions, a smattering of Dutch and English. His unwillingness to fully assimilate was also demonstrated in his faith. Tiong-ham never converted to Roman Catholicism, or any other religion practised by the Dutch but instead continued to observe most of the major Chinese customs, including ancestral worship. Even more telling was his inclination towards the patriarchalism that dictated the Chinese way of thinking towards marriage, gender, and inheritance – all of which we will get to in due course.

"Westernisation"

Fig. 4: Oei Tiong-ham.
Source: Yeap Chin-joo.

7
Is the East so far Apart from the West?

In old Chinese culture, a small foot was considered the height of female refinement. Anyone possessing a three-inch golden lotus would have an edge in the marital race. In European culture, the requirement was a lot less brutal. The young lady was only required to play a musical instrument, and if she managed to sing and dance as well, her marriage prospects would significantly improve. Without these skills, she was considered a social liability. So, it was imperative that Ms. Jones gave the Oei girls piano and dancing lessons, and a Cantonese actress was brought in to teach them to sing. As with French lessons, the girls showed an early aptitude for music worth nurturing. Tjong-lan proved particularly adept on the piano while Hui-lan found singing to be her forte. The Cantonese actress had another material influence over Hui-lan – she introduced her young protege to glamour and made her become "desperately stage-struck". There was just one problem – well-bred young ladies simply did not perform on stage, but Hui-lan somehow got her way.

In the summer of 1905, the family spent a few months in America and upon their return, made a detour to Singapore. The British colony was a second home for the Oeis. The girls spent many weeks in town engaging in their own activities while their mother shopped and their father attended to business. At the time they were in Singapore, there was a well-known Belgian soprano by the name of Blanche Arral who had been touring the Far East and subsequently made Singapore her home. Soon after her arrival, at the Raffles Hotel, she met a young American journalist by the name of Hamilton Bassett who was impressed by her singing. They began a relationship – he was first her agent, then husband. The couple organised regular performances at the Teutonia Club and later, the Belgian soprano ended up giving private lessons to well-to-do children in town. Blanche, who herself was taught by the famous Mathilde Marchesi, one of the world's best singing teachers of her time, took on a few budding pupils including the two Oei girls. After a few weeks of classes and seeing how much her pupils progressed, they decided it was time for them to perform in public.

At first, the event was meant to be held at the Victoria Memorial Hall but since the authorities were unable to guarantee stability of the electric lights, they shifted the recital to the Town Hall. Even that, apparently, was not large enough to accommodate an overwhelming audience who counted among them, Sir John Anderson, Governor of Singapore, and his entourage. The acoustics of the hall were also not up to expectations but despite that, the young ladies were able to put up a magnificent performance in December that year, two weeks shy of Hui-lan's sixteenth birthday. On the programme were works by Bizet, Faure, Mozart and Gelli. As the only two Asians in the ensemble, the Oei girls, who went by their English names of Gwendoline (Tjong-lan) and Angela (Hui-lan), were given two solo pieces each and two duets together. From the second they came on stage, the sisters were a sensation.

The following day came the proud news of their performance. *The Straits Times* announced excitedly that the Oei sisters had been "awarded exultant praise". *The Eastern Daily Mail* similarly sang tributes of the two sisters and of their performance of Faure's *La Charite* – "the timely blending of their voices, sweetly modulated, came as a delightful surprise to all present. Their rendition of a difficult duet was not only creditable to themselves, but a decided triumph for Madame." But it was Hui-lan who stole the show with her solo performance of Ettore Gelli's *Farfalla*. In the words of the paper, "[h]er effort captivated the audience, and but for the fact that encores were not allowed she would most certainly have been recalled. We have attended recitals great and strange in three capitals of Europe, but we must admit that this, the song of Miss Angela Oei, staggered us. We repeat the novelty in a nutshell: a Chinese girl from Sumatra singing a French classic in French to an English audience. Surely this is a world's record! Is the East, after all, so apart from the West?" For many Europeans and Asians, their performance was the first indication that the world was changing. Singaporean society was enthralled.

While the British colony was enchanted by the romantic notion of Chinese girls performing operatic pieces to an English audience, the reception back in Dutch East Indies was not quite the same. Just over a year after their debut performance, Henri Borel, a Dutchman with owlish spectacles who was also the advisor for Chinese Affairs, attempted to organise a similar concert in Semarang in August 1906. Suffice to say, it was overly optimistic of him to hope he could garner support from the various musical and literary forces in town to cooperate. Apparently, no one wanted to perform "with those Chinese".

Matters improved slightly when the community managed to get a concert going six months later to raise funds for the new THHK school. Hui-lan was the main attraction (her sister Tjong-lan was married by then). She was accompanied by her sixteen-year-old cousin and her twelve-year-old brother who played the piano. That evening, Hui-lan sang pieces by Gounod and Bizet in French before a large crowd who sat mesmerised by her presence and voice. When it all ended, they roared with approval. Henri Borel who had attended that evening published an account of the event which appeared on *De Telegraaf* – "A Chinese concert, but totally of European music, performed by two young Chinese girls and one young Chinese boy of just twelve years, is surely a sign of modern times, which everyone's attention was fixed on." Borel then turned his attention to the musical and literary groups who snubbed the concert, questioning whether the same people "would have been equally disgusted with Chinese money". The advisor on Chinese affairs further noted the handful of Europeans who attended were equally as insolent with one apparently shouting from the back – "I would rather have that bracelet!" in reference to Hui-lan's brilliant diamond bracelet. No doubt Borel was on friendly terms with Tiong-ham and perhaps was even on his payroll; no one refuted his observations. All he got after his article went public was a criticism from a fellow Dutchman who reminded him to be a little more "cautious" when writing about Europeans attending Chinese events considering the current tensions among well-to-do Chinese in the colony.

A similar reaction was stoked when Tiong-ham hosted H.R.H. Prince Valdemar of Denmark and his nephew, Prince George of Greece at Gergadji in 1907, the same year as the Semarang concert. The purpose of the royal visit was to establish trade relations between Kian Gwan and the Danish East Asiatic Company. In typical fashion, a grand dinner was hosted for the royal guests and a few high-ranking businessmen, with Tiong-ham as host and Hui-lan as hostess – a considerable honour for someone so young. That evening, Hui-lan was outfitted in a low-cut white evening dress wearing a diamond hair clip and pendant, a gift from her father which reportedly cost £8,000. Hui-lan sat to the right of Prince Valdemar and Tiong-ham, next to Prince George on the opposite side at dinner. Awe-struck, she later admitted that the young Prince George was her favorite and she never took her eyes from "this blonde giant who shared my [her] passion for tropical fruit". After dinner, the usual entertainment was laid out – a Javanese dance performance, a firework display and even a stroll into the stables to admire Hui-lan's horses. The royal party stayed the night at Gergadji before returning to their ship the following morning.

News quickly spread of the visit. *De Javabode* noted curiously how the Danish prince only contacted the Chinese but not Europeans when he visited the colony, then wished Tiong-ham well but remained suspicious of the visit. *Soerabaijasch Handelsblad* was amazed that the royal guests, against the advice of Dutch authorities and merchants, not only visited but also stayed the night with the former opium farmer. The paper then questioned whether the princes had any idea that Tiong-ham was involved in opium and whether the royals would extend an invitation back to him as guests of the royal palaces in Copenhagen and Athens. How easily the newspapermen forget – that opium farms had been eliminated almost a decade ago to be replaced by the *regie*, the government-controlled opium monopoly.

Such were the sentiments in the Dutch colony.

8
Dutch vs. British

We might pause here for a moment and consider why there was such a difference in attitudes between the Dutch and British colonies. How did things develop so differently in the Straits Settlements? One way of explaining these differences is to go back to the very beginning when the British first created the Straits Settlements. Before the arrival of the European imperialist, maritime commerce had always figured importantly in the region's economy, extending as far back as the 2nd century BCE. Indian, Chinese and Arab merchants sailed the trade winds connecting the islands and ports of Southeast Asia and established it as a distinct geographic zone.

To prevent the Dutch from monopolising the trade in the eastern archipelago, Britain began exploring the region around the late 18th century, with the aim of establishing a base in the Straits of Malacca. In 1786, the English counterpart of the VOC, the East India Company (EIC) managed to obtain the island of Penang from the Kedah ruler. Penang occupied a mere spot in the northern tip of the Straits, less than half the size of Singapore, and inhabited by just four Malay families. Over the next forty years, the British took possession of Singapore (1819), and then Malacca (1824). Under the British, the three settlements were consolidated into one administrative unit in 1826 with the seat of government in the Penang Presidency. From then onwards, this new colony was known as the Straits Settlements.

To develop their newly acquired possession, the British encouraged and welcomed all newcomers to remain in the Settlements by introducing a free trade policy – so that imports and exports could move freely without any taxes and levies. The British also offered its residents unrestricted immigration, unlimited economic opportunities and access to British and European goods. But most importantly, they gave these newcomers protection, equal rights and freedom from government interference or political suppression – concepts which many, particularly anarchists who had fled the wrath of the Imperial government, were not privilege to. They enjoyed almost total immunity in their new home.

Compared to the heavy handedness of the Spanish in the Philippines and the Dutch in the Dutch East Indies, what the British offered seemed far better. Soon enough, a steady stream of Chinese came and resided in the Settlements. The increase in numbers and their corresponding rise in wealth made the Chinese the most commercially formidable ethnic group for the British. In the meantime, China was rapidly degenerating. Droughts, famines, unstable political conditions, wars, rebellions, bureaucratic corruption and poor governance brought the Qing Government to its knees by the mid-19th century. Britain acquired Hong Kong in 1842 and forced open three other treaty ports of Canton, Amoy and Swatow. From there, it unleashed a wave of migration from China that lasted almost a century. It was the beginning of the Chinese diaspora and the most widespread series of exoduses by one nation the world had ever witnessed.

In 1852, the British began naturalising eligible migrants as permanent residents to further attract these able-bodied men to stay on and help develop the Settlements. By 1867, those locally born were granted the status of British subjects, whatever their skin colour or status. They were on equal legal footing as their colonial masters, a far cry compared to those born in the Dutch East Indies. Tiong-ham, his siblings and their children, even though born and bred in Java, were considered Foreign Orientals and subjected to differential treatments. Those naturalised or local-born in the British colony were referred to as Straits Chinese or rather more informally known as the King's Chinese. Becoming naturalised had obvious attractions: first, they did not have to revoke their Chinese nationality but could hold a second or third nationality if they so wished. Having a second nationality also offered them a sense of security under a foreign flag and more crucially, exemption from mainland taxes.

Despite these obvious attractions, the Settlements was not without problems. Being physically apart and scattered along the Straits of Malacca, the three outposts were difficult to administer. Adding to the inconvenience was the fact that the East India Company's headquarters was thousands of miles away, in Calcutta. Additionally, the Straits was infested with pirates from the Sulu Archipelago such that it had to maintain an effective navy, which tended to be an expensive undertaking. And while the British were successful in attracting settlers to their colonies, the difficulty with running a free trade colony was that it generated little revenue for the government. Further confounding the problem was the fact that the colonial authorities had little understanding in managing an alien population whose customs, traditions, manners and systems they had no conception of. The men of the EIC running the Settlements were seconded from the Indian Civil Service in Calcutta fresh from England and had not much experience. Although they depended on local headmen or *Kapitan* (Captain) to manage the different communities, these Captains in turn, reported to British officers who had to administer justice through their own discretions, inevitably leading to much confusion and inconsistencies.

With all these problems at hand, and in desperation, the local mercantile community petitioned for the Settlements to be placed under the Crown, under the Colonial Office in London. A Legislative Council was then formed in 1867 in the Settlements allowing laws to be made efficiently, thus all together bypassing its big sister in Calcutta. By so doing, it gave the local community more leeway in how things should be governed and best managed. But of all the advancements made in the Settlements, the most effective, arguably, was the establishment of a Chinese Protectorate in 1877. Realising their Chinese brethren were one of the main factors responsible for the rapid development of the Straits Settlements, the Colonial office in London created a government agency responsible for the protection and control of the Oriental population in the colony. The setting up of the Chinese Protectorate thus marked, for the first time, the transition from indirect to direct rule. It was a unique government institution with no comparable counterpart in the history of British colonial administration. As a result, the number of Chinese arrivals sky-rocketed, rising from less than 10,000 in 1877 to an average of 150,000 people annually over the next few years to the Settlements. This translated to over 98 percent of the total migration out of China. In other words, the bulk of people who left China during those periods headed straight for the British colony while the remaining two percent settled for Australia, Thailand and the Dutch East Indies. The Chinese Protectorate proved successful and a crucial factor in making the Chinese believe there was power to protect and keep them in order in the Straits Settlements.

It was for these reasons that many Chinese men, like Dr. Lim Boon-keng, strongly defended both their British and Chinese identities. The Chinese, whether in the Settlements or in the Dutch East Indies, were essentially the same people, but owing to the great difference between the British and Dutch systems of government and education, many preferred the Straits Settlements. In the words of Dr. Lim, it was "to the advantage of the Chinese born and bred under the aegis of the British flag".

All this reinforced Tiong-ham's decisions later in life and encouraged a number of his peers to follow suit.

9
Taboo

Just two years after the royal visitors from Denmark and Greece in 1907, Hui-lan's private life unravelled in another rather spectacular manner. She raised eyebrows again when news of her marriage emerged in Semarang society. She was to be wedded to an older man of Irish parentage. His name was Beauchamp Forde Gordon Caulfield-Stoker. Originally from Somerset England, Beauchamp came from a family of army men. His father, William Beauchamp Caulfield-Stoker, was a Captain of the 2nd West India Regiment and eldest son of William Beauchamp Stoker, a lawyer in Dublin whose father was Thomas Gordon Caulfield, Captain of the Royal Navy. The youngest Beauchamp worked for a Manchester firm and represented the British consular service in Semarang when he met Hui-lan. She was nineteen and he, thirty-one. Beauchamp was also a racehorse enthusiast and had rented a bungalow called Villa Djati on the grounds of Gergadji. It might have been through those connections that they became acquainted.

The outrage from town residents was not because Beauchamp was twelve years older, but because he was white. To put things in context, this was an age of eugenics – an age when ideas of selective breeding and the cultivation of superior beings were openly preached under the guise of scientific research. At first, the well-intentioned wish was to produce smarter and stronger people by encouraging good genes. But the idea became twisted when eugenicists began to exclude "inferior" traits in the gene pool so that poor people, people with disabilities, people whose customs, religion and sexual habits deviated from the norm; even people who dressed differently, spoke differently, and looked differently were labelled 'unfit' – all in the quest to form a perfect society.

As Equals: The Oei Women of Java

First coined and championed by Charles Darwin's cousin, Francis Galton in 1883, the modern eugenics movement began in England, then spread full force across America and the West at the turn of the 20th century. The ideas were endorsed by prominent public figures including Alexandre Graham Bell, Winston Churchill, Theodore Roosevelt, John Manyard Keynes and John D. Rockefeller Jr. Using mainstream media and popular culture as propaganda tools, they reached out to the masses. Newspapers, radio talk shows, films, books, magazines, public lectures, comic strips, popular art and music spewed out unverified notions of "Better Baby" and "Fitter Family". It was sermonised in churches, instilled at home, taught in schools, promoted at state fairs and even encouraged at fashion shows and baby contests. But suddenly in the 1940s, the movement fizzled out. Proponents went silent for a while – it seems they thought it wise to distance themselves from Nazi Germany.

Hui-lan and Beauchamp's announcement was approaching the height of this movement. Their union would have been perceived as radical and highly objectionable. Even worse, it would have been regarded as an act of contempt for the Dutch. Ann Stoler, Professor of Anthropology at the New School for Social Research in New York noted of such unions in colonies as "a dangerous source of subversion, it was seen as a threat to white prestige, an embodiment of European degeneration and moral decay". Such mixing called into question the very "criteria by which Europeanness could be identified, citizenship should be accorded, and nationality assigned". In other words, interracial marriages were destabilising forces in colonial society.

Indeed, not only were mixed marriages a taboo in the Dutch Indies but also considered illegal in many parts of the world. In America, at least fifteen states passed laws that banned Chinese from marrying whites. The Expatriation Act of 1907 could rescind the citizenship of an American woman if she married a foreign citizen, with extra consequences if the woman married a Chinese man. British and

American newspapers constantly ran headlines to warn its readers of "the evils of mixed marriages". As its opening line, the *Alaskan Daily* ran an article stating that "The marriage of a white woman to a Chinaman is more than disgusting, it is revolting". One went further by flagrantly describing John Chinaman, the English term for a Chinese man, as "not handsome either in native or European costume, nor is there anything dignified or even picturesque in his ugliness".

But it wasn't only John Chinaman that was deemed unsuitable husband material in the West. People of "colour" too were regarded as incompatible. In the German African colonies, mixed marriages between whites and blacks were forbidden by the government on the grounds that the offspring of such marriages inevitably degenerate. The children from these marriages were often referred to as mulattoes, quadroons, and octoroons. And when the Japanese Exhibition opened at Shepherd's Bush in London in 1910, the *London Opinion* thought it was worth repeating its warning concerning "the dangers to English women of inter-marrying with the colored races". The Asiatics were equally hostile to the idea of their countrymen mating with "foreign devils". China in 1909, made a rule which forbade its citizens from marrying foreigners. In Japan, the government had trouble acknowledging the validity of mixed marriages. In short, mixed marriages were universally condemned by all races.

Despite such deep-rooted oppositions, Hui-lan's marriage with Beauchamp forged ahead. For his son-in-law to comfortably provide a lifestyle to which his daughter was accustomed to, Tiong-ham bought over a London sugar dealer, F.C. Grein on Mincing Lane, renamed it Kian Gwan Western Agency, Ltd. and made Beauchamp director of the company. It was, as one paper called it, "a lucrative position" for his son-in-law. The following year, the newly-weds moved to London where Beauchamp started his new career as Kian Gwan's principal dealer. By then, Tjong-lan and husband, Dr. Kan Ting-liang, were also living in London. Tiong-ham had hoped that Kan would get involved in his sugar business, but the son-in-law wanted to become a doctor instead. So, the father-in-law sent him, his daughter, and their baby son to England where Kan could get a Western medical education. With her two daughters in London and possibly tired of her husband's constant romances, Bing-nio packed her Vuitton bags and headed for London, too.

10

The Yellow Peril

By the time the Oei ladies had moved to London, the city was at the twilight of the extravagant Edwardian era, the romantic golden age of long summer afternoons, house parties and cultural transformations. Edwardian Britain had been peaceful and prosperous, and London was at the height of its influence as the capital of the largest empire in history. It was also the largest and most influential city in the world, having asserted itself as possessing the greatest of everything – power, innovation and access to wealth. During his brief reign, King Edward VII led the fashionable elites that set the style influenced by the European arts and fashion. It was also during this era when women began to do away with corsets in their everyday life. Its residents were consumed with having proper manners and refinement, for they were considered essential elements of polite society. How you dressed, ate, spoke, and how you dealt with people and where you belonged mattered. The most prestigious manners were found in fashionable and aristocratic circles where people lived in great big buildings and ladies – both middle-class and aristocratic – enjoyed a much greater range of sociable opportunities than their Victorian predecessors. Luncheons, dinners, and balls were feminine activities while men found respite in gentlemen's clubs and leisure sports. Manners were also a means of making friends, and through friends, one gained influence and recognition.

But Edwardian London wasn't without conflict. Despite growth and general prosperity, it also marked the beginning of a nation in decline. Britain's world dominance had begun to wane. Extreme inequalities that had characterised Victorian London persisted. Urban poverty was on the rise – one in five children died in their first year, and hunger, illness and diseases were common. London also had a burgeoning suffrage movement. When New Zealand became the first country to grant women the right to vote in 1893, it spurred an even stronger women-only movement to fight for the same rights in Britain. Headed by Emmeline Pankhurst, a political activist born to politically active parents, the Women's Social and Political Union created havoc on the streets of England. They heckled politicians, held demonstrations and marches, intentionally broke the law to force arrests, smashed windows, set fire to post boxes and, when imprisoned, went on a hunger strike and endured force feeding. Adding to these internal pressures were territorial tensions from the Boer War and the Boxer Rebellion. At the same time, the country's economy was also increasingly under threat from America and the emerging German Empire. The confluence of all these factors began to take its toll on the nation. But for the Oei ladies, the chronic challenge in their new home was that London was abuzz with Sinophobia.

The same fear that stoked Holland's Ethical Policy in the Dutch East Indies, xenophobic fears against the Chinese had also fuelled fears in North America, Europe, and Britain. Even though the numbers in Britain paled by comparison to America, the Chinese, visibly and culturally different, with their odd hairstyles, funny coats and unscrupulous habits of gambling and opium smoking made the perfect scapegoat for whatever problems arose. British census in 1891 recorded just over 580 Chinese living in Britain that year. It remained a tiny community since the first Chinese set foot in 1830 on board the British merchant navy's ship. Their population rose to under 3,200 in 1911 – hardly alarming by any account and quite unlikely to generate the same level of hysteria as that in West Coast America. Yet reports by the press from the colonies and America fed into British minds.

Virulent anti-Chinese sentiment spread quickly among the city's white conservatives who were mainly responsible for spreading rumours about the moral and economic dangers of Chinese immigration. Just as in America and Europe, the fact they laid claim to certain professions, such as running a laundry business, left them detached from society at large, and therefore used as proof that they, the "almond-eyed son of the flowery kingdom", were unable to assimilate. Newspapers broadcast the threat, and so-called Chinese experts, like Captain Charles Etti, Director of the European Eastern Asia Traders' Association, loudly declared: "England is threatened by an invasion by thousands of undesirable Chinamen." Britain's anxieties escalated, crystallising into fears of the Yellow Peril. Remarkably, while this was happening, the daring Oeis – Hui-lan and her dear father, Tiong-ham – were radiating waves and attracting notice across Asia and Europe, whether in the company of European royalties, performing opera on stage or showcasing themselves in a Parisian floral parade.

Quite ironically, this peculiar fear began with the love of all things Chinese two centuries ago, in the 16th century, at an age when Sinophilia was in favour throughout the Western world. If the Oei ladies had arrived in London back then, they might have had quite a different experience. The Europeans were bowled over by the same things encountered by Marco Polo centuries before them. They were impressed with China's immense wealth, her ingenious inventions, large population, stable government and particularly, her age-old culture. Even foot binding was viewed favourably. Travellers of that era, people like the Jesuit missionary, Matteo Ricci, French historian Michael Baudier and Spanish friar, Domingo Fernandez Navarrete, thought that the age-old custom was a positive practice, something which their home country should adopt.

In Europe, chinoiserie sparked a following among polite society. Soon, they began engaging in a sort of fashionable one-upmanship by incorporating Chinese-inspired designs and imageries in almost everything – from porcelain to the decorative arts, to garden design, architecture, literature, theatre, music and more. China's ancient philosophies were also felt in Europe's intellectual discourse among philosophers. Not happy with just borrowing ideas from their Chinese brethren, the West wanted more. They began to compete for Chinese resources. The Dutch and Portuguese squabbled over Macao and the British, Spanish and Dutch over Taiwan. They also bought heavily into Chinese goods, and a lot of it – silk, porcelain and the innocuous Chinese invention called tea. Who was to know that it would be the British who took to drinking tea like ducks to water. Ever since that first sip, British import of tea ran into millions of pounds a year, eventually leading to a huge trade imbalance which they could no longer afford. The problem was that other than the Chinese, no one knew the secret of making tea leaves, and the self-sufficient Chinese weren't at all interested in buying anything British. British appetite for tea was on the verge of bankrupting the nation until the East India Company discovered a product which the Chinese wanted: opium – the sole merchandise that led to the Opium Wars, with the Chinese defeated both times. Humiliated and helpless, the Chinese were forced to open ports to British trade and ceded Hong Kong to the Crown. The British forcefully insisted on extraterritorial rights which gave them immunity to prosecution under Chinese laws. Next, they burnt the Old Summer Palace in Peking, and together with the French, looted everything in sight – over one and a half million objects including jades, porcelains, bronzes, Buddhist deities and golden stupas. It was around this time that Hui-lan's grandfather, Tjie-sien fled China with his brother and nephew.

Curiously, among the stolen objects were five Pekingese dogs, a previously unknown breed in the West. Four of the dogs were given away to the Duke of Gordon and the Duchess of Richmond. The fifth dog, the smallest and prettiest of the lot, was presented to Queen Victoria by Captain John Hart Dunne, the man who found the dogs and later credited with introducing the breed to Britain. The Queen renamed her Looty, then commissioned a young artist by the name of

Friedrich Wilhelm Keyl to execute a portrait of the pooch for the Royal Academy. As for the rest of the plundered artefacts, many ended up in private collections and museums around the world, among them London's British Museum as its seemingly chief culprit. These series of events – the Opium Wars and the destruction of the Summer Palace – were part of China's "century of humiliation", which gave rise to Chinese nationalism and the May Fourth Movement.

By the last quarter of the 19th century, or around the time when Hui-lan was born, sentiments changed drastically – from a keen interest to a deep dislike for Chinese culture. The admiration they once felt for the laws and government of China vanished. Sinophobic sentiments emerged in the West. The concern that the Chinese were barbaric and backwards, echoed throughout. But what really drove the message across the Western world was the aftermath of the Boxer Rebellion (1899-1901) which saw thousands of Europeans massacred. Investigative reports sent back to the West occasionally mixed fact with fiction, often emphasising the extravagant or the scandalous, which played explosively into the minds of its readers. The crux of the matter was that the villainous Chinese were brutalising their countrymen and the heart of that crux was that the West would be outnumbered by the East. And thus, the racist cultural stereotypical metaphor was born – the Yellow Peril. The West were made to believe the Chinese were mysterious brutes, as dangerous a force as electricity when the latter was first introduced. Also, by then, India had started a thriving tea trade, thanks to a Scotsman by the name of Robert Fortune who secretly stole information on tea cultivation from the Chinese. Fortune then introduced Chinese tea plants to the British colonies of India, Sri Lanka and British Malaya.

11
Birthplace of the Most Recognisable Chinese

Nowhere did these Sinophobic fears flame more fiercely than in East London Docklands known as the Limehouse district, Europe's first Chinatown. When Hui-lan arrived, there were less than thirty Chinese shops and restaurants in Limehouse, of which four were the notorious opium dens or "hop joints" as they were called. These dens of infamy, mysteriously seductive, had become famous thanks to the media's unrelenting obsession to write lurid accounts about them, directly feeding into the intrigue of the newspaper-reading public of Britain. Since 1890, the nation's newspapers produced more articles about these dens in Limehouse each year than there were Chinese residing in the country. The ratio was almost two to one, that is, two articles to one Chinese. By one estimate, British newspapers collectively ran on average three articles per month on opium dens between 1890 and 1894. If John Chinaman could read, he would think much ado about nothing, so much paper wasted on a subject which only concerned a trifling minority.

Given all this attention Limehouse attracted, it was no surprise the district became the birthplace of the world's most recognisable Chinese – Dr. Fu Manchu, a fictional character who *Vanity Fair* called "the most exotic and diabolic of contemporary villains in the annals of crime" and for decades, "the imperial propaganda machine". Fu Manchu was supposedly the most evil man in the world, intent on the downfall of Western civilisation. He was secretive, crafty, with a first-class criminal mind. With long fingernails, a droopy moustache, arched eyebrows and a yellow face, this fictional character was created by Sax Rohmer, an Englishman who had never set foot in China nor studied Chinese history. Born as Arthur Henry Ward in Birmingham in 1883, Rohmer earned a living as a freelance writer during a time when sensational journalism was becoming popular. In conjuring his fictional character, Rohmer admitted he drew inspiration from two sources, the Boxer Rebellion and tabloid tales of London's Chinatown, Limehouse district.

In 1911, Rohmer was sent to Chinatown to research a shadowy drug and gambling boss named Mr. King. Although he found nothing, Rohmer maintained he saw a tall Chinese man with a beautiful Arab girl which gave him the idea of Fu Manchu. There was another account claiming his luck changed when he consulted a Ouija board, which spelt the word C-H-I-N-A-M-A-N. In any case, when his first novel, *The Mystery of Dr. Fu-Manchu* was published in 1913, Rohmer catapulted from an obscure writer to a sensational novelist, a recognition which lasted almost half a century. In total, he published thirteen highly successful Fu Manchu novels, with over twenty million copies sold during his lifetime. As one historian puts it: "Rohmer's strongest talents lay in deliberately playing to the racial prejudices and desires of white bourgeois audiences. The image of Oriental hordes invading Western nations yielded a malleable literary formula that became the cornerstone of Rohmer's commercial success." Even Rohmer himself attested that the evil doctor was the "Yellow Peril incarnate". So, there we have it, a fictional villain whose devious plans for global dominance became Edwardian Britain's perception of Chinese people. And that is the context of the London where Hui-lan, her mother, sister, and brother-in-law lived.

While Rohmer was carving out a lucrative position for himself, the Oei ladies were trying to ease into London society. Discrimination was not something they were unfamiliar with. It was part of life in the Dutch East Indies. But as overseas Chinese, they were even more socially at a disadvantage because mainland Chinese regarded them "provincial" and when they travelled, they were not entitled the same treatment by the Chinese diplomatic core as would a mainlander.

One way to dodge the taint of Chineseness was to loudly proclaim whiteness – and the Oei ladies did so magnificently. The women lived a rather lavish modern lifestyle in their new home. The Caulfield-Stokers settled in the quiet suburb of Wandsworth south of the Thames, in a house on Lytton Grove which Tiong-ham bought so that Hui-lan could take her proper place in society. The leafy street was later home to the fashionable set of society, one of whom was Ettienne Bellenger, Managing Director of Cartier, Messrs. Cartier jewelers of Bond Street. Hui-lan's mother lived with her sister in a bigger house called Grayland's on Augustus Road in Wimbledon, also bought by Tiong-ham. When in London, they resided in a stylish townhouse in Mayfair on Grosvenor Street, also owned by Tiong-ham. The sons-in-law too enjoyed "the great flow of money that came effortlessly from Papa to Mama" and to the girls – access to a fleet of cars, cushy jobs, and a generous allowance. They hired a retinue of liveried servants, including footmen and a chauffeur to drive the Rolls-Royce for their mother. Hui-lan preferred to be independent and drove her grey two-seater Daimler about London, often seen threading through traffic rapidly. The right clothes too, played a key part in creating the right image. A substantial amount of the allowance went into buying clothes from London and Paris' most popular dressmakers.

Just like in Semarang, lineage was a prerequisite for status in Edwardian London. And since society in their new home was unfamiliar with their *cabang atas* hierarchical rankings, the ladies took on trappings of European gentry by bestowing aristocratic titles onto themselves. Mother and daughters went by the title Countess. Bing-nio was referred to as Countess Bing, her eldest daughter was Countess Kan and Hui-lan was known among her friends as Countess Hoey Angela Caulfield Stoker. She was, as one journalist from *The Sketch* breathlessly reported, an oriental countess, "a descendant of the famous house of Count Oei (Vei) Ham, a great nobility in the money market of the Far East". The journalist went on to note, "Before her latest marriage, Countess Hoey was lady-in-waiting to the late Dowager Empress of China." Though not quite European peerage, they might have gotten away with the aristocratic title in view of their *cabang atas* status. But the "lady-in-waiting" assertion is harder to justify. Perhaps the journalist had her confused with Princess Der Ling, a woman of mixed-heritage whose father was a Chinese nobleman, her husband an American and who did indeed serve as lady-in-waiting to the Empress Dowager. In any event, mystified by Oei ladies' title, an American journalist did some digging around but could not find their names anywhere in the almanac of British nobility.

About two years into her marriage, in May 1912, Hui-lan gave birth to a son, Lionel Montgomery Caulfield-Stoker. But life was about to get terribly complicated for their young family. As the year passed, baby Lionel's parents grew increasingly estranged. Beauchamp left his job in Kian Gwan Western Agency and obtained commission in the Royal Army Services Corp in 1915. As his first posting, he was sent to Devonport. When Hui-lan attempted to visit him, he discouraged her, constantly making up excuses. He paid a visit to his family at Christmas that year but insisted on taking a separate room. By the time Lionel was four years old, his parents were living permanently apart. His father moved out from their home in the spring of 1916. A month later, Beauchamp wrote to his wife about the War and again discouraged her from visiting. In his letter, he said "It is ridiculous your coming down to Devonport (as she proposed). It would do no good, you coming down here for a few days to get gaped at. I should apply for leave, and certainly should not stay here." It would seem he was uncomfortable having her presence around.

Adding to their personal strain was a growing uneasiness among Beauchamp's people. Despite all the wealth that came with the marriage, a marriage between a British husband and a Chinese wife was their bone of contention. Differences in personality was the other. The couple was obviously gawked at when together and, when they were not, people talked. Once Beauchamp wrote to his wife citing that their lives and ideas were so far apart it made it impossible for him to return to her. Feeling humiliated and dejected, Hui-lan took refuge with her mother and sister at their Wimbledon Park home in autumn of that year and stayed there till Christmas. She wrote to Beauchamp expressing surprise that he had not come to see her, and he responded with a telegram the following day which annoyed her. She drove all the way to see him in Grove Park where he was quartered, then drove him to London where they had a bitter argument. In the two years after that, they grew even further apart.

While Hui-lan was dealing with marital woes in England, her father Tiong-ham was engaging in another conjugal arrangement in Semarang – wife number seven.

Fig. 5: A picture of Lucy.
Source: Yao-hua Tan

12

The Great Cobarry Aeas Tree

Lucy Ho

12
The Great Cabang Atas Tree

Tiong-ham was a generous man, generous with gifts and generous at entertaining. He took delight in eating well and was a great adventurer with food. He enjoyed gambling and riding bareback on horses. He displayed a fondness for tailored suits and handmade shoes. Dogs and breeding horses also played a big part in his life. But most of all, he loved women. Even though he publicly displayed a fondness for the occidental lifestyle, Tiong-ham kept his private life rather traditional, and monogamy was not part of that way of life. Before we go any further, some clarification is required regarding his wives. Sources rarely agree on just how many wives and children he had in his lifetime – it was in the vicinity of between eight to eighteen wives and twenty-six to forty children. The difference in numbers lies with who was recognised as wife and who, a concubine or mistress. Presumably, eight wives went through a ceremonial ritual with Tiong-ham and were therefore, acknowledged as his spouses. He might also have indiscriminately recognised them as wives because they bore him sons.

Polygamy might not have seemed odd back in the Chinese *kamp*, where maintaining a harem of women was customary practice. But in Dutch society, the commonly accepted norm was a stable monogamous marriage within the household. Dutch laws furnished women far greater autonomy than the Chinese-speaking world did. Even the British did not treat their women as equally as the Dutch had at that time. A Dutch woman could have legal recourse and file claims against a man. She could own property and retain control of it after marriage. Before 1882, British women upon marriage had to surrender their assets and properties to their husband, including their identity. She ceased to exist, legally speaking. Dutch women also enjoyed other freedoms compared to their English sisters. They could borrow money, own and operate a business, and make contracts in their own name, and all that was required was the husband's consent. Dutch laws also allowed their women to make their own will and continue to use their maiden name even after marriage, if they so chose.

On the opposite end of the legal scale was the Chinese wife. Chinese society had traditionally been patrilineal, that is, the most important relationships were those derived through the man. It was this relationship which provided the basis for rules on inheritance and ancestral worship. Marriage was patrilocal, which meant, once married, the bride left her own family and lived with the family of her husband. Her primary duty was to serve and please every single member of her husband's family, especially her new parents-in-law. She had to conform to the social norms of a filial daughter-in-law, submissive wife, and caring mother. Polygamy was legally and morally accepted. A man was allowed to marry as many wives as he could support. It was rare for an Emperor to take less than four "head wives". Most took around 75 to 100 "assistant wives", otherwise known as secondary wives or concubines. The first wife had precedence over the others. She was also considered the equal of her husband but the inferior partner. If a woman lived with a man but did not go through the formalities of a wedding, she is more likely to be a kept woman, therefore a mistress. A mistress has lower status than the first and secondary wives with no proper wedding to bind their union. A typical Chinese wedding has many rites for a couple to be considered legally married. But over the past 150 years, many of these wearisome rites have been discarded, making matrimony less cumbersome and cheaper for young couples. Nevertheless, a few remain, the most important being the tea ceremony. Without it, nuptials might be considered null and void. Its significance is also reflected by the fact that the custom is also observed during Chinese New Year. But even if a Chinese bride went through the tea ceremony and became an official wife, she had little, if any, power to divorce and was subject to expulsion for seemingly indiscriminate reasons. If she was physically abused, she could, at best, go to the local *yamen* (administrative office) to file a complaint. In the Dutch East Indies, however, there were no such avenues, not even a Chinese consulate to protect the interest of its citizens. In other words, Chinese wives in the colony had hardly any rights.

Yet, Chinese women in the Dutch East Indies were far more important than anyone would care to admit. When they bore sons, for the Chinese, that meant everything. Women were also important for another reason, particularly among the *cabang atas* community. Just like the monarchs of Europe, they were able to seal alliances. In the Dutch East Indies, revenue farmers and Chinese officers were drawn from the *cabang atas* community. With so much at stake, those who controlled lucrative revenue farms kept their bloodlines and seats of power firmly intact through intermarriages. They married their daughters off to powerful allies for stability and to accumulate and protect wealth. Matrimonial arrangements also kept family members gainfully employed for generations. The Be family married into the Tan, Tjoa, Kwee, Goei and the Liems, and the Goeis into the Ho.

No one better exemplified this crucial matrimonial link than Tan Ndjiang-nio. Born into the most powerful Chinese family in the colony, she was the granddaughter of the first Majoor der Chinezen (Major) in the Dutch East Indies. Her father served as the second Major of Semarang. Her brother had also risen as a Major in Semarang. She married Be from Bagelen, who was the son of a Major Titulair. Thanks largely to her family connections, her husband later earned himself the title of Major and prospered substantially through that association. Her only child, a daughter, married a Liem who later succeeded his in-laws as Major of Semarang. By the time of her own death in 1870, Ndjiang-nio had become the titular head of a large and powerful clan that included many powerful men. She was the only woman in the colony to be able to lay claim to being the granddaughter, daughter, sister, wife, daughter-in-law, and mother-in-law of Majors in Semarang. Historian Liem Thian-joe aptly described her as *Kim Ki Giok Hiap*, a tree with branches of gold and leaves of jade, while James Rush, history professor at Arizona State University, recognised her as the most celebrated *peranakan* woman of her day.

Not to be left out in the status struggle, upstarts like Yam-lo also engaged in arranged nuptials with women from a certain lineage. His marriage with a Goei not only ensured his standing in society but also the beginning of a business dynasty that would be renowned throughout the Dutch East Indies. Tiong-ham's father, also a newcomer himself, linked three of his daughters by marriage into established families. One of his sons-in-law was The Tik-gwan, a descendant from an old Hokkien family in the colony. Tik-gwan was a fifth generation *peranakan*. His father was a merchant who owned sugar factories and real estate. As for his son, Tiong-ham, marrying into blueblood wasn't so much a convention as a compulsion. Of his eight official wives mentioned in his will, Tiong-ham married into not one, but three powerful families. Among them was Lucy Ho, our second protagonist. Her story begins in the following chapters.

13
Mesdames Oei Tiong-ham – The Wives

Tiong-ham's first wife was Goei Bing-nio. Just like Yam-lo, he took a wife from the established Goei family. The first Goei to set foot in Semarang was born in 1765. Great-ancestor Goei was a merchant-mandarin who also served as an estate master and later appointed as a lieutenant in the colony. He was married to a girl from the Tjoa family. His great-grandson also married into the Tjoa family. From that union, they produced eight children. The eldest boy from the eight also married a Tjoa girl. Bing-nio was the fourth in the family, and was considered the prettiest of the daughters. She inherited her father's small frame, not quite five feet tall, her mother's ivory complexion and fine features. Her father was a short stout man while her mother was a tall, slim woman who kept to a vegetarian diet and insisted on eating her meals in solitude. In 1884, at seventeen, her father made an agreement with Tjie-sien, to unite their children in an arranged marriage. Tiong-ham was just a year older than his bride. The young couple wed in the traditional Chinese way in Semarang and produced four children – two girls, Tjong-lan and Hui-lan, and two boys. The boys died at infancy.

Young, virile, handsome, and rich, Tiong-ham proved irresistible to the fairer sex. It wasn't long before he began his philandering ways in his quest to sire sons – shortly after Hui-lan was born, to be more precise. Tiong-ham preferred young maidens from good families above other credentials. Since Chinese females were not allowed to emigrate before 1893, the ready pool of available maidens was fairly limited in the Dutch Indies. Making his selection even tougher was the fact that he was expected to pick his brides from a small circle within the *cabang atas* community, and even then, he had to be strategic because most elite families did not get along or were in competition with each other. It was perhaps for these reasons Tiong-ham took girls from the same family, usually around fifteen or sixteen years of age, from good but impoverished homes. He provided them their own establishments – the more loved they were, the bigger their homes. The women politely addressed each other as *hsiao hsi* (minor stars) and took turns to care for Tiong-ham, but overall kept socially apart. He hardly appeared with them in public and often returned to the main family house with Bing-nio and their two daughters at night. When he got tired of them, he pensioned them off – a few remarried but lived quite happily on their income supported by Tiong-ham.

His second official wife was a young widow named The Khiam-nio. Mrs. Khiam, as she was referred to, was previously married to a man whose surname was Ong. How he died, no one really knows, but they produced a daughter named Tjiang-tjoe. When Mrs. Khiam was taken in by Tiong-ham, she brought along her two-year old daughter and her own sister, Tjik-nio, who was just ten. Mrs. Khiam was extraordinarily devoted to Tiong-ham, tending to his every need and grateful to be living under his generosity. But when she couldn't produce sons for him, he evidently demoted her to a housekeeper and took her sister Tjik-nio who, by then, was fifteen or sixteen years old, as his third wife.

Tjik-nio grew up to be irresistibly attractive, presumably like her older sister. A photo of Tjik-nio shows a charming slim girl with large brown eyes, well-formed lips and a rather pleasant face framed by her hair tied in a neat bun. For the next ten years, Tjik-nio blessed him with nine children, of which five were sons. The sons were exceedingly handsome. Tiong-ham was happy with his favourite wife and remained faithful for a while. The office staff soon addressed Tjik-nio as the second wife, side-stepping her older sister's rightful position in the marital hierarchy. Tjik-nio's boys were given the generational name of Tjong while the girls shared the common name of Nio. In that brood, Tiong-ham seemed to have favoured the second son, Tjong-swan, over the first son who was spoilt rotten by his mother. Under the tutelage of his father, Tjong-swan was eventually groomed to take over the family business.

Meanwhile, Mrs. Khiam had not completely fallen off from Tiong-ham's carnal radar. She fell pregnant by him when her attractive sister was into her first trimester with her fifth child. Mrs. Khiam produced a child for Tiong-ham, but alas, it turned out to be a girl. For Tiong-ham, producing sons took precedence over considerations of affection and happiness, and that conviction seemed to have applied to Mrs. Khiam. From then on, she was relegated to keeping an eye on the children and the domestics. Mrs. Khiam died on 29 March 1932. Her obituary appeared in the *Bataviaasch Nieuwsblad* stating her age as sixty-three.

Not long after the birth of Mrs. Khiam's daughter, Tiong-ham took up with another girl thirty-odd years his junior. Her name was Ong Mie-hwa, his fourth wife. She was believed to have come from up country, from the mountains. Tiong-ham seemingly duped her into marrying him but never went through the proper motions of a conventional wedding. She was naïve and simple but too ashamed to return to her family when she realised there was not to be a wedding. Her story turned out to be an unhappy union. Despite being the new girl, she felt very much out of place and was generally miserable. In any case, she produced four sons and a daughter for Tiong-ham – falling pregnant around the same time as Tjik-nio, attractive wife number three. Mie-hwa's eldest son, Tjong-hauw also came under Tiong-ham's wings to learn about the family business. Eventually, his father got tired of his mother and swapped her for a younger maiden. But before she left, Tiong-ham apparently made her sew the mosquito canopy of the bed for another woman. After the War, two of her sons emigrated to New York and brought her with them.

Overlapping with Mie-hwa was another girl which Tiong-ham took as fifth wife. She was a familiar face in the Oei household, Mrs. Khiam's daughter by her first husband, Tjiang-tjoe. When she came of age, Tiong-ham took fancy to her. She would have been around sixteen and he, forty. Technically, Tjiang-tjoe was his stepdaughter but conventions at that time were a lot more accommodating than today. Since she was not a blood relative, no one could object. Even if they did, there wasn't much they could do. There might have been an undercurrent of gossip within the household and across town, but it never surfaced to become an issue. Tiong-ham was at the height of his career, majestically unperturbed by what his prudish Dutch neighbours might have to say. By then, he was fraternising with the elite and counted among his friends the Dutch Governor General who was the personal representative of Queen Wilhelmina in the Indies. He presided over a glorious business empire making himself and those that dealt with him, ridiculously rich. The women in his life were financially liberated, never required to do another day's work. His infidelities hardly ignited anything except expensive gifts to those he had upset. Even wife number four, Mie-hwa, was a recipient of Tiong-ham's munificence, no matter how brutal he was to her. In any case, Tjiang-tjoe gave him two daughters, Noes and Ida. And just like Mrs. Khiam, Tiong-ham withdrew his affections and she eventually retreated to Penang in British Malaya to live quietly with her daughters, who by then were married to sons of Tiong-ham's business partner.

Wife number six appeared sometime in 1915. We know very little of her, nothing about her background or what she looked like – suffice to say she was noteworthy enough to be acknowledged as his wife. Like wife number five, she did not produce any sons and only gave Tiong-ham a daughter. By the time wife number six came along, Tiong-ham's favourite wife number three, Tjik-nio, had passed away.

Shortly after wife number six, Lucy Ho, Yam-lo's great-granddaughter, appeared in Tiong-ham's life. Lucy was different from the other wives.

Out of all the wives, she was particularly intriguing. She was well-born, well-connected, well-spoken and above all, well-educated. She was also significantly younger than Tiong-ham.

Of the eight, the least known wife of Tiong-ham was wife number eight who brought him a connection to the Tan family, even though by then Tiong-ham was already a very rich man. They were descendants of a major opium farmer from the mid 19th Century. The Tans were also connected by marriage to the powerful Be family. Almost nothing is known about this eighth wife of Tiong-ham – where she came from, what her educational background was, only that she bore him a baby girl and was not kept for long. Now that we have established the background of Tiong-ham and his wives, let's move on to Lucy's story.

14
Lucy

Born in Semarang in 1901, a year before foot binding was outlawed, Lucy Ho was the eldest in a family of ten children. Tiong-ham took her as his seventh wife in 1916 when she was just sixteen and he, fifty. Of the wives, Lucy's pedigree was perhaps the most notable. Her grandfather was the eldest son of Yam-lo, and her father, Sie-sioe, was the youngest of seven children by him.

On her maternal side, Lucy came from a long line of strong women – a fact that would prepare her for her future role as matriarch to a rather complex extended household. Her maternal grandmother was from the Liem clan, a family of sufficient wealth. Great-grandfather Liem and his brother made their fortunes as merchants in the import-export business with close contacts to Dutch merchants. Despite being the oldest child, Grandma Liem never inherited the business from her father because she was born female. It went to her youngest brother who was spoiled from an early age and never amounted to much later in life. Instead, Grandma Liem received a house in Ketandan and a bit of capital as dowry when she married an employee of her father, a rather apathetic fellow. When the laid-back husband died years later, inheritance, like everything else to do with marriage, was incredibly one-sided in favour of men. The family home, which was given by Great-grandfather Liem as her dowry, went to Grandma Liem and her sons but not the daughters. And upon her death, her share was handed over, again, to the sons. Indeed, in law a wife had no rights at all beyond those her husband chose to accord her.

With the small capital from her father, Grandma Liem set up a *batik* (printed textile) business, a trade usually associated with women and part of the classical arts of court life culture in Central Java. Grandma Liem ran the business successfully. She supervised staff, watched over the printing process, managed supplies, dealt with callers and customers, arranged deliveries and all the rest, while her listless husband sat in front of house as cashier and lazed his days away. There was hardly a detail that did not involve her decisions at work. The business flourished thanks almost entirely to her enterprising and industrious disposition, and it was enough to comfortably support the entire family, an especially remarkable achievement for a woman back then.

The couple had ten children – seven sons and three daughters. In the same way she ran the business, Grandma Liem, who had grown to be a hefty *sireh* (betel leaves)-chewing woman, was also expected to devote herself to childrearing, managing the household and ensuring her children had a good start in life. Most of her children married well and despite her adept skills in negotiating dowries, her sons somehow eventually squandered everything away. Nevertheless, it was under Grandma Liem's influence that led to the most prominent nuptial in the family's history, that of Tiong-ham and Lucy. Evidently, it was Grandma Liem's decision that carried enormous weight in sealing the deal. Apparently, Tiong-ham was ever so grateful that he often paid her regular visits as if she was his own grandmother.

Grandma Liem's daughter, Khing-nio (Lucy's mother), inherited her mother's qualities and was equally industrious at making her way in the world. Khing-nio was one of two daughters. She married Lucy's father sometime in 1900. The couple lived in Kranggan, part of the Chinese *kamp* in Semarang, in a typical Chinese-style residence with a courtyard in the middle. They engaged a single maid who had to cook, clean, and occasionally keep an eye on the children. Right from an early age, the children endured the hardship of character building. Each one had chores assigned to them and were expected to carry it out straight after school, obediently and without any fuss. The boys cleaned lamps every Sunday while the girls helped in the kitchen.

When her husband became financially indebted, Khing-nio stepped forward and held the family together, selling biscuits and whatever she could to bring in money for the family. Khing-nio was also forward-thinking and ahead of her time. Most women in her generation were traditionally-oriented, viewing superstitions and age-old customs as solutions for everything. Khing-nio, on the other hand, was remarkably modern, preferring Western medicine for cures. She chose to give birth in hospitals by Western-trained doctors instead of at home by midwives. Even more notable was how she managed to put her children through a European school.

While most Chinese households accepted that the home was the woman's domain, Khing-nio not only raised her children but also managed the family's affairs and finances. Like her mother, she passed her work ethics and talent to her daughters. Khing-nio was exuberant. She was the soul of the family and there was never a dull moment when she was around. In contrast, her husband was a recluse and hardly spent time with the children. What all these meant for Lucy was that she was brought up in a world that was quite independent of male supervision. Furthermore, the conventional assessment so widely held by the Chinese that women were not capable of absorbing knowledge and that they must not study clearly did not apply to their household. Lucy was, in fact, among a very small growing number of girls who had begun to receive a Western education.

In 1900, a year before Lucy was born, her father Sie-sioe and his brother established a trading firm together, dealing with European textiles and garments. They could not have chosen a worse timing to set up a business. Between the late 1890s, right through to the mid-1910s, hundreds of firms in Java succumbed to bankruptcies. A severe drop in export prices coupled with recurring outbreaks in crop and cattle diseases precipitated a long drawn economic slump resulting in spiraling debt levels and shrunken markets. Adding to everyone's sufferings was the government's heavy-handed tightening of existing laws after the introduction of the opium regie. For the regie to be effective, the authorities restricted movement of Foreign Orientals by making it tougher for the Chinese to travel. A few years following that, they further tightened the residential restriction which required people to stay within their own zones – effectively a lockdown. At first the laws were introduced in Batavia, and many assumed their towns would be spared. It was after a while that it dawned on them just how sweeping the controls would be. Any slight breach led to heavy fines. Almost immediately, Chinese businesses crumbled. The loss in sales hit businesses hard, resulting in a wave of loan defaults and bankruptcies. But just like many laws in the colony, the restrictions had loopholes and those with influence could get away with it. At least one man did – Tiong-ham. Again, through Van Heeckeren, they submitted a formal request to the authorities to allow their directors, commissioners and agents of Kian Gwan free travel passes to move around to where the company had an interest.

By the time the restrictions came to Semarang, the Ho brothers found themselves among the casualties and unable to honour what was due to their European suppliers. By 1905, they liquidated the business, and both were declared bankrupts. Sie-sioe, the younger of the two, living in chronic debt with a large and growing family, entered into a pecuniary arrangement with Tiong-ham, who was by then Asia's richest man. Sie-sioe and his wife had eight children – three girls and five boys – with another on the way. Tiong-ham gallantly offered to settle Sie-sioe's debts and provide an annual recurring income of 50,000 guilders in exchange for the hand in marriage with all three daughters. Upon hearing the news from the Chinese press, the Dutch paper, *Sumatra Bode*, disparagingly concluded it as a "trade in yellow slave girls". However, as it turned out, one daughter was too young, while another eloped with a young man she had fallen in love with. In the end, only one daughter ended up with Tiong-ham, and she was Lucy. She was not only twelve years younger than Hui-lan but also younger than five of Tiong-ham's other children. No doubt the age difference might have created some awkward relationships but, then again, perhaps not. A big part in the lives of many rich Chinese men was to have as many young wives as one could afford. She was expected to produce heirs to carry on her husband's legacy. Infant mortality was high too, so some marriages that were not so prolific produced no direct male heirs to inherit.

There was no account of a wedding ceremony. Tiong-ham fetched Lucy in his limousine one day and accompanied her to his hill residence in Salatiga. Located between Semarang and Solo (Surakarta), Salatiga was about 3,000 feet above sea level with a temperature that was constantly cool. It was a small village whose main economy was supplying Semarang with raw commodities like coffee, rubber, cacao, cotton, tobacco, and spices for processing. The house in Salatiga was spacious, but decorations were kept basic with rattan and bamboo furnishings. Perhaps the only decadent feature was the marble flooring added by Tiong-ham's first wife, Bing-nio, who had a taste for opulence. But because Bing-nio only used the house during the dry seasons, she kept the interior rather restrained. Tiong-ham enjoyed spending time in Salatiga and often used the house as a rest place when he visited his plantations. Occasionally Van Heeckeren, his wife and two daughters would meet up with him as they too had a country home there. With its charming verandah surrounding the property, cool breezes, and magnificent views of Mount Merabu across jungle land, Salatiga was a comfortable retreat and the ideal home for young Lucy. It was also away from prying eyes and social routines, but more importantly, the undercurrents of gossips in major towns.

15

Dollar Princesses

As news of Tiong-ham and Lucy's union condescendingly unfolded in the Dutch East Indies, the same marital arrangement continued its popularity in the West: rich American heiresses marrying into cash-starved British nobilities. Announcements of these transatlantic marriages were widespread with *The San Francisco Call* describing such arrangements as an international marriage tree that had "sprung up and developed wonderfully". American girls, or dollar princesses, as they were better known, bought into social status by entering into marriage "settlements" with British noblemen who had no money, or at best, measly allowances and, often, highly in debt. In exchange for a title and entry into an elite social world, all these Gilded Age heiresses had to do was part with some railroad cash and mining stocks.

By one estimate, these well-heeled young ladies were thought to have invested the equivalent of a billion pounds into the British economy. The phenomenon occurred in the early 1860s when America increasingly began farming its own food. As a global exporter of agricultural produce, England suffered badly from this trend. Its rural population dropped and so did the fortunes of the landed gentry and British nobilities whose lives were supported by their agricultural holdings. Forced into a similar conclusion as the Ho family, many distressed heirs were compelled to dispose of possessions that had been part of the great houses for generations in order to fix a leaky roof or a crumbling wall. Museums and rich foreigners bought into heirlooms – centuries old paintings, jewellery, porcelain, silverware, rare collectibles such as stamps and books – in exchange for cold hard cash. Then came a few willing rich American damsels offering financial support in exchange for marriage rather like Tiong-ham's to the Ho family. Even more blatant was a publication called "Titled Americans", which made its debut in the 1890s, listing down heiresses who had married into nobility as well as eligible bachelors with their titles and alleged fortunes to facilitate such unions. By the turn of the 20th century, Britain saw more than a third of titled noble men from the House of Lords marrying dollar princesses. In the 1910s, the decade when Tiong-ham took Lucy as wife, there were at least close to sixty wealthy American socialites who married into the European titled nobility and peerage.

The first of such unions was in 1874 when a wealthy heiress from Brooklyn named Jennie Jerome married Lord Randolph Churchill, whose family belonged to the highest level of British aristocracy. As third in line, Randolph had not much money of his own but enjoyed the trappings of life and a fondness for gambling. Added to his dilemma was the notion that British gentlemen do not work for money. Following his younger brother's footstep, George Charles Spencer-Churchill, the 8th Duke of Marlborough too traded his title for cash when he married Lily Warren Price, a widow with a handsome bank account in 1888. Though Randolph's wife, Janine, did not bring in as much money to the family as his brother's, she did give Britain one of her most famous sons – Winston Churchill.

Not to be left out, George's son Charles, the 9th Duke of Marlborough, landed himself with the finest catch of the century when he married Consuelo Vanderbilt, the only daughter and eldest child of William Vanderbilt. Charles inherited an almost bankrupt dukedom when his father passed away and was compelled to find a quick fix-it solution. He entered into an arrangement with Consuelo's parents for the much-needed financial support to ensure a continuation of his family line and maintain the lifestyle which he was born into. The transaction included a handsome dowry of 50,000 shares of Beech Creek Railways, the full refurbishment and maintenance of Blenheim Palace and the construction of a brand-new London home, Sutherland House – a deal purportedly worth well over ten million dollars. Consuelo, who had secretly entered into her own arrangement by getting engaged to an American named Winthrop Rutherfurd, shied away from the idea. But her vehement mother did everything she could, including faking her own illness and threatening to kill Rutherfurd, to make sure her daughter made her way to the altar of St Thomas' church. The news of their engagement gripped both nations, sparked a fad which led others to follow, but also marked the beginning of their loveless marriage which ended in divorce. In America, *The Herald* called it "an important commercial transaction" while the *Buckingham Express* in England dubbed it "The Ducal Wedding. A Brilliant Ceremony". For weeks, newspapers throughout the West covered the wedding preparations in exhaustive detail. Oddly, not one headline reported it as a "slave trade".

16

An Educated Woman

Concubinage fosters female rivalry. Whenever a man brings another woman into the family, friction inevitably arises – indeed even more so when the woman is young and comes from one of the most respected families in Semarang. Not only were Tiong-ham's wives envious of young Lucy, his children were too. Hui-lan once mentioned that her father never seemed to stay with one wife until "Lucy Ho came into his life, and I can only suspect age had something to do with his settling down then". When we consider Lucy's background and who she was, we may safely assume that perhaps age wasn't the only factor that made her the envy of many, but more importantly, why Tiong-ham chose her above others. Lucy was quite obviously an opposite to the other wives.

Physically, she was not as dainty and striking as Tjik-nio, Tiong-ham's favourite and wife number three. Lucy had her mother's downturned eyes which at times made her look sombre and demure. She also inherited her mother's bone structure and from her father, his height. From her maternal grandmother, Lucy, without a doubt, inherited a pragmatic mind. Even her taste in fashion differed from the other wives. Whereas Tiong-ham's first wife, Bing-nio, was extravagant and decadent, racking up stupendous bills at fashion houses in Europe, Lucy was modest and discreet. Her apparel was confined mostly to understated below-knee-length drop-waist cotton dresses instead of *sarong kebaya* or the modish flapper-inspired dresses. She hardly ever wore jewelry or makeup nor had she any impulse to adorn herself with anything frivolous. Instead of spending hours on her hair, she wore it tied up in a loose bun. On the face of it, there was a rational disposition about the way Lucy dressed and carried herself. There was also her family name and wealth before Tjiauw-ing's downfall and how masterfully Tiong-ham took over the Ho family opium farms and thwarted her uncle's attempt from securing them back.

And then there was the other matter that distinguished Lucy from the rest – the family home, Gergadji. Gergadji was built by her great grandfather, Yam-lo – a circumstance which implicitly gave her more clout than the other wives. In 1910 when Bing-nio moved to England, Tiong-ham replaced her position with favourite wife number three, Tjik-nio, as the new mistress of the house. By then Tjik-nio had produced several sons for him, but she tragically died seven or possibly eight years later. Expecting to fill her position, the other wives were gravely disappointed when Tiong-ham selected Lucy instead. It would seem Gergadji now had its rightful mistress, Lucy Ho, to preside over the house. But Tiong-ham's decision certainly gave rise to petty jealousies and bickering, leading to apparent bursts of jealous rage, making life miserable for young Lucy.

Torn between an upbringing of sober principles, then suddenly hurled into a large, complicated family where the women seemed to have a distrust of each other, it was unquestionably a strange world for Lucy. Right from the time she moved in, Lucy turned to her mother and grandmother for help. Not only had she to take charge of her own child and the other unmarried children of Tjik-nio, who were not much older than herself, but also deal with the rivalry and different personalities of the other wives. They counselled on every aspect of her complex household from childrearing to servant management and health care, fussing over every detail. Even more extraordinary was Tiong-ham who, seemingly aware that his young wife needed time to gain confidence in her new role, sent her to a well-known dress shop in town to buy herself a new wardrobe. If there was anyone who knew how clothing played a critical part in creating the right image, it was he. When she arrived at the shop, Lucy discovered to her dismay that everything carried an exorbitant price tag, and so she ended up only buying one dress. But as soon as she returned home, Tiong-ham brought her back again to buy an entire wardrobe. Even more thoughtful was his decision to take her on a trip to meet his younger sister, Maud, and her husband, Tik-gwan in Surabaya. For Lucy, the trip was a coming-out party, and for him, it was a way to formally introduce her into society as his wife.

Perhaps her most defining quality that set her apart from the other wives was that she was unusually well-educated for a woman of the time. Lucy was a star student – conscientious, articulate, well-versed in Chinese, Dutch, Malay, and English, and excellent in maths and book-keeping. In all likelihood, it wouldn't have been surprising if she had pursued a university education before heading for a career of some sort if she had not been married to Tiong-ham. During her time, schooling for girls was rare and, even if they were lucky enough to receive one, it would only be up to thirteen years of age. Before 1854, the Dutch had no publicly funded education for the native residents in the colony and when they did, they excluded Chinese children from the programme. The Chinese were forced to set up their own schools, with the first being established in 1792. According to one estimate, there were just 2,000- odd Chinese students in 1900 out of a population of over 30 million in the colony. Of that, only 120 were girls.

Lucy's education would be considered rare among locals but what made it even more exceptional was that she was among a handful of Chinese girls who attended the Hogere Burgerschool, the Dutch East Indies' top European school – all thanks to her dexterous mother. There, she was accorded a modern education, one which offered studies relevant for the duties of an operative life, the same kind that would prepare young people for careers or roles in the public realm – yet without denying their special responsibilities to home and family. It was also one of her virtues that Tiong-ham was immensely proud of. He once commented to Hui-lan that "his affairs were being managed better than ever before, for much of his personal bookkeeping was being done by Lucy Ho who, unlike his other concubines, was an educated woman". And he went further by telling her that "You and your mother would be better off if you could keep books as well as Lucy Ho."

Lucy bore Tiong-ham their first son, Jack, in 1918. By then, the other wives had stopped producing children for Tiong-ham. The last was a son in 1916 by the fourth wife. In January 1921, she gave birth to their only daughter, Lovy. Three months later in April that same year, Tiong-ham, Lucy and their two young children vanished – quite unexpectedly it seems. Rumours of his disappearance began circulating a few months later. Local papers were rife with speculations. *De Sumatra Post*, much excited, claimed he fled Semarang to Singapore because of an overdue tax debt. The Chinese press *Warna Warta*, possibly attempting to cover up his disappearance, reported that Tiong-ham was taking time off in Penang to see if the town was a suitable place for retirement. The paper further reassured its readers that it was just not thinkable for him to leave in such a secretive way when the bulk of his assets were still in the Dutch Indies. *De locomotief* speculated his son, Tjong-swan, had also disappeared to Singapore while *Sumatra Bode* claimed that the "lost sheep" had returned to Semarang in November of that year. For months, everyone was left guessing what happened to the great Oei Tiong-ham.

An Educated Woman

Fig. 6: Lucy (far right) with Maud, Tik-gwan and friend in Holland.
Source: Yao-hua Tan.

Fig. 7: Tan Khing-nio and Ho Sie-sioe, Lucy's parents.
Source: Poppy Kwee.

17
A Question of Domicile

When War broke out in 1914, businesses in the Dutch Indies were making extraordinary war-time profits. Import and export firms sprouted like mushrooms. Banks were liberal in extending credit and overtrading took place. Meanwhile, since the Europeans were busy fighting each other, major beet producers in Germany, Austria and Russia halted sugar exports which immediately drove up demand for Java sugar. Britain and France placed large orders with the traders in the Indies to guarantee sufficient supply. With Europe out, the Indies dominated the Asian market – from India to China and Japan. Exports jumped fourfold between 1918 and 1919. Sale prices for sugar increased by approximately 50 percent in a period of three months towards the end of the War, then doubled again in the middle of 1919. For a short while, importers, exporters, and producers in the colony enjoyed a period of unprecedented prosperity. But by 1921, their windfall gain ended – value of exports plummeted by well over 60 percent within a year.

At the height of this development in 1921, the colonial Dutch Government launched a series of taxes, amongst which was one known as the war profits tax. Assessment took a while to implement, and when it did, it taxed not only on the gains by a company, but also on the dividends received by the company's shareholders. Allied with the war tax was a new bill to increase export duties on nearly every staple product in the Indies including sugar, coffee, tea, oil, and bark. The taxes naturally aroused protests and bitter resentment not only by local producers but also foreign investors who had previously ploughed significant investments into estates in the colony. The British threatened to withdraw their investments and to divert their funds to more congenial climes. Chinese merchants rushed to remit funds across to Hong Kong and trade associations came together and petitioned the government that the taxes were unjust and that they had greatly imperiled both commerce and the economy. Industry observers were convinced that the colonial Dutch Government was aiming deliberately at expropriation.

So why the sudden need to raise revenues? Apart from the War, there was another reason. Back in the Netherlands, a change of opinion regarding the role of the state in society led to escalating expenditure on education, public housing, social care, and public health. At first, the government drew part of its revenues to fund these activities from income tax, but as its initiatives and expenses multiplied, it began looking at other taxable sources. And so, to cover its shortfall, they decided to milk its colony.

The problem with the windfall gains in the Dutch East Indies was that it was an aberration – a one-off event. Because shipping routes were disrupted during War years, goods could not reach markets, resulting in the escalation of prices. In the meantime, stocks began to pile up. When the whole world reverted to normality in 1920, forced sales from huge stockpiles depressed markets, triggering huge losses for exporters and speculators who had signed forward contracts at high prices. Such taxes, argued the observers, would have been justifiable if Java and Sumatra had themselves been involved in a costly war. What made matters worse was the fact that the taxes were made retrospective – that is, based on income of former years. Instead of income tax being based on a three-year average, it was based on only one year, 1919, the most profitable year.

Among the many burdened by the taxes was Tiong-ham and his group of companies. In the Dutch East Indies, income tax was payable by companies and by shareholders, and if a man owned all the shares in a company, he paid twice. In Tiong-ham's case, he owned all the shares in ten companies. Before 1920, income tax in Dutch East Indies was moderate at a maximum of six percent for both individuals and companies. In 1920, the rate was raised from six to eleven percent because of the war profit tax. At the beginning of 1921, it became known that taxes were going to be raised further, and indeed the increase came into force in May that year. Personal tax was raised from 11 to 25 percent while company tax also increased materially.

For months, Tiong-ham and his team of lawyers met to discuss this predicament that was clearly troubling him. Lead counsel was W.G.F. Jongejan, a profoundly serious looking Dutch man who later became the chairman of the General Syndicate of Sugar Manufacturers. Jongejan laid out two scenarios for him: the first option was for Tiong-ham to pay the war profit tax which his accountants had estimated to be about 40 percent of his personal earnings or roughly 350,000 guilders for that particular year. There was no certainty, warned Jongejan, that the rate would remain the same the following year, but what was certain was that the tax was not going to go away anytime soon. The second option was to avoid paying altogether and the only way for that to happen, said Jongejan, was to change domicile. That meant Tiong-ham was to give up his home and position in the Dutch East Indies and acquire another in a foreign country.

Having made his decision, Tiong-ham went to Jongejan's office one Friday afternoon in the middle of April 1921 to draw up his will in Dutch before a notary public. In the will, all his wives and children were provided for. He was 54 years old at that time. They discussed in detail who would administer his estate, how his assets were to be distributed and who was to take the lead of his business empire. He stepped down as head of his colossal conglomerate and appointed his heirs to come on board. Jongejan also provided him with a set of clear instructions on what he should do when he arrived in Singapore. The two men never discussed the possibility of his return to the Dutch East Indies even when taxes were lowered. They both knew his life there

A Question of Domicile

was winding to an end. That evening, he had his suitcase packed, and early the following Saturday morning on 16 April 1921, he boarded his ship bound for Singapore. That was the last anyone heard of him for days. In the meantime, Lucy had the entire household effects in Salatiga packed, including her belongings. She had the house closed, then took the next boat headed for Singapore with her two young children and her stepdaughters, against the advice of her own mother. Defiant, she responded to her mother, "He has been so good to us, why do I have to abandon him now that he is in trouble?"

18
To Congenial Climes

In the same year he left, Holland further raised income tax from 25 to 30 percent while company tax went up to 20 percent. The Municipality of Semarang kept completely silent about how long the tax was going to last but most in business and the legal world feared that it would be a very long time before it was lowered. In less than twelve months, taxes in the colony multiplied by almost ninefold or close to 900 percent. Others burdened by the same assessments soon followed Tiong-ham. Van Heeckeren took off with his family to Europe and retired to Cannes in the South of France. Kwik Djoen-eng, a prominent sugar merchant, whose company was assessed with a war profit tax of nine million guilders, fled for Hong Kong and assigned his property holdings to his eldest son. The Tik-gwan, Tiong-ham's brother-in-law, absconded from the Surabaya tax authorities who wanted to hold him accountable for his enormous tax debt. Disguised as a coolie, Tik-gwan boarded a ship heading for Singapore a year or so after Tiong-ham.

A question many in Semarang began to ask: did Tiong-ham decide on the spur of the moment to leave because of the high taxes, or had he been thinking of leaving the Dutch East Indies and taken time to plan his exit? The answer seems clear when we consider what he had been doing over the past decade.

Singapore, part of the Straits Settlements together with Penang and Malacca, had a population of less than a million at the turn of the 20th century, tiny by comparison to the Dutch East Indies. Like Semarang, it was a seaport under colonial rule. But unlike their own town, Singapore had a few key attractions for the Chinese of Semarang, one of these being that they would notice the sheer volume of Chinese people in the Settlement. More than half the population was Chinese, compared to a mere one percent in Semarang or for that matter, the whole of the Dutch Indies. Malays made up about a quarter, while Indians formed a sixth of the population. Europeans, who controlled most of the Settlements' trade and administration, amounted to less than one percent of the total.

Had they gotten in trouble with the authorities, they would find the laws of the Straits Settlements applied equally to all. Dr. Schoppel, Austrian Consul in Batavia, in his 1907 publication titled *The Commercial Handbook on the Netherlands Indies,* drew a parallel between the two colonies. Dr. Schoppel opined, "The laws of the Straits Settlements know of no distinction between Europeans, Asiatic or natives and make no distinction between British and non-British, the same legislation holds good for all." In the Dutch colony however, Schoppel noted, "a great deal of distinction is made between Europeans, natives and non-Europeans". The Europeans had their own civil and penal laws and so did the natives.

Another notable difference, but one which may not be apparent to a visitor, was that the Straits Settlements had its own Constitution with its own Legislative Council to make laws. It also had a Municipal Commission to look after public health, urban planning, sanitation, and local government work. The Dutch Indies on the other hand was governed by the Dutch Parliament in the Netherlands but had no representative there. The Colonial Budget was prepared and approved by the Dutch Parliament, resulting in the colony having very little say in fiscal matters.

The limitations placed on land rights were also quite restrictive in the Dutch colony. Land laws were enacted partly to alleviate welfare of the natives as well as to expand private capitalism in agriculture. The Dutch achieved this by facilitating a lease arrangement of land under native rights. Europeans were forbidden to buy land from the natives. Alongside this law, the government issued a rather thick guidebook that explained in much detail the rules and procedures for anyone interested in leasing land. As one can reasonably imagine, the application process was tediously slow and demanding. The British, on the other hand, took a slightly different approach. They opted for free competition. Anyone who wanted to cultivate land or engage in any industrial pursuits could do so with few or no restrictions. Singapore was also blessed with one of the finest harbours in the region and an ever-constant supply of industrious labour. Thanks to these factors, the city was able to grow into a bustling cosmopolitan seaport.

Attracted to the city's business prospects, Tiong-ham had started doing business in that part of the world since the turn of the 20th century, but it wasn't until the early 1910s that he took a more considerable position in the British colony. In 1912, he assumed control of the Heap Eng Moh Steamship Co Ltd. through an equity swap, then transferred his own fleet in Semarang into the Singapore entity, thereby concentrating all his shipping interests under the British flag. From its office on Teluk Ayer Street in Chinatown, Tiong-ham managed his business affairs in Singapore. Two years later, he appointed Lee Hoon-leong (grandfather of Singapore's first Prime Minister, Lee Kuan-yew) as managing director of the company. Hoon-leong started off as a purser aboard one of the steamers belonging to the company and worked his way up to management. He also had an able assistant in Kum Cheng-soo who acted on his behalf during his absence. From there, new opportunities became available in the British colony.

Singaporeans, too, began noticing the rich "*Major* from Semarang" and greeted him with enthusiasm when he made generous public donations towards education by buying over the residence of a well-known Chinese lawyer then donating it to the Toh Nam Hokkien School. He was also a great benefactor of the Convent Girls' School, the Chinese High School, St Andrew's Medical Mission and even the Japanese Earthquake Relief Fund. When War came, he contributed handsomely to the Prince of Wales War Relief Fund and when the

British needed to raise more funds, Tiong-ham again made news when he subscribed 250,000 straits dollars in the FMS war bonds, making him the largest single individual subscriber from Singapore. The bonds which paid an interest of six percent with a maturity of five years were issued by the colonial government to help Britain's war efforts. His next purchase on Singaporean soil was his investment in the newly formed Overseas Chinese Bank. Dr. Lim Boon-keng, the Edinburgh-educated medical doctor, founder of two other Chinese banks and a Straits Chinese leader, persuaded him together with two other merchants from Java to subscribe to the shares. His fellow shareholders included several well-known Singaporeans in the rubber industry including his soon-to-be future in-law, Lim Nee-soon. Tiong-ham's munificence seemed endless. In 1920, a year before his exit, Tiong-ham again made headlines when he donated a rather handsome sum of 150,000 straits dollars toward the construction of the reception hall of Raffles College, an institution conceived as an embryonic university in the centennial of Raffles' founding of Singapore.

Perhaps nothing says more about Tiong-ham's longer-term plan than a piece of news reported by the Bandung-based newspaper, *De Preangerbode,* began to surface sometime at the end of 1916. The paper reported that a large Japanese sugar entity was in discussions with Tiong-ham to acquire the latter's sugar factories – Krebet, Ponen, Pakkies, Redjoagung and Tanggulangin. According to the paper, an offer of 45 million guilders was put on the table and negotiations were ongoing. The news seemed plausible for two reasons. First, as an importer of sugar in the 1880s, Japan had become a major producer of refined sugar by the turn of the 20th century. Sensing enormous opportunities from their growing urban middle-class, Japan's *zaibatsu* (conglomerates), notably Mitsui and Mitsubishi, poured significant resources into setting up sugar refineries in the country. They were soon exporting to neighbouring China and competing with the British firms, and when War broke out, they went on an acquisition spree. The

As Equals: The Oei Women of Java

War gave Japan the opportunity to spread its commercial network in Southeast Asia. In the Dutch Indies, major Japanese banks and trading companies including Yokohama Specie Bank, Mitsui Bussan, Taiwan Bank and Gosho began to appear on the scene while existing trading firms (Ogawa Yoko, Nanyo Shokai and Choya & Co) expanded their networks rapidly. At around the time when news of negotiations with Tiong-ham surfaced, Japanese firms had owned five out of the one hundred and eighty sugar factories in the Dutch East Indies. As historian Roger Knight puts it, "Indeed, by the early 1920s, the Java sugar industry had become, in effect, an outpost of the Japanese sugar 'empire'." Tiong-ham was well-connected and had long-term links with the sugar industry in Japan which too made it probable that he would be among one of the contact points in the Dutch East Indies. Kian Gwan had a branch in Kobe at the turn of the 20th century that supplied raw sugar directly from the Dutch East Indies via China through his shipping company. In any case, the deal fell through for unknown reasons and came to naught, but this piece of news offers some insight into what he might have been thinking at that point in time.

19
Singapore

Under Jongejan's carefully drawn instructions, Tiong-ham did as he was told when he arrived a few days later in Singapore. He did not go to the Dutch Consulate to register himself as he would normally do when he visited the city. By failing to do so, he had effectively relinquished his Dutch Indies nationality. Next, he had to establish a permanent residence. His office in Teluk Ayer Street made arrangements with an agent to lease a bungalow for him and his family on Scotts Road, an upmarket residential area in the heart of the city, but that was only to be a temporary arrangement. Jongejan impressed upon him that permanent residency was imperative as it was seen as a change of domicile under the law of the Straits Settlements. So, for the next few months, he and Lucy set about looking for a home. The agents presented them with a few properties to view but in the end, they settled for a comfortable house on Dalvey Road called Omdurman. Omdurman was located in the European neighbourhood of Tanglin not too far away from Sentosa, a second home that Tik-gwan kept on Stevens Road.

Apart from Tik-gwan and his wife Maud who left Semarang for the same tax reason as Tiong-ham, there were a few other family members who had chosen Singapore as their new home. Forced to leave by the elder Oei (Tjie-sien) for raking up huge debts, Tiong-ham's brother-in-law and wife, relocated to Singapore. Three other sons from favourite wife number three had also made Singapore their home. So did Tiong-ham's fifth wife, Tjiang-tjoe and their two daughters, Noes and Ida.

Like Tjandi, Tanglin was a relatively hilly neighborhood which had initially been plantation land in the 17th century. Its fertile and well-drained slopes made it suitable for growing gambier, nutmeg and pepper. By the 19th century, Tanglin gentrified and became a popular residential neighbourhood among European and Teochew planters. Though not as grand as Gergadji or Salatiga, Omdurman was a fine property. It sat on just over two acres of freehold land, with six large bedrooms with separate verandas and en-suite bathrooms. It had a decently-sized drawing room and dining room, a tennis court, and stables. The previous owner purchased the property during the War in 1916 for $13,600 from H.S. Arathoon, an Armenian merchant. Six years later in 1922, Tiong-ham paid $50,000 for the same property. He would have liked a bigger residence, but having been hard-pressed to quickly find a home and with not much available on the market, they decided to take Omdurman.

Apart from its size, the house also had a few irritating problems by Tiong-ham's standard. It lacked the conveniences of a modern home which he had been accustomed to. There was no flushing toilet. Most of Singapore's residential homes still relied on the night soil bucket system which was introduced in the 1890s. Although the bucket system was a great improvement in hygiene from previous methods, it was still antiquated and unsanitary. Tiong-ham and Lucy appointed the island's pioneering architects, Messrs. Swan and Maclaren to gut out the existing drainage, install plumbing that had enough pressure in the pipes to get the water to the upper floor. Bathrooms also had hot water and flushing toilets. A septic tank was added to the back of the property. Tiong-ham also requested for additional stables for his horses while Lucy's request was a new modern kitchen with piped-in water, a gas stove, pantry, and miscellaneous cupboards.

While renovation was taking place, Tiong-ham set out on a real estate shopping spree in the city. He had already owned a few properties in Singapore but was looking at ways to safeguard his capital by putting them in prudent long-term investments such as real estate. After forty years of steady economic and population growth coupled with the rising cost of living after WW1, Singapore faced a severe housing shortage, forcing rents up and sending land prices spiralling. The Public Works opened new areas, laid out miles of roads, sewer, and water pipelines. Municipal housing schemes aimed at the middle to lower classes were launched in areas such as Geylang and Havelock each year, yet supply could not meet demand. Investors like Tiong-ham, convinced that prices would continue to boom, bought heavily into real estate. Most of his acquisitions were commercial shophouses located near Boat Quay, the island's first development project. Boat Quay was where the city's entrepot trade took place. Nearly half of its imports and a quarter of the exports were handled from there. Merchants, retailers, and real estate investors clustered, their warehouses and shophouses hugging as close to the river front as possible, driving up prices of properties beyond the reach of many but the most well-off. A shophouse close to the riverfront fetched an average price of 20,000 Straits Dollars while something similar slightly further away might sell at below 10,000 Straits Dollars. Within less than three years, Tiong-ham had amassed a substantial real estate holding worth between 2.6 million to 2.7 million Straits Dollars. By one estimate, roughly 80 to 100 properties were mostly located in this thriving commercial enclave.

Just when it must have seemed to Tiong-ham that his tax liability issue was beginning to fizzle out, the Dutch authorities ignited it again. In early January 1922, they pressed his son Tjong-swan, whom the father had entrusted the business to in the Dutch East Indies, to pay the father's continued liability for income tax. Tiong-ham immediately sought the advice of his Singapore attorney, A.P. Robinson of Messrs. Drew and Napier, who explained to him the principals of an usher's writ – a document recognised in Dutch law by which a person gave notice of his intention to change his domicile. He promptly took out the writ and sent it to Jongejan in Semarang to hand it to the Dutch authorities. At the same time, his attorney executed a new will for him in English, declaring his domicile to be in the British colony on 26 January 1922. The question of naturalisation also crossed Tiong-ham's mind but both Jongejan and Robinson advised him that by doing so, his assets would, in case of his death, be administered according to English law. So, he dropped the idea. At around the same time, Tiong-ham purchased a house in Gulangyu island, an international settlement in Amoy, China. It could have been part of his game plan to repatriate to China and take up naturalisation there, but what his intentions were, we will probably never know now.

By June 1923, when the renovations of Omdurman were completed at an outlay of 20,700 Straits Dollars or almost half as much as the property itself, the family moved in with furniture that Lucy had packed from Salatiga, which included Tiong-ham's favourite armchair. By this point Lucy was proving to be quite a capable woman, not only as a doting mother and an attentive wife but also as a disciplined individual. They lived a relatively modest life and got by with just a handful of household staff unlike the extravagance of Gergadji. The family celebrated most of the important dates in the Chinese lunar calendar and observed some Chinese customs but other than that, the children were fairly Western in upbringing. They addressed and spoke to their father in Hokkien, referring to him as *Tiah* (father) while they spoke to their mother in Dutch and called her by the more endearing Dutch term, *Mam*. Lucy would prepare the meals and in the evenings after dinner when the children were asleep, she spent time with Tiong-ham, helping him with his letters and documents. She helped translate Dutch letters into Malay for him. She would also write and type his Dutch letters. Lucy was also a competent book-keeper and diligently kept his personal books in order.

As Lucy, Tiong-ham and their children settled in Singapore, Hui-lan was making headlines in London, yet again.

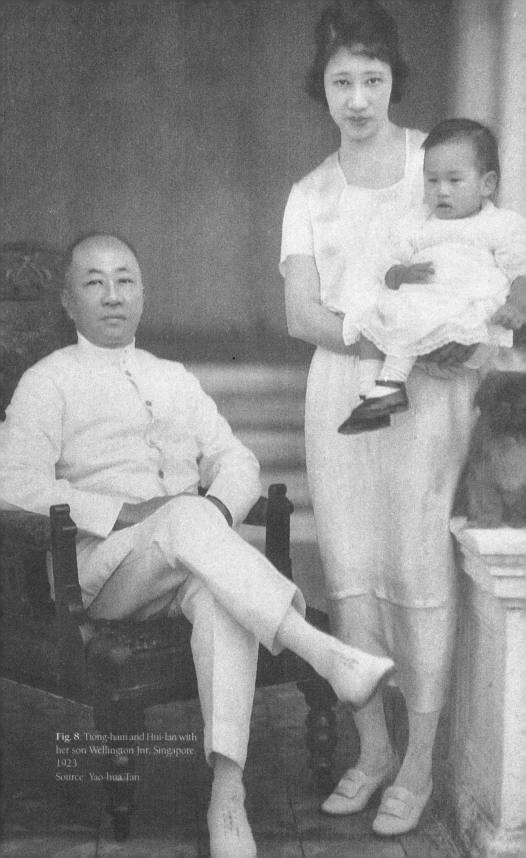

Fig. 8: Tiong-ham and Hui-lan with her son Wellington Jnr, Singapore, 1923.
Source: Yao-hua Tan.

Oei Hui-lan

20

May Fourth Movement

In the spring of 1919, 3,000 students took to the streets in Peking to protest against decisions made at the Paris Peace Conference to officially end World War I (WWI). Angry mobs poured through the streets, hurling rocks, burning houses and assaulting China's minister to Japan. Though initially dominated by the student masses, the movement quickly reached out to the working class and a newly rising national bourgeoisie. Continued pressure in summer that year culminated in the nation boycotting Japanese goods and labour strikes which drove major cities, including Shanghai, which was the sixth busiest port in the world, to a standstill for nearly two weeks. In the end, the government yielded and responded to the demands of the protestors by condemning the Treaty of Versailles. They sacked corrupt officials and released those imprisoned.

What brought this on was a series of events that dated back to 1898, three years after China's crushing loss in the Sino-Japanese War. In humbling defeat, China was forced to give up territorial concessions to Western powers. Britain claimed Hong Kong and Kowloon. Germany took Jiaozhou Bay in Shantung. Russia ended with up Liaotung Peninsula and Dalian. France secured Guangzhou Bay. These powers also claimed spheres of influences in other parts of the country: Britain in the Yang-tse River Valley and Canton, Japan in southern Manchuria, Fukien and Kwantung Province, Russia in northern Manchuria, and France in Yunnan Province. They carved the country into buffer zones, then instituted imperialist systems whilst maintaining a military presence to protect their turfs. The whole fiasco turned China into a semi-colony – the first in its very long history. The nation which was once one of the greatest civilizations the world had known, now swamped by "foreign devils".

Exasperated by the spread of foreign influence, a secret organisation called the Society of the Righteous and Harmonious Fists led an uprising in northern China in what became known as the Boxer Rebellion of 1899–1900. The rebels sieged the foreign districts of Peking until an international coalition which included America was brought in to crush the rebels. China ended up having to pay foreign powers an indemnity of USD333 million, or roughly USD10 billion in today's money, and was forced into accepting unequal treaties.

When WWI broke out, China remained neutral for the first half of the war, but decided to join the allied forces in 1917 with the hope of resolving their diplomatic issues with Japan and Germany at the post-War conference. With the support of America, they thought they could win back Shantung, put an end to extra-territoriality and revoke Japan's exploitative demands. But instead, none of their demands were taken seriously by representatives of the allied powers at the conference, one of whom was American President Woodrow Wilson. Not only were they ignored, but Japan was allowed to retain territories in Shantung.

In any event, the protest that spring afternoon set off what came to be known as the day that propelled China towards modernity. It was an epochal event in modern Chinese history. Starting off as what Mao Tse-tung described as a "bourgeois-democratic revolution against imperialism and feudalism", it soon developed into a widespread rethinking and critique of Chinese culture. Many believed the only possible way to save China was to learn from the West as Japan had done decades ago – to separate from the past and embrace modernity. In consequence, a number of intellectual theories were put forth by the so-called New Culture Movement. They urged every citizen to reject Confucianism and archaic practices such as those that the cotton farmer girls would have had to painfully endure. Instead, they maintained that China would be better off adopting modern Western beliefs such as science, democracy, individualism and equality.

One of the key concepts used by new culture intellectuals as an example of modernity was the idea of New Woman, an archetypal figure who personified someone modern, educated, political and intensely nationalistic. In fact, the term was such a novel feminist ideal that it had only been coined the same year as Hui-lan's birth. The very opposite of New Woman was Old Woman, equated to enslavement and a weak China. Proponents of New Woman even went so far as to describe what she looked like, how she behaved, her beliefs and attitudes. Constantly appearing in periodicals and popular media, the idea of New Woman caught on with the youth and soon became the core focus for reform-minded intellectuals to push forth their ideas of transformation.

On 14 May 1919, just ten days after the May Fourth Movement exploded on the streets of Peiking, Hui-lan did a rather valiant thing – she had obtained permission to fly a plane at the famous Handley-Page aerodrome at Cricklewood, England. In doing so, Hui-lan scored an inspiring double achievement. For one, she would have been among a handful of female aviators in history to fly, well ahead of even Amelia Earhart, the American who championed the advancement of female aviation. But more importantly, Hui-lan would have been the first Chinese woman to do so. Over the next few months, as the May Fourth intellectuals and reformers expound their ideas of modernity and of New Woman, there was Hui-lan, a true-to-life modern Chinese woman, soaring in the clouds a few thousand feet above the ground, like a shiny winged bird in the Western sky.

Little did the world realise how quite symbolic her feat was then.

Fig. 9: Hui-lan and her son, Lionel, by Beauchamp Caulfield-Stoker, 1919.
Source: Mary Evans Picture Library
© Illustrated London News Ltd/Mary Evans.

21
Marital Melodrama

Even before she conquered the skies, Hui-lan had been capturing London's attention. She had begun asserting a newfound sense of independence in the city, not merely as a married woman, but as her own person. Columnists took relish in reporting on the social activities of this fun-loving oriental countess. She took part in pageants. She took part in plays. She raised funds for charities. Portraits of her were featured in society papers, often describing her as *haute noblesse* (high nobility). She threw dance parties at her Mayfair home. She hosted and participated in fashion shows, occasionally showing off to London's fashionable set traditional Chinese dresses. "Countess Hoey Stoker's gorgeous native gowns with their fringe hats inspired many guests at her Wimbledon and Mayfair houses to follow suit." No longer seen as hideous and antiquated, Hui-lan charmed her guests with the colours, tactile qualities, and fine workmanship of these exquisite Chinese outfits – indeed, a breath of fresh air compared to the sober and muted colours or wartime garments. One of her greatest fans turned out to be Baroness d'Erlanger, a larger-than-life personality, patron of the arts and the most important society hostess of her time. Impressed and inspired by Hui-lan's style, the Baroness had her music room redecorated in an Oriental theme. For a while, Hui-lan captivated London's high society, but only so long as there were little hints of her marriage to an Englishman.

Then, in the spring of 1920, she made a shocking announcement which got the whole city excited. She filed for divorce. Divorce, just like interracial marriages, was socially unacceptable. It was regarded as a sexual transgression and detailed reporting of it created much anxiety over how such stories would affect public morality. And all this could not have come at a worse time. News of her divorce coincided with the birth of tabloid newspapers, and the slightest information of her tainted marriage brought her right into media limelight – a stupendously rich Chinese Countess, mixed marriage, and infidelity – racy news that would sell. Hui-lan engaged one of England's top barristers, Sir Edward Marshall Hall, a man who had gained a reputation for successfully defending several high-profile cases and thus, had become known as "The Great Defender". For the next few weeks, London devoured every scandalous detail of her unhappy marriage with Beauchamp. The divorce petition noted Beauchamp's infidelity and desertion. On a Saturday evening that Beauchamp had been scheduled to call on Hui-lan, she caught him at a theatre with a lady in evening dress. He later wrote back to her telling her a completely different story – that he had taken out for dinner a brother officer who was going to India and was short of money. When she wrote asking for Beauchamp to return to her, he replied that although she would consider his refusal cruel, their lives and ideas were so far apart that it was impossible. The suit was undefended. Beauchamp admitted to adultery and oddly produced evidence that he had stayed at a hotel with another lady. After leaving Hui-lan and his son in the spring of 1916, he never intended to return to his wife. The court granted Hui-lan a divorce and custody of eight-year-old Lionel. When the story went public, one newspaper, *The Leeds Mercury*, pointed a "strange resemblance" to Joseph Hergsheimer's novel, "Java Head", which had an unhappy ending "just as this real-life story has had." Another, *Birmingham Gazette*, unkindly mocked the marriage with the headlines "Love Laughs at Wealth and Devotion – Ideas Far Apart."

Her divorce wasn't the only one that the tabloids were focused on. There were a host of others. With so much detailed coverage and unsavory marital scandals swirling about, it was bound to create displeasure. And it certainly did – from King George V. The royal concern was that such reporting not only humiliated well-to-do divorce litigants, but also provided amusement to the man on the street, in so doing, undermining the legitimacy of the social hierarchy. Legislators debated the issue and promptly introduced a new law that forbade the publication of salacious details from the testimonies in divorce cases. The law, Judicial Proceedings Act, was enacted in 1926. It provided discretion not so much as to protect the individual's privacy from public scrutiny but moreso to preserve the public decorum crucial for the "maintenance of hierarchies of class, gender, and age". Apparently, revealing too much about divorces had become a public evil and a danger to society.

In any event, as news of Hui-lan's divorce faded from the headlines in London, another attention-grabbing marital melodrama was brewing in the background for her. This time, across the Atlantic and over to America. Just less than two months after the court granted her divorce, Hui-lan, her mother, and young son bade farewell to her sister and brother-in-law, boarded the Adriatic from Southampton and sailed across to New York in summer of 1920. They were accompanied by six English maid servants and Lionel's governess. They were about to start a new life.

22

The Career Diplomat

Into this developing chapter in Hui-lan's life emerged a distinguished gentleman by the name of Koo Vi-Kyuin (Gu Weijun) or better known as Wellington Koo. Born into a merchant family in the treaty port of Shanghai in 1888, Wellington and his siblings grew up in the Chinese section of Shanghai, and later moved to a mansion in the city's International Settlement district. His father was a successful businessman who started off as a deputy purser with the China Merchants' Steam Navigation Company, later starting his own hardware shop, then becoming a tax collector before serving as President of the Bank of Communications. His mother was a traditional Chinese wife with bound feet. She had never travelled further than Peking and knew very little of the world outside her own sphere. Young Wellington was initially given a classical Chinese education where he was taught to memorise the Five Classics. When he turned fifteen, his father enrolled him at St John's College, an American missionary school in Shanghai.

The city of Shanghai was the most accessible and alluring to foreign colonisers in semi-colonial China. It was easily the most cosmopolitan. Although not a colony like Hong Kong, Shanghailanders (foreigner residents) controlled the metropolitan even though there were more Chinese than there were them. While Shanghailanders seem to have enjoyed the cultural diversity and vibrancy the city offered, the city was without its problems. Shanghai was segregated. Racial discrimination was endorsed by the unequal treaties and formed part of the fabric of Shanghai society. Chinese people were barred from the main elevators and had to use a separate elevator in commercial buildings. They were banned from the first-class compartments of French-controlled trams.

Foreign social clubs flatly denied them admission as members. The city's Public Garden (Huangpu Park) and other recreational grounds were off limits to the Chinese even though they helped pay for its upkeep. Fifty percent of all taxes and fees in the International Settlement were paid by the Chinese. Despite their contributions, they were banned from the city's top medical facilities and had virtually no say in how the settlement was governed.

Growing up in the foreign settlement, Wellington, like Hui-lan, experienced the prejudices and foreign privileges of the Shanghailanders. One of his earliest boyhood encounters was being punished for mistakenly riding his new bicycle on the pavement when only a few seconds before him, a British boy had done the same. Instead of ticking off the British boy, the policeman abruptly halted Wellington, impounded his bicycle and fined him five yuan for breaking the law. The incident left an unforgettable impression on extra-territoriality for young Wellington. Later in life, he told his daughter, "The first fifteen years of a child's life make a deep impression upon him and more or less set the mold in which his future life is to be cast, as far as character, habits, taste and viewpoints are concerned."

In the summer of 1905, the same year when Hui-lan delivered her impressive concert performance in Singapore, Wellington was admitted into Columbia's School of Political Science where he read liberal arts. He was seventeen. While many of his contemporaries went to Japan for further education, Wellington chose America because St John's offered him alumni connections which gave him the chance to study at the alma mater of some of his American teachers. America also provided one other attraction – exceptional academic faculties in the study of politics and international law. Before he left, he had his queue cut off, paid the barber twice for the effort, then tied a ribbon and wrapped the hair in paper before presenting it to his mother who broke down into tears.

In his seven years at Columbia, Wellington became one of the most brilliant students at the institution, earning himself three degrees, including a Ph.D. in international law and diplomacy with a particular focus on extra-territoriality. There, he immersed himself into American culture, actively participating in social functions and activities. He edited the campus newspaper and worked for the *New York Herald* which gave him an understanding of the power of the press and propaganda to influence public opinion. Wellington also honed his debating and oratorial skills, wining numerous prizes as a student. His formidable linguistic skills got the attention of the president of the university who personally congratulated this impressive young man. His classmate described him as Columbia's best orator "largely because of his successful use of the debating technique of offering his opponents polite Oriental concessions and then demolishing them with a sly and devastating thrust of logic". It was his time in Columbia when he made the decision to become a diplomat. Diplomacy, he felt, presents a more peaceful alternative as opposed to heavy-handed military force – and international law formed part of his arsenal to wield in diplomatic warfare.

After completing his education, Wellington embarked on a career that was impressive to say the least. In a nutshell, he started off as English secretary to President Yuan Shi-kai, then quickly promoted to counsellor with the Foreign Ministry before becoming China's minister to the United States, and, later, to Britain. In between, he was appointed as the Chinese delegate to the Paris Peace Conference (1919) and the Washington Disarmament Conference (1921–22). By the second half of the 1920s, his diplomatic accomplishments won him the portfolio of Foreign Minister in a newly-appointed cabinet. He returned to Peking for his new post where he continued to push for policies to revise the unequal treaties but always peacefully. During the warlord era in the late 1920s, Wellington went out of favour briefly. Chiang Kai-shek issued an arrest warrant, forcing the young minister to go into exile for two years before bringing him back to become the premier and Finance

As Equals: The Oei Women of Java

Minister of China. By the early 1930s, China had become increasingly important in Western affairs and so, the Foreign Ministry was raised to an Ambassadorship. Wellington then served as the Chinese Ambassador to France (1936–1940), then to Britain during World War II (WWII) and finally to America (1946–1956) where he focused on maintaining the US–China relationship. Wellington was also one of the founding members of the United Nations. After an extraordinary career spanning over forty years of China's most tumultuous time of war and revolution, he retired from diplomatic service in 1956.

Fig. 10: Dr. Wellington Koo.
Source: Library of Congress.

23

A Proposal

Wellington's personal life, however, did not achieve a parallel success. After completing his undergraduate studies, he returned to Shanghai one summer to fulfil a promise made on his behalf of his father. The bright young man was to enter an arranged marriage with the daughter of his father's friend, Dr. Zhang. The girl, Chang Jun-e, was a sheltered lass, raised the traditional way, unexposed to the world and had nothing much in common with her brilliant groom. When Wellington returned to America to begin his postgraduate studies, he brought his new wife with him but rented a separate boarding house for her while he spent almost all his time at Columbia. The loveless marriage was never consummated and ended in divorce three years later.

In the summer of 1912, roughly six months after his divorce, Wellington married the second time around. Her name was Tang Pao-yi, also known as May Tang. She was the daughter of Tang Shao-yi, the first Prime Minister of China and the man who offered Wellington his first job as English-language secretary to the Republican President. Just like Wellington, May was both Western and Chinese-educated, receiving most of her education in America and a graduate of Bryn Mawr in Philadelphia. But her American experience, interestingly, went farther back to the time of her youth. During the outbreak of the Boxer Rebellion in Tientsin, her family home was shelled by mortars, which caused great damage to the property. In an act of selfless heroism, their American neighbour and his wife who were themselves under siege, stumbled through debris and smoke in search for survivors. There, they found three of the Tang children huddled together. The wife took care of the older two while the husband carried little May out of the

A Proposal

house. As it turned out, the kind American later became the 31st President of the United States, Herbert Hoover. His wife, Lou Henry Hoover later described their time in Tientsin as "the most exciting time of her life". The story was recounted back to Wellington almost sixty years later by the ex-President himself when Wellington paid him a courtesy call.

Wellington and May's union was a well-matched marriage. The couple returned to America when Wellington was appointed Chinese Minister to the US in December 1915. Life was happy for a while for the Koos. May took her duties as the new minister's wife very well and bore him two children – Wellington Jr and Patricia. But tragedy struck in 1918. One afternoon, in early October that year, May made a trip to Philadelphia to watch a film by Lady Tsen-mei, a Chinese movie star in a patriotic propaganda film called "For the Freedom of the East". Wellington was in New York for the China Day celebration. When May returned, she fell gravely ill and within a week, passed away at a young age of twenty-two. Her body was sent back to China for burial. What took her life was the influenza virus that killed fifty million people worldwide. As WWI drew to a close in November 1918, the flu pandemic, known to us today as H1N1, exploded ruthlessly throughout the country. Philadelphia became the hardest hit American city when, in September of 1918, organisers of the Liberty Loan Parade went ahead with the event despite concerns from medical experts. To support the war efforts and boost morale, the city put together a two-mile long procession to raise funds. Some 200,000 people thronged Broad Street, cheering wildly as the procession went past. Little did they know that lurking amongst them was the deadly virus. Within a week, half a million people in the city of almost two million had contracted influenza. An acute shortage of medical personnel left the city partially vulnerable. Over a quarter of the city's doctors and an even greater number of nurses were occupied with the war efforts. Six weeks later 12,000 would be dead. May Tang was among them.

Wellington had not much time to mourn in private. In January 1919, less than three months after May's tragic death, he was appointed as one of China's plenipotentiaries to the Paris Peace Conference – of which, as we already know, the outcome ignited the May Fourth Movement. Heading the five-member delegation was Lou Tseng-tsiang, one of China's best known and experienced diplomats. The rest included C.T. Wang, representing Dr Sun Yat-sen's opposition party; Alfred Sze, Minister to Great Britain, Wei Chen-zu, Minister to Holland; Hu Wei-te, Minister to France and Wellington, Minister to the United States. At the age of only thirty-one, Wellington was not only the youngest, but also one of the most articulate spokesmen representing a nation at the conference. Shantung was one of the hottest topics in Paris and all eyes were on the Chinese delegation. Complicating matters for the Chinese delegates were three pressing internal issues: The first was that domestic politics back in China were spectacularly chaotic. Over the past few decades, China had been torn up between numerous interest groups – power in the country fell into the hands of some two hundred warlords while a dozen European powers determined to cling on to their concessions on Chinese territories. Even among themselves, the five Chinese delegates were at loggerheads with each other, which eventually led to a leadership struggle. Finally, and probably the most contentious, was that prior to the Conference, Peking had signed two secret agreements which gave Japan political and economic rights over Shantung. This was done without the knowledge of the delegates, Wellington's, in particular. They simply did not know that the Shantung issue had already been settled by their governments. When the conference was leaning in favour of Japan over the Shantung, Wellington was pushed into the limelight as its official spokesman with no inkling that a private agreement had already taken place.

Thoroughly familiar with the West and able to apply Western logic to China's international problems, Wellington delivered the greatest speech of his career in "perfect English, and in cool, lucid and logical

A Proposal

argument which carried the members of the Council right along with him". He argued that for the Chinese to willingly give up Shantung, the "cradle of Chinese civilisation" and the home province of Confucius, would be like asking the Christians to abandon Jerusalem. Wellington concluded that they (the Chinese delegation) would be false to their duty to China and the world if they did not object to paying their debts of gratitude by selling the birthright of their countrymen, and thereby sowing seeds of discord for the future. Despite his poignant speech, the conference ruled in favour of Japan. Protest erupted back in China and under significant pressure by the May Fourth protestors, Peking bowed down and could only direct its delegates to abstain from signing the Treaty of Versailles. Later that afternoon, Wellington walked alone on the deserted streets of Paris, thinking that "28 June 1919 must remain in the history of China as the day of sorrow". He had failed in Paris but back home, he was regarded a hero for standing up for his country. The outcome of the Conference was met with immense disillusionment, turning many Chinese intellectuals away from the West. America was seen as hypocritical. Believing that they were betrayed at Versailles by America and its European allies, men like Mao Tse-tung and Ch'en Tu-hsiu, future founders of the Chinese Communist Party, looked to Soviet Russia for an alternative political model.

And in the midst of all this heated dispute and enormous tensions, Wellington proposed to Hui-lan.

As Equals: The Oei Women of Java

Fig. 11: Participants in the Paris Peace Conference meeting in the Salon de l'Horloge (Clock room), Quai d'Orsay, French Ministry of Foreign Affairs, Paris, France. President Poincaré of France is shown giving his opening address, 18 January 1919. Source: Library of Congress.

24

Paris Courtship

They met over a dinner party hosted by Hui-lan's sister, Tjong-lan, in Paris in the autumn of 1919 or, just around the same time as the final stages of the Paris Conference. Hui-lan and her mother had been enjoying a summer tour of Europe when Tjong-lan, who had taken a short-term lease of an apartment in Paris, sent letters out to them to quickly return to Paris, for a young man was interested in meeting Hui-lan. The young man turned out to be Wellington. Who initiated the meeting remains unclear. Suffice to say, the chief matchmakers from both sides saw tremendous value in the union. Mother and older sister were definitely keen on Hui-lan settling down with someone of Wellington's stature. Even though he may not have had a big bank account, Wellington had more distinctive attributes – respectability and status. At thirty, with one child and separated from her husband, Hui-lan seemed to be heading towards a life of disrepute as far as society was concerned, so her mother and sister waged a campaign to land her a man of distinction. Conveniently, just two months after the orchestrated dinner party, Caulfield Stoker sent a letter to Hui-lan with proof of his affair with another woman. They were officially divorced in April 1920.

Wellington was obviously equally agreeable to the union. In fact, it was unlikely for a man to go to such great lengths to woo a woman for love given the intense global political pressure he faced at that time, coupled with the fact that his own wife had just passed away no more than a year earlier. Wellington had apparently "fallen in love" with a photograph of Hui-lan, but beyond looks, there was undoubtedly something else that had caught his attention. It wouldn't be altogether surprising that that something might have been Hui-lan's maiden flight from Handley-Page aerodrome as she took to the British sky the same week as when the May Fourth Movement erupted. "A fair aviatrice: Who has recently been up in the clouds" proclaimed the *British Tatler*. "Countess to fly", announced the American *El Paso Herald* which also added "England's Chinese countess was among the first to take advantage of permission for civilian flying". For the world, airplanes were a symbol of a futuristic modernity. The romance and allure of it can hardly be imagined now, but back then airplanes were viewed as prophetic machines and aviators were considered quasi-messianic. The news of a true-to-life modern Chinese woman flying transfixed Europe and America – surely it too would have gripped Wellington's interest.

Tjong-lan had invited a few guests, including some of the delegates from the Paris Conference that evening. Dressed in a pair of green chiffon Turkish trousers with a gold lame bodice and a brief yellow jacket, she wore a triple strand pearl necklace from Cartier and adorned her hair with matching gold and green flowers. Looking absolutely stunning, Hui-lan was seated next to Wellington. Her initial impression of him was that of a small man, neatly dressed, with thick hair cut *en brosse*. He was not quite her idea of romance – that of a "tall exciting young man, handsome as a moving picture star" and neither was she impressed with his reserved nature. Still, they engaged in polite conversation in English throughout dinner. Just before dinner ended, their guests made plans, to spend the following day at an outing together at Fountainbleau which Hui-lan and Wellington agreed to follow along. The next day, Wellington sent a car for her, and they spent the day together. For the next week or so, her new suitor showered her with as much attention as his time would permit. He accompanied her shopping, carried her parcels, waited patiently for her as she had her manicure done, sent her orchids, bought her candies, magazines, and books and finally, on the tenth day, popped the weighty question – will you marry me?

It seemed Hui-lan needed more time to think, so the Chinese contingent from the embassy stepped in to help her with her decision. General T'ang Tsai-li's wife talked to her about her duty to the country. Another statesman, Dr. C.T. Wang, sang praises of Wellington. But the most persuasive was Madame Wei Tao-ming, the only Chinese woman at that time to be decorated with the Legion of Honour. To Hui-lan she stressed that it was the duty of every Chinese man and woman to work for his or her country and that Hui-lan, with her fine education and material advantages, could do a great deal for China. It was difficult for a woman to work alone. Hui-lan would prove much greater value if she combined forces with the brilliant Dr. Koo. It seemed Tiong-ham opposed his daughter's marriage to Wellington on the grounds that he was twice married, this coming from a man with eight wives! In any case, Hui-lan made up her mind and accepted his proposal. Their engagement was officially announced the same year on 10 October, the same day as the Double Tenth Celebration, China's National Day.

When the Peace Conference ended in January the following year, in 1920, Wellington transferred his post in US for London, much to Hui-lan's delight, for she felt that London with its glittering court life had more appeal than "unglamorous" America. The transfer was to facilitate Wellington's work as China's spokesman in the League of Nations. Meanwhile, the couple decided for Hui-lan to temporarily remain in Paris while he returned to Washington to make the necessary arrangements. Two days after he arrived in New York, he leased the Gaither estate located on the beautiful Severn River, near Annapolis. It was to be their summer home. From there, he could commute to Washington while his new fiancée's family together with his two children could live there, away from the prying press. They had to keep the whole arrangement a secret for the sake of Wellington's diplomatic career. But as soon as Hui-lan and her entourage landed in New York on the *Adriatic* six months later, the press announced their arrival – "Countess Bing Oei Tiong-ham, of the Chinese nobility, who was accompanied by her daughter, Countess Hoey Oei Tiong-ham, and the latter's son, Master Lionel Stoker. The party which was attended by six English maid servants and a governess will make a tour of this country."

For the next few months, the Oei ladies and children managed to keep a relatively low profile hiding in their comfortable summer house while Wellington attended to important matters in Washington. It wasn't until September 1920 that the press got whiff of what was going on when the entire family was seen at one of the grandest hotels in Atlantic City, the Ambassador. A favourite summer vacation home among the rich and famous, guests of this Gilded Age hotel included the likes of Enrico Caruso, Fanny Brice, Sir Arthur Conan Doyle, Harry Houdini and even mobsters such as Al Capone and Lucky Luciano. Even within the hotel, the family kept pretty much to themselves, seldom appearing in public spaces. They chose to have their meals served in their suites and employed their own Chinese chef to cook for them.

Fascinated but confused, the press strove hard to find answers about this rather intriguing woman and her mother who had suddenly appeared in Wellington's life. Immediately, they began to probe – were they married? Was she of British nobility? Was she of mixed parentage? Impressed by the retinue of staff the ladies had with them, *The Washington Herald* reported the ladies "lived many years in England with small armies of servants". Whenever Hui-lan appeared in the lobbies, "there was a suppressed hush, for her beauty seemed to affect every nook and corner of the great lounging rooms. Her clothes were the most expensive that European designers could produce. Despite her wealth, which is said to run into the millions, and the position she held as the wife of the ambassador of a foreign power, Madame Koo wore only one jewel, a massive sapphire ring in a tiny platinum band." That ring, a Kashmir sapphire, was the engagement gift from Wellington.

Efforts by newspaper men to find more information from attaches of the embassy in Washington turned futile. No one was willing to talk. Before more salacious news was uncovered, the family left for London and by November 1920, Wellington and Hui-lan were secretly married at the Legation in Brussels. She wore a fabulous Callot Soeurs gown, but only her mother was present from her side of family. Tjong-lan had fallen ill and was too sick to attend. Troubled by tax issues, Tiong-ham never made it to her wedding, but made up by paying a lot for wedding gifts, which included a gold and silver dinner service for Hui-lan and three Rolls Royces: one for Hui-lan, one for Bing-nio and another for Tjong-lan. Apart from Bing-nio, the other parties at the civil marriage ceremony were the Chinese minister to Belgium and the minister to Spain and their wives. After the ceremony, Wellington hosted a luncheon for forty guests and made a surprise announcement that they were to leave for Geneva on the night train because the Assembly of the League of Nations was opening the next day. If it had been left to Hui-lan, the wedding day might have turned out very different, but Wellington was a man with a mission. Even the private alone time that Hui-lan had hoped to spend with her husband after the low-key celebration was dashed. Wellington worked throughout the rest of the day and when they reached Geneva the following morning, he was off to attend to his duties, leaving Hui-lan to spend the day with her mother shopping. In her own words, "it was like not being married at all".

Hui-lan's first legation as wife to the Chinese minister was in London in 1921 and her first official duty was to accompany Wellington to Buckingham Palace for him to present his credentials to Their Majesties, King George V and Queen Mary. Their royal visit was just a few months after John Hart Dunne – by now a General and in his mid-80s – presented a photograph of Looty, the dog, to Queen Mary. There is a

As Equals: The Oei Women of Java

Fig. 12: Dr. Chung-hui-Wang, Mrs. Koo, Wellington Koo. [Between 1921 and 1924]. Source: Library of Congress.

certain irony in the thought that the one common connection that brought Looty's photograph to her Majesty was also the very same element that had weakened China and thrust Wellington into a diplomatic career, while at the same time enriching Tiong-ham, who in turn, financed Hui-lan's extravagant lifestyle, which drew Wellington to her – that common connection was, in fact, opium.

25
China

In 1922, a year after London, Wellington and Hui-lan left for China. He was to serve as the new Foreign Affairs Minister. The homeland they arrived at was a rather different place from when Wellington left it seven years ago. His success from saving Shantung from the Japanese occupation saw him returning to a hero's welcome, but also to a chaotic nation marred by constant conflicts and civil wars. After the death of President Yuan Shikai and without a clear successor, China disintegrated into many factions, each controlled by power-hungry warlords who

Fig. 13: Hui-lan, her newborn and step-children, with her string of English servants at the steps of the Chinese Legation in Washington, D.C. on their departure for China in 1922. By the time the baby returns to London, he will have travelled at the rate of 1,0000 miles for every week of his life. Source: United Archives / Topfoto.

knew only to plunder and oppress. What followed was one of the swiftest historical evolutions known in human history. Over the next two decades, China would witness a series of major shifts – from a four-thousand-year-old monarchy to a republic; from authoritarianism to egalitarianism; a semi-colony to a sovereign state; farming community to industrialisation; and from Confucian classics to modernity. Never has there been a more muddled and perplexing age. And it was in China where Hui-lan spent most of her time as wife to Wellington Koo.

They were greeted by Wellington's family in Shanghai when they first arrived. His mother had not met Wellington's new wife or his children. Even though Wellington was western-educated, mother-in-law Koo had an old-fashioned disposition and was naturally anxious to meet her modern daughter-in-law. "I was quite beyond her understanding...as if we had been born a few hundred years apart", recalled Hui-lan. Her mother-in-law came from an entirely different generation with an innate suspicion of anything new and unconventional. Despite Hui-lan speaking several languages including Mandarin, her mother-in-law only spoke Shanghainese. Not only could they not communicate but even their physical appearances were different – Hui-lan's mother-in-law and sister-in-law had bound feet. Even more baffling to Hui-lan's mother-in-law was the fact that her grandchildren were all cared for by English servants. And if that wasn't enough to shock the living daylights out of the poor lady, she soon found out the little ones too could not speak a word of Chinese!

Peking became their new home. The Koos were loaned an old palace in the middle of the capital city as their official residence. Built in the seventeenth century by a general for his concubine, the property had clearly lost its lustre but as soon as Hui-lan entered the gates, she fell "completely under its spell". Set on a 10-acre plot, the palace was a series of villas comprising 200 rooms, connected by roofed corridors with lacquered beams. So enamored with her new home, Hui-lan made a trip to Singapore to see her father. Tiong-ham was evidently shocked

China

to hear that Wellington did not own a house in China, so he gave his daughter the funds to purchase and refurbish the property. In her usual style, Hui-lan brought new levels of elegance and luxury to it. She added modern bathrooms, running hot and cold water, a grand ballroom, reception rooms and even a complex coal-fired central heating system, which was a real luxury for its time. Every square inch of the palace was meticulously planned out. Hui-lan and Wellington had their own separate wings, while the children were given their own quarters. Guests and visitors, depending on whether they were close or important, were allocated different pavilions. When the renovations were finally completed, like Gergadji, it became one of the most admired homes in the capital and a preferred venue for entertaining. The number of guests swelled over the years – from European royalties, foreign dignitaries, religious leaders, fellow cabinet members, wives from the diplomatic corps, warlords, military dictators, puppet presidents. Even the venerable Dr Sun Yat-sen spent his last remaining days there. Hui-lan cherished her home and described it as "my one real possession, the symbol of security, peace and the background I wanted my sons to remember."

Indeed, it was a happy and exciting world Hui-lan found herself in. As wife to the new minister, she was required to call on the other spouses of powerful men, many of whom had great influence over their husbands. But whenever the political wheel turned, which happened quite often, Hui-lan had to "re-acquaint" herself with the new First Lady. Strict protocols had to be observed. More importantly, tact was essential, for sometimes their own domestic situation complicated matters – especially when the powerful husband had more than one wife.

One of the most novel social customs in Peking around that time was an informal gathering introduced by the American minister at which mixed alcohol was served. First initiated in response to the Prohibition (1920–1933), liquor-based mixed drinks became the principal drink in America, and with it a new form of merrymaking: the cocktail party. At first, it was seen an oddity because it was neither a reception nor a meal. The hours, too, were unconventional and so were the rather odd "seating arrangements" – there were simply none. Guests either stood or, if held outdoors, sat on the stone steps sipping cocktails. Hui-lan and Wellington found this social side of Peking life "delightful". They saw it as a way to stay in touch with the foreign community and to get an idea of their reactions to the political developments and activities of the Chinese government. Gradually, cocktail parties became a hit because they were often held after office hours, which meant that there was no need to dress up for the occasion and people could come and go as they please. The fact that it was an informal gathering and that numbers were kept moderately small made it easier for guests to have one-on-one conversations. Compared to the formal dinners and receptions which could drag on for hours, putting a severe strain on people's comfort, cocktail parties became an enduring part of diplomatic life.

As with life in London and elsewhere, Hui-lan fascinated many people in China. Her domestic staff treated her like a goddess, devoted to her needs, treaded around her unnoticed but appeared in a flash when beckoned. Her ability to speak several languages drew her to many circles including the diplomatic corps, which meant her social obligations were more frequent than other political wives. Even the warlords were intrigued by her. Two created such a boorish entrance, making them almost certainly the most unforgettable people she had to receive. Chang Hsueh-liang, often known as Young Marshal, was the son of Chang Tso-lin, leader of Manchuria. Young Marshal had never met a modern Chinese woman before and upon learning that Hui-lan had taken a suite at the Peking hotel, requested for his aide to arrange for him and his roguish friend, Chang Tsung-chang, known as Dogmeat General, to meet her. Hui-lan politely declined – several times, it seems. Both men were well-known for cavorting around Shanghai's glitzy nightlife. The fact that Dogmeat General had the most notorious reputation amongst all the warlords might also have swayed her decision. He was once dubbed by Time magazine as "China's basest warlord" and for good reason too. At six-foot-six, this giant of a man was infamous for brutally cracking heads of enemies with rifle butts. Adamant to make her acquaintance, Young Marshal and his gigantic buddy took matters into their own hands. They barged into the hotel with a revolver, threatened the servants, demanding to see her. Caught off-guard, Hui-lan kept her composure and bravely received the men with great decorum and civility. She offered them tea. Her graciousness must have humbled them such that they "behaved beautifully" throughout the afternoon. It must have been quite an extraordinary sight to see two tough guys sipping tea and minding their Ps and Qs in polite company. Upon leaving, Young Marshall gallantly offered Hui-lan the use of his bodyguards for protection should she ever require them. A friendship had been struck between them ever since.

Being a career diplomat, Wellington was not affiliated to any political parties and continued to hold his position as Minister of Foreign Affairs even during the regime changes. But that isn't to say his position was always secure. The Koos received their fair share of threats throughout the anarchic years. The first was just a year after they moved to Peking. An attempt was secretly made on their lives when their food was laced with arsenic. The poison was targeted at Wellington but because Hui-lan was pregnant, the effect it had on her almost turned lethal. Doctors pumped her stomach out and it took several days before she began to recover. Fortunately, she and her baby were unharmed. Even before they could get over the terrifying incident, a second attempt occurred. A bomb was delivered to Wellington, disguised as a gift with a curious tag labeling the contents as precious antique gold seals from the Han Dynasty. By a stroke of luck and apprehensive premonition, Wellington instructed for the parcel to be discarded. Instead, the curious servant disregarded the order and took upon himself to open the parcel, detonating a fatal explosion which tragically took his life. The delivery man was caught but managed to escape without revealing the mastermind behind the act of terror.

The third harrowing experience was during a coup d'état by Feng Yu-hsiang, the Christian General, who turned traitor and broke establishment by seizing Peking in the autumn of 1924. Wellington, as a member of the ousted regime, was forced to flee but Hui-lan decided to stay, taking cover at the Peking Hotel, hoping things would settle. It was her first taste as a political outcast and an experience which she described as having "punctured her flourishing ego". It was also around the time when Young Marshal and Dogmeat General burst into her hotel suite and ended up having tea with her. The unannounced imposition turned out a blessing, for it was Young Marshal who later smuggled a letter to her, warning of the dangers if she continued to stay in Peking. Terrified, Hui-lan promptly packed her children and servants in her Rolls Royce and got a Canadian friend to drive them out of the city to meet her husband. When the Koos finally returned to Peking after the Christian General was kicked out, they found their beautiful home ruined, but the capital was now under the control of Young Marshal's father, Chang Tso-lin, the Old Marshal.

Four years later in 1928, Wellington found himself on the wrong side of history again when General Chiang's Kuomintang (KMT) army marched into Peking and overthrew Old Marshal. Wellington and Hui-lan had first taken refuge in Tianjin but when it became too dangerous for him, Wellington fled to Weihaiwei and sought asylum with the British – ironically, after having fought so hard for the removal of foreign concessions and unequal treaties in his country. Wellington was regarded a puppet for the northern warlords by the KMT and a warrant for his arrest was issued, but by then, he had left for France, and later, Canada on a fishing trip. Hui-lan's palatial home again was again confiscated. The local *tang-pu* (Party headquarters) turned it into Dr Sun Yat-sen's Memorial Hall, had the walls plastered with glue and without due consideration, undertook many ghastly alterations.

With the husband exiled, Hui-lan took charge. She returned to Peking and was completely dismayed to find her palace ruined. Without informing Wellington, she called the Mayor of Peking in disgust and "expressed her indignation that her private house could be taken over without even consulting the owner", as Wellington explained. The mayor responded emphatically that he would not raise any objections if she decided to restore the palace and further added – though rather sheepishly – that she should tell no one that he had given his consent. On that note, Hui-lan took back the property and restored it once again. No one said a word, apparently.

Meanwhile, KMT government attempted to reassert its authority by claiming the treaties between China and Japan were invalid. Up north, Old Marshal likewise took a firm stance against the Japanese by refusing to yield to their pressure for further concessions. Peeved, the Japanese had Old Marshal assassinated so that his son, Young Marshal, could succeed him to become ruler of Manchuria. They thought the young man could be easily manipulated. But Young Marshal deflected Japanese hopes and silenced his opposers by first, purging Japanese influence within his inner circle and executing two of his father's lieutenants who were pro-Japanese. The young ruler then raised the revolutionary flag in support of the KMT government. All this pleased General Chiang tremendously and as a reward, Young Marshal was made Vice-Commander-In-Chief. Soon, others began to hail him a "Hero of History" for his gesture to reunite China.

At this point, Wellington was about to give up on his political career and diplomatic life when Young Marshal offered him protection in Manchuria. While in Europe, Wellington had gathered crucial information about the military potential of Soviet Russia. Although Russia adopted a policy of restraint towards the West, their strategy for the Far East was not as forgiving. Concerned that the young Manchurian warlord might be pushing Russia to a "trial of arms", Wellington immediately sent a telegram to Young Marshal's advisor, warning him of the potential dangers of provoking the Russians. Within days, he received a message from the advisor with an invitation from Young Marshal to act as his consultant. Wellington initially declined and had his reasonings penned down, but before his letter could reach Manchuria, he received another telegram with a stronger plea for his return. Eventually, Wellington accepted the invitation and made his way to Mukden, or Shenyang as we know today. The two men spent much time together discussing politics and playing golf. One thing led to another, and Young Marshal having gained the trust of General Chiang, pressed for Peking to cancel Wellington's arrest warrant. Yet when it came to Wellington's warnings to him about Japanese encroachment in the north, the young ruler turned a deaf ear. Just about a year later, on a Friday autumn afternoon, a staged bomb detonated close to a Japanese owned railway line in Mukden. The false flag attack gave an excuse for the Japanese to invade Manchuria. Overnight, they seized Mukden and the rest was history. Rattled, Young Marshal sent for Wellington who by now was back in Peking. The KMT army could not offer any military assistance as they were too preoccupied with fighting the Communist in the hinterlands. With little option, General Chiang wired Wellington, made him Minister of Foreign Affairs and reinstated his diplomatic career. It is impossible to say exactly how crucial a role Hui-lan played in getting Wellington and Young Marshal together, but it was certainly a good thing she offered tea to her warlord friends that afternoon at the Peking hotel.

Hui-lan continued her friendship with the swashbuckling Dogmeat General, often playing poker with him and the other warlord friends. Despite his notorious reputation, she found him "delightfully outrageous". Likewise, he seemed to have a fondness for her, "the way a large, fierce animal might grow fond of a little bird". Towards the end, Dogmeat General sought Wellington's help for a passport when things got bad but was shot dead before he could leave China. Young Marshal too had a sincere fondness for her. She became close to his family life and saw both his wife, the uncrowned Queen of Manchuria, as well as his mistress, Edda Ciano, daughter of Mussolini, often – but never together. As the years progressed, Young Marshal and his wife became deeply addicted to narcotics, a habit which almost cost him his career. But perhaps his biggest mistake in life was to kidnap General Chiang and force him to agree to fight the Japanese. Young Marshal's impetuous action led him to be placed under house arrest by the KMT and under constant watch for the rest of his life. Life for him would never be the same again.

Whenever there was a power shift, Hui-lan would spend time in Shanghai. With the ongoing power struggles, Shanghai inevitably become the epicenter for everything – commerce, finance and cultural life. It was also the most cosmopolitan of all cities with many young Chinese mingling freely with foreigners. Strongly influenced by Hollywood and their newfound freedom, the new generation Chinese smoked, drank, bobbed their hair, dressed skimpily and mirrored the mannerisms of celebrities. Streets were always crowded. Fashionable supper clubs were popular, and so were big hotels and American jazz bands. There as everywhere, Hui-lan made friends – from lawmakers to gangsters to movie stars, to American magnates, European aristocrats and more. It was also in Shanghai that Hui-lan and Wellington's life began to drift apart. When they were in the city at the same time, they lived separately – she stayed in their house and he, with his family. But officially, they carried on as a couple for as long as Wellington remained a diplomat.

For all the excitement that was China, it is worth noting a small but telling reversal on Hui-lan's perspective on life. Many who saw her as the very essence of modernity were amazed to discover that she had also become the most devoted bastion of all things Chinese. No longer obsessed with foreign objects and culture, she developed a taste for old embroideries and silks as opposed to imported fabrics; imperial jades to diamonds; Chinese food to French cuisine and old architecture to modern shiny homes. Even her taste in pets shifted from thoroughbreds to the ancient Pekinese pooches. But perhaps the most out of keeping with the modern age was a change in her style of dressing. Right from the beginning, she took to wearing the unfashionable Manchu loose fitting long gowns, reveling in its simplicity and elegance, but adapted it to her own style by first shortening it to the ankle with slits a few inches up each side. Then, entirely by accident, she raised the slits all the way to the knee before altering the gown's length, fit, sleeves and trimmings to suit the occasion. At first, her experiments upset Shanghai's fashionistas who aspired the look of the European *beau monde*. People weren't sure what to think of these adaptions but soon enough, they began to imitate her with "flattering frequency". Whether she can lay claim as the first woman to cultivate this new style of dressing is a matter of conjecture, but Hui-lan certainly was at the forefront of securing Shanghai as the birthplace of the modern-day *qipao*. Coincidentally, just a few years later, General Chiang and Madame Chiang would launch the "New Life Movement" – a programme to reform social habits by reviving old virtues that had been lost during the transitional period of chaos and confusion. China was on its way to becoming a new nation.

Fig. 14: Lucy and her son, Hervey.
Source: Yao-hua Tan

Lucy Ho

26

Farewell to the Sugar King

Back in Singapore...

Tragedy struck in the early hours of a Sunday morning, on 3 June 1924. Quite suddenly, Tiong-ham had a cardiac arrest. He collapsed and died at home, five months short of his 58th birthday. Tiong-ham had always been considered a healthy man and never once complained about his well-being. In fact, the day before his death, he was discussing business matters with a friend, so his heart attack came as a total shock to everyone. News of his passing quickly circulated amongst the press the following days. Lucy's mother was among the first to arrive to lend support. Lucy was heavily pregnant and had four other very young children between the ages of six to one. With her mother's help, they began to prepare the funeral arrangements.

Nearly everything about the wake was non-conforming in the eyes of the Straits Chinese in Singapore, but then nearly everything about the Oei family was non-conforming anyway. Instead of appointing a Chinese funeral parlor, the family engaged the Singapore Casket Company, a newly set up European establishment in the city. Its manager, Mr. C.B. Webb, was himself an experienced undertaker and in all probability, extremely honoured to have the Oeis as a client. Unlike traditional Chinese funerals which can be exhaustingly comprehensive, Webb planned out a simplified but refined service. The wake was held at the family home and lasted for about a month as it took time for other family members from afar to make their way to pay their last respects. Hui-lan arrived with an American friend and her secretary, but without Wellington, who was dealing with a looming crisis back home – Tiong-ham had passed away four months before Christian General schemed his way and captured Peking. Curiously, her sister Tjong-lan and mother were not present either. Perhaps Tjong-lan was embroiled in her own divorce proceedings with Dr. Kan that kept her away from her father's funeral.

In the meantime, Webb arranged for a twelve-foot-long coffin made entirely of lead. It was common for European monarchs to be buried in lead-lined coffins, but extremely unusual for anyone, royalty or otherwise, to have a solid lead casket. Lead-lined coffins keep out moisture and preserve the body for up to a year while slowing down the decomposition process. They weighed an average of a quarter-ton. By comparison, Tiong-ham was laid to rest in a magnificent structure which weighed an immense five-tons, twenty times heavier than its lead-lined cousin, so heavy that a specially designed hearse had to be built from scratch to carry it. Javanese craftsmen were brought in to add etchings and the final touches to the coffin. The whole affair was kept private though newspapers tried their very best to report to the reading public how much the "Richest Chinese in the World" had left behind. In the meanwhile, Lucy gave birth to her fifth child.

On the Saturday morning of 2 July, exactly a month after his passing, Tiong-ham's coffin made its way back to Semarang. Adorned with grey silk draping, the magnificent grey coffin was carefully placed on the custom-built hearse mounted on a Clydesdale motor chassis which Webb himself drove. The cortege, which included a dozen cars of mostly family members, traversed Orchard, Stamford, and Robinson roads before heading to Tanjong Pagar port where *Giang Seng*, the same steamer Tiong-ham had arrived in three years earlier was docked. While the cars went ahead, Tiong-ham's sons, dressed in black suits as pallbearers, followed behind the hearse on foot. The journey to Tanjong Pagar took them three hours. A newspaper noted how unusual the entire procession was as there "was no crashing of cymbals or the medley of sounds which usually accompany processions of this nature, so that the cortege passed through the streets practically unnoticed".

Tiong-ham gave prior instructions that there should be no elaborate rituals, priests and public display at his funeral. Even the mourning garments were pared down considerably without the different graded mourning colours to determine the canon of relationships between the departed and the living. More noticeably, no one wore the melancholy burlap overcoat, with its equally gloomy looking headgear and footware popular amongst the Chinese in the Straits. No wonder the procession went by discreetly. By the time the pallbearers reached the wharf, it was almost noon. Waiting for them there was a large crowd who gathered for the final send off. Captain Dunlop, skipper of the *Giang Seng*, had the ship painted with a fresh coat of paint and a special enclosure was built on the main deck for the coffin. The following morning at 3am, *Giang Seng* set sail for Semarang with Tiong-ham's sons accompanying the coffin while the women boarded a different vessel.

The funeral took place the same day the coffin arrived. It was only then that Hui-lan met, for the first time, some of the other wives of Tiong-ham and their children. She noticed that all, except Lucy, were "exceptionally cheerful" and "full of giggle and gossip". Lucy seemed "genuinely sad", she thought. Swarms of people crowded around as they unloaded the weighty coffin from the boat to a beautifully draped hearse with an arrangement of flowers above the canopy. But there was one detail which appeared odd – instead of lion figurines positioned on top of the hearse as an indication that the deceased was a man, Tiong-ham's hearse had four cranes at each corner of the canopy – cranes, typically representing the female gender. Why that was so, no one knows. As the hearse made its journey, a cortege followed behind with his sons and daughters in the first row, followed by the rest of the family members. The convoy travelled through Semarang city to the hills of Simongan. By the side of the road, tens of thousands of people from around Java turned out to watch and pay their last respects.

The ceremony in Semarang was in keeping with Chinese customs. Procession flags and banners were carried in great numbers behind the cortege. Relatives who came within the five degrees of relationship wore white. Tiong-ham's sons appeared in the customary Chinese *changpao* and a white cotton band across their forehead. The eldest sons from each respective wife were further distinguished by holding a mourning staff – a wooden stick with a piece of white cloth attached to one end. The attire of the wives and other female members were confined almost entirely to a local dress code – *sarong kebaya* in full white with matching covered slippers. Not surprisingly, Hui-lan's choice of clothing stood out, not because of its richness or extravagance but because of its simplicity. What she wore was at the forefront of Chinese fashion, the New Culture attire. Appearing in a white top with bell-shaped elbow-length sleeves coupled with a midi-length white skirt with stockings, she was the only woman dressed in that fashion. The style evolved from the traditional *qipao* after the May Fourth Movement, thanks to New Culture female students who preferred a more practical and comfortable form of dressing. It became so iconic that the Chinese Government labelled it as "national attire" some years later. Something else set Hui-lan apart from the other female family members – she was the only female wearing a white cotton band across her forehead, a basic piece of accessory, but one which positioned her at the same rank as sons.

At length, the great procession reached the resting ground. The massive coffin was hoisted to a solid wooden footing above the tomb. When the last ritual was carried out, the funeral director shouted out "take up the coffin", a signal that the burial was about to reach its climax. Forty strong bearers wrestled with the ponderous coffin while another group hurried to remove the hefty footing underneath it. The funeral director took charge of their motions. On every directive he shouted out, the entire chorus of bearers responded with bellows like those of sailors heaving a stubborn anchor. As the coffin was slowly lowered, the cries and high-pitched wails from the mourners intensified amid the heaving roars. The cacophony of sounds reached a crescendo then died down when the coffin reached the ground. To anyone who has never experienced a Chinese burial, the sight and sound of this very last act would have been a moment of soul-stirring spectacle. Like a great symphonic piece with its various movements of joy, sorrow, glory and despair, Tiong-ham's life had finally come to an end. The remains of Asia's Sugar King was at last laid to long rest on Monday, 6 June 1924 in the Pengillin cemetery, next to his father.

Farewell to the Sugar King

Fig. 15: The beautifully draped hearse carrying Tiong-ham's remains with his sons, daughters and wives standing beside it. Hui-lan standing fourth from right and Lucy, standing next to little Jack.
Source: Audrey Oei Siok-lian.

Fig. 16: The elaborate coffin of Tiong-ham at the burial ground, Seen here with family, friends and associates paying their last respects.
Source: Audrey Oei Siok-lian.

27
Asia's Largest Estate

Needless to say, the great estate of Asia's richest man drew much interest from all sides – from disowned sons, from wives and daughters who were left *sans le sou* (penniless), from ex-in laws and even a disgruntled in-law who had not even met the deceased. Even the colonial government pressed their claims through the courts for a share of Tiong-ham's magnificent estate. One paper estimated that with a value of about 50 million Straits Dollars the death duty would be the "biggest amount" assessed by the government of the Straits Settlements. For context, the paper also noted that "next to the Sugar King's was that of the late Mr. Lee Choon-guan which amounted to about a quarter of a million dollars". Lee Choon-guan was a prominent businessman philanthropist, founder of the Straits Steamship Company and co-founder of the Chinese Commercial Bank in Singapore.

The multitude of legal battles gave newspapers plenty of stories to sell papers and lawyers ample opportunity to earn splendid fees. In the first four months, when the first legal action began, newspapers in Singapore and the Dutch East Indies ran over two hundred stories. The trials lasted fifteen years, involved dozens of lawyers and spread across three countries – the Dutch East Indies, the Straits Settlements and the Netherlands. From her relatively sheltered sphere of domesticity, Lucy found her life thrust into yet another radical world – the male-dominated world of estate management and the law. Tiong-ham entrusted management of his estate to three executors, Lucy and her two stepsons, Tjong-swan and Tjong-hauw. At just twenty-three, she was, together with her two slightly older stepsons, administering one of the most onerous and richest estates in Asia – quite a feat for a supposed "slave girl". What can be said for certain is that her appointment must have reflected Tiong-ham's confidence in her. Lucy was also dutiful and honest, qualities that came to seem all the more important in her role as executor. Tiong-ham wanted her to ensure the estate was dealt with according to the law while at the same time, carrying out his wishes.

Tiong-ham had eight official wives. One died before him and what happened to another remains uncertain. From these wives, they bore him twenty-six children – thirteen boys and thirteen girls. In his will, he would convey his vast holdings to nine sons, two daughters and one wife – but left five wives, four sons and eleven daughters portionless. Typical of the patriarchalism that dominated Chinese attitudes toward property and male descendants, Tiong-ham bequeathed the bulk of his estates to nine sons from three different mothers (wife number three, wife number four and wife number seven, Lucy). He also appointed three executors, one to represent each branch. The first executor was Tjong-swan from Tjik-nio, wife number three. Tjong-swan's mother gave birth to four sons but two sons, Tjong-tee and Tjong-yoe, were disinherited while another son was cut off with just $200,000. The second executor was Tjong-hauw whose mother was Mie-hwa, wife number four. He acted on behalf of his three brothers from the same mother. The third executor was Lucy who represented her four minor sons. Tiong-ham apparently knew of the rivalry between the two older sons, Tjong-swan and Tjong-hauw, and that there was a possibility they would gang up against Lucy who did not have an executive role in the business. A three-person executor structure, according to various sources, would serve as a balancing factor for decision-making purposes. Much to everyone's surprise, Lucy and her daughter would inherit nothing, but as executor of the estate, Lucy received a fee, enough for her and her children to be economically secure and live comfortably, until the boys came of age. Tiong-ham also left a million each to his two oldest daughters, Tjong-lan and Hui-lan and a million to their mother, his first wife Bing-nio, revealing his loyalty and affection for this branch of the family.

Exactly three weeks after Tiong-ham was laid to rest, the first legal action began when probate was sought by the executors but opposed by Tjong-tee and Tjong-yoe, the two disinherited sons. The executors hired Robinson, Tiong-ham's lawyer, to act on their behalf of the estate while the two defendant brothers each appointed their own lawyers. Tiong-ham made three wills over a period of three years – one, in haste, just before he left the Dutch East Indies in April 1921, a second in January 1922 and the final one in April 1923. The first will was in Dutch which apparently provided for all children and wives. Eight months later, in the second will, Tiong-ham made the decision to disown two sons and cut another off with just a token sum, a fraction of what the estate was worth. Tjong-tee and Tjong-yoe were under the father's payroll acting as his attorneys in Singapore and represented his interest in various businesses. According to family sources, both were disinherited for various reasons including getting involved in unscrupulous business dealings and marrying a Dutch woman, which Tiong-ham disapproved of. So furious was Tiong-ham that he refused to see Tjong-tee when he turned up at the Scotts Road residence. And when he tried to appease his father by appearing for his birthday the following year with the new wife, Tiong-ham refused to have the wife upstairs.

Both sons blamed Lucy for their disinheritance, claiming that she exerted undue influence on their father when he made his final will in Singapore. They further argued that the domicile of their late father was not the Straits Settlements and therefore contended the last will was invalid. Over the next few months, witnesses were called in to testify – Jogenjan, Tjong-swan, Tjong-tee and Lucy had to take the stand. Singapore feasted on the trial. Tiong-ham's absurdly huge estate, his disinherited sons and the excessively high war profit tax of the Dutch Indies were reported with relish by the newspapers. One paper noted how the English could not figure out why the Dutch Government, by raising taxes so high, would "slaughter the goose that laid the golden eggs". The case finally concluded four months later in November 1924. At the Supreme Court, Chief Justice Sir Walter Shaw delivered his judgement – that by purchasing Omdurman, by taking out an usher's writ, by instructing Jongejan to submit the writ to the Dutch authorities and by explicitly declaring his domicile in his final will, Tiong-ham had clearly shown his intention to permanently cut himself from the Dutch East Indies. Probate was therefore granted.

Still not satisfied with the judgement, Tjong-yoe took the initiative to appeal. Three weeks later, the Appeals Court dismissed the case on similar grounds. Even more greatly dissatisfied, the disowned sons, along with those who were left unprovided for, sought further legal advice. By 1926, their lawyers devised a strategy that would leave all of them 400,000 guilders richer in their pockets. They contended that according to the law of the Dutch East Indies, Tiong-ham could only freely dispose of one quarter of his estate and that they would be entitled to the remaining three-quarters, their legitimate portion. Under Dutch laws, sons and daughters inherited equal portions of the family estate and there were restrictions on cutting off a son, whereas English laws allowed the testator to do as he pleased. They threatened to bring the suits to enforce their claims in the Dutch court. So rather than going through another round of litigious dispute, both parties compromised and reached a settlement where the executors agreed to pay those who were left unprovided for 400,000 guilders each. The monies came from the nine male heirs, each contributing a million guilders as part of the compensation.

28
Femme Sole

Lucy, meanwhile, moved back to Semarang into Gergadji with the children and put Omdurman up for rent. While her sons remained minors, she performed virtually all the tasks that would have been managed by her husband, collectively making decisions regarding the vast estate and defending the family's interest in lawsuits. She soon found her legal and financial know-how publicly magnified and scrutinised. She hired her older brother, Paul, as attorney to represent the boys' interests. In her usual diligent and determined style, she enrolled herself and her two younger brothers, who were still in their final years of school, for typewriting classes. At the same time, Lucy and one of the younger brothers took up a course on stenography, presumably to better prepare themselves for court documentation work. They passed the exams and became some of, if not the only, Chinese in the Dutch East Indies to be qualified as office stenographers.

Her newly-acquired skill was put to good use when the following year in 1927, Lucy and her two other executors were dragged back to court. An in-law, Dr. Kan, husband of Tjong-lan, went to some lengths to lay his hands on his ex-wife's inheritance. According to Dutch laws, a wife had no authority to act or litigate without the consent of her husband, with two exceptions: first, a wife could litigate on the grounds of her husband's absence and second, on account of her husband's contrary interest. Tjong-lan then filed for divorce from the Dutch Cantonal Court in Amsterdam in June 1926, and in so doing, managed to get the legal permission she needed. Dr. Kan twice appealed, claiming that for their children's sake, he was the rightful person to manage the million-dollar legacy, but was ruled out each time. The ex-husband maintained the wife was extravagant with luxurious tendencies and "not a proper person to have control of the moneys". He then appealed against the divorce, then tried his luck in the Singapore Court by applying to be included as a party in the estate, but that too failed. Nevertheless, that wasn't the end of the in-law problems. Years later when Lucy was living in Holland, the same Dutch wife of Tjong-tee, who was by then a widow, found Lucy's name on the phone directory and decided to file a lawsuit against her as executor of the estate. Even though the judgement was found in favour of Lucy and the case dismissed, the constant stress and anxiety of preparing for court work would have taken a toll on Lucy.

Perhaps the most high-ranking legal battle was the one against the Commissioner of Stamps in Singapore concerning probate duties. Before the testator's assets could be distributed, probate needed to be obtained at court and to do that, duty had to be paid on the estate. The Commissioner valued Tiong-ham's estate at over 35 million Straits Dollars – the bulk of it, or roughly 80 percent, consisted of movable assets outside of the Straits Settlements. The remaining 20 percent were movable and immovable assets owned by him in the Straits Settlements. Duty was set at 12 percent of the value of the estate, which came up to roughly 5 millions Straits Dollars – a fabulous windfall for the Crown and by far the largest amount ever to be assessed in the history of the Straits Settlements. The executors could pay the duty in ten annual instalments, at an interest of four and a half percent per annum. By 1931, the executors had paid out a sum of 3.8 million but decided to take up a case against the Commissioner for what they believed to be a wrongful inclusion in the valuation by the Commissioner. They claimed that estate duty should only be payable on the movable and immovable properties located in Singapore which were valued at slightly over 7.7 million Straits Dollars and the duty on which would be a little over 930,000. These were mainly Tiong-ham's real estate holdings, shares in the Overseas Chinese Bank and the shipping company. The executors maintained that the remaining movable assets of twenty-seven million were outside British jurisdiction and therefore should not assessable under the provisions of the Stamp Ordinance.

Just before they took the matter to court, Tjong-swan, head of the Oei Tiong-ham Group, sold his entire shareholdings to the other eight heirs. He stepped down from the Group as director in January 1931, relinquished all responsibilities and left with his family to Holland where they settled in Haarlem. Whether it was a power tussle between him and Tjong-hauw or whether he sensed troubles ahead that led to his stunning decision cannot be verified, but his move rattled the business community as well as the family. From nine, the group now had eight shareholders split into two equal groups. Tjong-hauw stepped up as the new chief and Lucy held power to the other half of the business. As the family later acknowledged, after Tjong-swan exited the business, there was no longer a balancing factor. All this meant that there was a good deal of tension in the air. Tjong-hauw was in a much stronger position than Lucy and attempted to further strengthen his position by changing the Company's articles of association. When she found out, she hired lawyers and successfully fought it out in court. Although she might not have had similar powers as the chief executive, she was still a notable force, controlling fifty percent while the rest, just twelve and a half percent each.

The pressing case against the Commissioner, meanwhile, came before the Supreme Court in August 1931. The presiding judge, Justice Terrell, delivered his judgement which completely shocked the government. It ruled in favour of the executors and held that the Commissioner of Stamps was required to repay the excess duty plus interest as well as legal fees back to the estate – all of which roughly came up to three million Straits Dollars. From a financial point of view, this was a critical case for the government. Just over a year earlier was the onset of the Great Depression. Consumer spending and investment plummeted, causing steep declines in industrial output and employment. Government surpluses dwindled, land values continued to drop, and the value of foreign trade declined drastically as commodity prices collapsed. The once crucial opium revenue which used to contribute roughly half of government revenues had also been on a steady decline so much so that by the end of 1931, government coffers faced a deficit of $20 million. To plug the shortfall, the Legislative Council urgently looked at various sources, from raising income taxes to duties on liquor, tobacco, and petrol to counter the decline. The last thing they needed was to have to repay a substantial sum with money which they were already short of.

In December 1931, lawyers acting for the Commissioner appealed against the decision, but the Supreme Court's finding was unanimously upheld. The Commissioner then applied for leave to appeal to take the matter to the colony's highest court, the Privy Council, but leave was refused. They tried again and applied for special leave as the case was deemed to be of high public importance. The Commissioner's persistence paid off and in March 1933, the case was taken to the Privy Council. To the delight of the Crown, the three-member panel at the Privy Council reversed Justice Terrell's decision and ruled in favour of the Commissioner of Stamps. So instead of suffering a loss, the Crown now gained an extra million in addition to the $3.8 million it had already collected. Even though it was only a quarter of the total sum payable, the amount was still so large that it was cause for a mention by the Colonial Secretary in the *Annual Report on the Social and Economic Progress of the People of the Straits Settlement* of 1933. In retrospect, things could have been worse for the beneficiaries. During Tiong-ham's time, estate duty was comparatively modest at twelve percent on estates exceeding 1.5 million Straits Dollars. Recognising how reliable it was as a revenue source, and so minimal was its political cost, Britain raised the rate to twenty percent in 1931 and again in 1940 just before WWII, to sixty percent. It is quite ironic to think that back in the Dutch East Indies, Foreign Orientals, like the natives, were exempt from estate duties.

As executor who had half control on the wealthiest estate in Asia, Lucy's status within the family and society was elevated to that of a *femme sole* (a woman possessing legal independent standing). We also know the kind of responsibilities and the tremendous strain she endured in administering the estate – engaging in countless activities inside and outside the courts which demanded a great deal of vigilance. She dealt with kin, employees, lawyers, accountants, creditors and government officials, while, at the same time, confronting litigants and court officials. She would have had the financial competency to make critical decisions on what asset to dispose of to raise funds for legal disputes. These transactions involved a great deal of money, often drawing up millions of guilders at a time. Through her work as estate administrator, she demonstrated a familiarity in legal and financial matters which allowed her to navigate in her own right and manage her own affairs even as she drew upon multiple sources of influence available to her. This gave her immense legal and financial authority within the family and society.

Despite not having worked at Kian Gwan or any of Tiong-ham's companies like Tjong-swan and Tjong-hauw, Lucy did nevertheless show good working knowledge of the business and financial transactions. She spent a good deal of time with Tiong-ham, acting as translator and personal bookkeeper for him in the last three to four years before his death. She would have cultivated certain financial knowledge and expertise along the way but more importantly, gained incredible insights into certain dealings and Tiong-ham's line of thought. The years she spent by his side prepared her for the financial responsibilities of widowhood.

29
Matriarch

In town, Lucy was known as Mrs. Oei Tiong-ham-Ho, but at home, she was affectionately called Sisi. Even when court proceedings were at its busiest, she found time to manage Gergadji and the children. As a single parent, she assumed the added responsibility of not only feeding, nurturing and training but also of fulfilling the duties of the father as breadwinner and disciplinarian. Lucy was firm and resolute in the way she raised her children. The children were reminded to never flaunt their wealth, to show humility, and to be independent, hardworking, dutiful and above all, honourable. Lucy made it a point to find out from other mothers how much they gave their children as allowance, then provided the same to her own children. She would make them write down what they spent every day and why they spent it. While other children from wealthy families were chauffeured to school, Lucy's children were encouraged to cycle – an over-two-kilometer ride down Holle Weg (Jalan Kyai Salleh) and into Randoesari (Jalan Pandaranan) before turning into Bodjong (Jalan Pemuda) and into school.

Lucy's children were also close to Tjong-hauw's children who lived just down the road at the corner of Randoesari and Holle Weg. They were around the same age and went to the same school. Two of Lucy's stepdaughters, Nini and Gerda, lived with them in Gergadji. They were Tjong-swan and Tjong-hauw's sisters from two different mothers. The children played together, their families met for meals, and while some felt differently, there was an implicit understanding that Lucy was the matriarch of the Oei family. This held true for the Ho side of the family as well. Lucy assumed the familial role as financial provider for the entire family. She paid for the education of her siblings and some of her nieces and nephews. She supplemented her parents' income every month and absorbed major costs for renovations and maintenance of the family home in Kranggan. They practically relied on her for financial aid.

But it must be said that the money she gave came from her own source of income as administrator. Nothing was drawn from her children's legacy, not even to pay for their upbringing. In fact, she was remarkably principled such that she made her daughter enter a contract with her brothers to voluntarily waive any rights that may arise from lawsuit against the estate. That was Lucy's honest devotion to her job.

If there was one thing Lucy embraced with great enthusiasm in life, it was education. For her, learning was the gateway to the future and that girls should also be accorded full and equal educational rights as boys. Perhaps her interest in education might have also stemmed from her own responsibilities managing her husband's estate, compelling her to continuously improve herself. It was for this reason that she decided to give her children a first-class education in Europe. In December 1933, three months after the legal tussle with the Commissioner of Stamps ended, the young family boarded the *Melchior Treub* and headed for Holland. They waved to family and friends who came to see them off. Many sent bouquet of flowers to wish the family bon voyage. Jack, her eldest son, was already in Holland, having been sent there two years earlier to attend school. Also on board were Lucy's mother and brother Paul. They accompanied the young family as far as Singapore before parting ways.

Europe was liberating, away from town gossips and public scrutiny that seemed to tail the family everywhere they went in Semarang. No one really knew who they were, and they could get on with life in serene anonymity. Lucy found a large brick house in an old neighbourhood on Parkweg 19 in the Hague. The house had a neatly landscaped garden as most houses there did, five bedrooms, a separate living and dining room and a generous kitchen with a large bay window. Nearby was the

Scheveningen woods, a large, forested park with walking trails surrounding a pond and roughly sixty kilometers away was Tjong-swan's family house in Haarlem. Parkweg soon became the heart and the family home for friends and relatives visiting from Semarang during summer months. Lucy was welcoming and generous to her guests, inviting them over for meals, offering them board and extending her home to members of family who came to Holland for further studies. Nowhere were the family dynamics more perfectly illustrated than during Nini's marriage. Nini, who had been under Lucy's care in Semarang and Singapore when Tiong-ham was alive, migrated to Holland to live with her brother, Tjong-swan. When Nini decided to wed, the family agreed for her to have her reception in Parkweg, the family house. To Western eyes, this may not mean much, but for the Chinese, what all this meant, rather interestingly, was the acknowledgement of Lucy as the head of the Oei family – even by Tjong-swan, the eldest heir and blood brother to Nini.

After having spent Christmas in St Moritz with her children one year, Lucy decided to switch their education curriculum and sent the younger four to Switzerland for schooling. Being the metropolis of the colony, life in Holland was not what Lucy had expected and felt that it was not the right environment to bring up her children. The following year, she put the boys into the Lyceum Alpinum Zuoz, one of the most prestigious boys' school in the world, near St Moritz, and enrolled Lovy into an equally famed boarding school for girls sixty kilometers away, the Hochalpines Institut Ftan. When her eldest son Jack came of age in 1940, he returned to Semarang to be properly installed as a shareholder of the group. Lucy completed her role as administrator when the youngest son graduated as an aeronautical engineer and took his position in the family business in Semarang. She was, needless to say, an exception – never once flaunting her wealth nor her position, guiding and sustaining her family as honourably as she could and when the time came, stepping aside, having fulfilled her role in keeping the family fortune intact. What's even more unusual was that even though she was close to her children, she chose to spend her life independently, pursuing personal fulfillment and autonomy, in quiet obscurity in the southern city in Switzerland's Italian-speaking Ticino region.

Switzerland, a tiny nation in the heart of Europe, has no natural resources but had qualities of what she held dear. Among them was a superb education system. The schools of Switzerland were renowned for their liberal and democratic approach to education, both of which have played an important role in building a prosperous, progressive, and peaceful nation. Lucy enrolled herself in vocational courses in Lugano learning languages and all she could to develop herself. The little country was also a prime example of cultural pluralism, a distinct asset which afforded people from different cultures to live happily together. With its four diverse subcultures of German, French, Italian and Romansh, Swiss society could reliably prosper in an orderly manner and co-exist together in harmony. By then, she had developed a more resolute philosophy; it was no longer travelling which made her happy. She had discovered that it was solitude itself that gave her comfort. Lastly, there was one other thing that materially influenced her decision to settle in Switzerland – a lower tax system, something which Tiongham would have gladly approved.

Lucy passed away in 1963, aged sixty-four.

Matriarch

Fig. 17: Lucy (second from left) with her son Jack, Maud and a relative.
Source: Yao-hua Tan.

Fig. 18: Source: Yeap Chin-joo

30

Ida

30
Ida

The youngest Oei to inherit from the settlement of Tiong-ham's vast estate was Ida, the second daughter from wife number five, Tjiang-tjoe, and our third protagonist. Ida was only ten when Tiong-ham passed away. She barely knew her father, a circumstance that almost certainly applied to most of his children. Young Ida grew up in a different age from Hui-lan and Lucy. She was a whole generation younger than her famous sister and twelve years younger than her stepmother. By the time she was born, the world had changed. Foot binding was outlawed, and so was keeping a queue. Throughout the world, industrialisation offered women more opportunities to leave home, go to school and get a job. More women were stepping forward into public spaces and actively questioning the traditional place of a woman in society. Crucial for them was intellectual freedom – to be able to think, express and discover themselves and their identity. For Chinese women, however, the world became cloudy, slightly vague, somewhat ambiguous. Not only were they confronted with the question of what it meant to be a modern woman but more precisely, a modern Chinese woman.

Ida spent most of her childhood in Singapore. Her older sister, Noes was married off to Yeap Kim-hoe, a Straits-born Chinese whose father was Tiong-ham's business partner, Yeap Chor-ee. Chor-ee, a Hokkien who came to Penang in 1885, first worked as an itinerant barber before starting a small trading business. Towards the end of 1900, he met Tiong-ham who by then had gone into the manufacturing of white sugar in a big way. Chor-ee bought Tiong-ham's sugar on consignment, then sold locally and to distant markets. By the turn of the 20th century, he accumulated so much capital that he single handedly funded the establishment of his own bank. With a reliable business associate, the next most natural thing to do was to marry their children and seal future relations with one another. And so, in true Chinese fashion, arrangements were made between Tiong-ham and Chor-ee for Noes to marry Chor-ee's son, Kim-hoe. The children, of course, had no say in the matter. So, in October 1923, six months after Tiong-ham drafted his final will, Noes and Kim-hoe performed the tea ceremony and became man and wife.

The newlyweds had a house on Tiverton Lane, the Chinese mercantile part of town, where they lived together with young Ida and their mother, Tjiang-tjoe. Ida was sent to the Convent Girl's School in Singapore of which her father Tiong-ham was a great benefactor. Both Noes and Ida were multilingual and could speak English, Malay, Mandarin, Dutch fluently, as well as some French. As the years progressed, Ida was exposed much to Singapore's fast-changing lifestyle. Singapore, being the centre of cosmopolitanism in the colony, saw the birth of new public spaces, mass media and the rise of a consumer culture in the mid 1920s. Periodicals and magazines began providing women with new cultural content, focusing not only on etiquette and beauty but also encouraging women's rights and introducing them to the notions of education and equality. Cinemas, dance halls and coffee shops boomed while a new type of women's press overtook the humdrum of radio. Movies which had become the world's most popular form of entertainment further fortified this feminine appeal through its leading ladies. Typical of this new age was a subculture of women called flappers – young fashionable women who embodied the idea of a free spirit and embraced a life viewed by many as disdainful. They were modern and independent and often pushed barriers in economic, political, and sexual freedom. Such independence brought with it other rights among which was the right to choose to be married and the right to choose one's husband. Hollywood stars like Clara Bow, Olive Thomas, and Anna May Wong, the first Chinese Hollywood movie star, glamourised the image of flappers. Women's lives were also presented with another modern development – electricity. By 1920s most houses in Singapore had electricity which meant homes could have new appliances like irons, fridges and sewing machines which, in turn, gave women more leisure time. Against this backdrop, clever entrepreneurs from the cosmetics and hairdressing industries began to tailor their products to women, aggressively marketing the idea of glamour and beauty as a form of attraction to the opposite sex – a craze which quickly led to the sexual objectification of women. As Anna May Wong once said, the sure way to flapperism was "real make up, short skirts, fast patter and an attempt to be blasé".

Just as the world was getting friendlier to women – more liberation, more education, more say and more rights – an opposing undercurrent was fermenting in the background to bottle them up again. The general concern in Singapore was that the youth had abandoned themselves to wayward behaviours, more specifically, to the irresistible forces of Westernisation and partly to the influences of local culture. There was a need to contain the degeneration and so a few prominent members of society, including Dr. Lim Boon-keng, responded by launching a series of social programmes of a moral nature to redefine the Chinese identity. They called the programmes cultural self-assertion which had similar aspirations as the New Life Movement spearheaded by General and Madame Chiang in 1930s. On the one hand, they believed in reviving several important Chinese traditions, such as preservation of the Chinese language and retaining Confucianism as a religion and social ideology. On the other hand, they wanted to eliminate "useless customs", archaic in nature, in Chinese rituals, especially those relating to marriage ceremonies, funeral rites, and mourning rules so that it became less tedious to get married or to die.

Again, women were recognised as agents of change. The reformist believed that women's influence in molding the new generation of Straits Chinese proved crucial. But first, women needed to be educated, because if they were uneducated, they would be ineffective to social reforms. Women should be educated but should not pursue a career for if they did, they would take away jobs from the men. Education was only to help them in their roles at home and not for them to function in public. It was not meant for them to gain knowledge, but rather, to instill character and develop maternal instincts for them to be good wives and good mothers. Women were also required to dress in traditional Chinese attire instead of adopting a modified version of the Malay dress, the sarong kebaya. They should learn to speak Chinese rather than Malay so that they could pass on the language of the "mother tongue". All these requirements were parcelled together with the notion that Chinese women must be shielded from the debauchery and liberal temperament of the West, namely, flappers. Too much individualism was not in the best interest of the community, asserted the reformists. And it was in this puzzling conundrum around gender roles that Ida became acculturated with it.

Ida grew up to be a high-spirited, vivacious, and intelligent girl with a taste for travel, fast cars, and horses. She also enjoyed the outdoors, played tennis, golf and learnt how to ride horses. Ida was also fashion-conscious from an early age, always clad in pretty dresses and wearing her hair in different styles – bobbed, long or permed. By all appearances, she was exceptionally pretty with an engaging smile, thick dark hair, attractive eyes, and a petite physic just like her mother in her younger days. Ida was also immensely sociable and had a winning charm, a stark contrast to her sister Noes, who was a lot more reserved. But then, something happened to her early on in life which she might not have been fully aware of. When she was just ten years of age, she was betrothed to Noes' younger brother-in-law, Hock-hoe. He was nine.

As Equals: The Oei Women of Java

Fig. 19: Yeap Chor-ee's wife, sons and daughters-in-law. Standing from left: Ida Oei, Noes Oei, Yeap Hock-hin, Yeap Kim-hoe, Yeap Lean-seng, Yeap Hock-hoe. Seated from left: Lee Cheng-kin, Yeap Chor-ee. Early 1920s. Source: House of Yeap Chor-ee.

31
An Arranged Marriage

The Yeaps and Oeis shared some similarities but were quite different in many other ways. Chor-ee migrated during the great diaspora, at a time when hundreds of thousands of Chinese poured out of China and to lands afar. Chor-ee was illiterate, but he was hardworking, trustworthy and honest, qualities that drew Tiong-ham to him. Both men were around the same age. Both were Hokkien – Chor-ee came from the neighbouring district of Lam-oa (Nan'an), slightly northwest of where the Oeis originated in China. But unlike Tiong-ham, Chor-ee grew up in a household that was impoverished. He started life as an orphan, in circumstances quite unfortunate. When he arrived in Penang, quite ironically, he made a living in a trade which Tiong-ham was not overly excited about – that of shaving and plaiting the queue. Both shared similar ambitions and entrepreneurial spirit, but they differed in the ways they managed their businesses. Tiong-ham preferred Western methods whereas Chor-ee relied on the conventional Chinese kinship arrangements to conduct his business. Chor-ee was notoriously thrifty. He would not, for instance, appear in a carriage decked with flowers and youthful maidens on parade along the streets of the most fashionable capital in the world. Even more ridiculous was having to pay good money for it. One other striking difference that separated them – Chor-ee was deeply conservative. He was exceedingly traditional in his thinking that for the sake of progeny and lineage, he would subscribe to posthumous marriages. He had a daughter-in-law from China brought into the family as a bride for one of his sons who died at an early age. Unsurprisingly, the young bride had bound feet. Any other modern girl would surely have objected to such arrangements.

Ida's future husband, Hock-hoe, was at the other end of the personality spectrum from her. He was, by all accounts, a solitary and watchful young man. He was also the only son from Chor-ee's youngest wife, Cheng-kin. Chor-ee married four times – his first wife was Kim-hoe's mother, but she continued to live in China for the most part of her life to look after the ancestral tablets. Chor-ee's second wife was sister of a respectable merchant in Penang who, shortly after the marriage, ran off with a Chinese sorcerer after giving birth to two children while the third wife died soon after giving birth to a son. When Chor-ee married Cheng-kin, she was just fifteen and he, forty-five. Their marriage coincided around the same time when Lucy became Tiong-ham's wife. A year later, Cheng-kin gave Chor-ee a daughter, then a son. As the only natural-born son for Cheng-kin, Hock-hoe led a protected life. Although he grew up in a privileged household, his father's frugality and austere disposition was legendary. Chor-ee was not an indulgent parent, despised idleness and forbade his children to engage in any vices including gambling, smoking, or drinking. Almost the moment they were born, they were expected to be obedient, dutiful, filial, and hardworking. Young Hock-hoe grew up under this grave Confucian bearing of his illustrious father.

He was sent to Penang Free School, the oldest English-medium school for boys in the country but was at best, a mediocre student, neither academically inclined nor sporty. While several affluent Chinese families sent their children to England for further studies, Chor-ee wanted his son close by and chose Singapore for his college education instead. A well-told story was that because of his matched future with Ida, Hock-hoe was held back from going abroad, which became a source of resentment that he later recounted in life. When he returned from Singapore, he worked as an assistant at his father's bank. Unlike his older stepbrother, Kim-hoe, who was suave and had an effortless charm about him, Hock-hoe was self-contained and a serious young man. Kim-hoe played polo while Hock-hoe would prefer to watch from the

An Arranged Marriage

grandstand. In contrast to his brother, socialising was not Hock-hoe's strong suit and he chose to remain close to a small circle of friends throughout his adult life. Despite his inhibitions, Hock-hoe was a dashing young man and with his family wealth, he was, to many, an irresistible catch. When Ida turned eighteen, Kim-hoe, her sister Noes and mother all moved to Penang and made the island their new home. She was to prepare for her new life as Mrs. Yeap Hock-hoe.

The wedding was set on 22 November 1933, six days short of Hock-hoe's nineteenth birthday. Ida had just turned twenty, two months earlier. It was by far the most extravagant wedding Penang had ever seen for a while. The Great Depression left thousands abruptly broke and unemployed. Morale plunged. Residents were deeply disenchanted and any cause for celebration was a welcome change. The newspaper, much excited, called it "Wedding of the Year". Those who were invited were equally thrilled for the wedding was to be held at the Homestead, a recently purchased piece of real estate by Chor-ee, two doors down from his family home, The Aloes on Northam Road. Known as the grandest mansion in the colony, Chor-ee bought Homestead from a shipping and real estate investor in the early 1930s. Bankrupted by the economic slump, the owner, had in turn, inherited the property from his late father who commissioned the architects Messrs. Stark & McNeil to build this mansion in 1919. The firm was well-known for helping the rich spend money by building houses for them of sumptuous grandeur and Homestead was among the few on Northam Road. The property was also the first to hit the market when the economy collapsed. At first, Chor-ee was not interested but after much persuasion from the wife, he yielded and reportedly paid $600,000 for the mansion. The family added a new extension and a pavilion with a small theatrette by the sea and moved in a few months before the wedding day.

The Yeaps and Oeis families agreed and settled on a type of ceremony known as the Reformed Wedding – a cross between traditional Chinese and English weddings. Chor-ee and Cheng-kin would have favoured a traditional wedding for their son, but times were changing and their new daughter-in-law was not likely going to settle for anything less. Held over just a day or so, nuptials often involved a handful of rites – the most important being the tea ceremony. The high point for the young bride was not having to wear the antiquated Chinese wedding costume and its equally outmoded head dress. For fashion-conscious Ida, this suited her very well and in true movie-star style, she appeared in an exquisite white laced wedding gown which flowed out into a trailing train. On her head, she wore a juliet cape veil with beaded floral lace and accessorised with a sumptuous, studded crystal handle ostrich fan. Escorted by a handsome Hock-hoe in tuxedo, they both looked absolutely stunning. Family and friends were invited to witness the tea ceremony, the symbolic act of marriage in a reformed wedding and the signing of the registry, the legal form. In true Western custom, the ceremony ended with the cutting of the cake.

Even guest entertainment was a hybrid blend of East and West. Chor-ee invited over three hundred of the family's local guests for dinner the night of the ceremony. The caterers, staff, and extra hands laboured throughout the day to ensure the evening went smoothly. Food and drinks were lavished freely. Guests mingled but also found the opportunity to view the mansion and its grounds. Many of them had never seen the interior and back gardens of the famous house. Ronggeng, a dance culture of Javanese origin was staged to entertain the guests and there was a mix of popular tunes for enthusiastic dancers until late into the night. The following evening, a different kind of celebration was given by the host. This time, seventy of their European guests were invited to an elegant sit-down dinner in the formal dining hall of Homestead. Although not knowing much English himself, Chor-ee sat through the evening watching the guests indulge themselves. Champagne was flowing, speeches were made and a three-course dinner was served.

There is no doubt that Ida and Hock-hoe's extravagant wedding

An Arranged Marriage

was a display of how much Chor-ee and Cheng-kin approved of the union. By acquiring Homestead, getting it ready and putting on an elaborate ceremony at a time when the global economy had slumped to an all-time low, it was undoubtedly the most lavish marital affair the family had ever hosted. None of Chor-ee's other sons had been so sumptuously honoured. Noes and Kim-hoe's wedding, by contrast, was a modest affair. Their ceremony was held in a terrace house on Tiverton Lane in Singapore without much pomp and splendour. Aside from a simple announcement of the date and venue of the wedding, nothing else was mentioned by the press – all fairly low-key in retrospect – despite the presence of the father of the bride and Chor-ee's esteemed business partner, Tiong-ham. After the wedding, Ida moved into Homestead as Hock-hoe's wife. The newly-weds occupied the main wing of the mansion and so began their new life as husband and wife. Chor-ee and Cheng-kin resided quietly in the humble apartments of the new extension and spent their leisure time indulging in Chinese operas, Chor-ee's passion from boyhood. The in-laws had hoped for their new daughter-in-law to learn the social attitudes and expectations of her new family, and to pass it on to her children when the time came.

But while the in-laws remained hopeful, the newly-weds felt quite differently. They were thrust into a marriage against their wishes and compelled to follow an arrangement that had been planned over a decade ago.

Fig. 20: Homestead, Penang.
Source: House of Yeap Chor-ee

An Arranged Marriage

Fig. 21: Ida and Hock-hoe. 1933.
Source: House of Yeap Chor-ee.

32
When Two Poles Apart

At 5:40pm, on a Sunday evening of 8 December 1940, almost seven years after the marriage, Ida gave birth to her first child, a baby boy. Chor-ee who was already 72 years old at this stage and had not been blessed with any grandchildren from Hock-hoe. In a society where pedigree and lineage counted for a lot, the birth of a son mattered because the family line could only be perpetuated by boys. Boys also supposedly bring honour to their ancestors. Girls, once married, must bid farewell to her father's ancestors, and embrace those of her husband's. All this followed from the patriarchal Confucian teachings that dominated Chinese thinking. Added to the fact that this baby boy was born in the Year of the Dragon, the mightiest of the Chinese zodiac signs, and more importantly, a grandson of Oei Tiong-ham, his birth would have been the most eagerly anticipated in the Yeap family household.

But alas, it wasn't so. In one of the most intensely dramatic turn of events Northam Road had ever recorded, or for that matter, the whole town, the baby boy turned out not to be Hock-hoe's, but another man's. What can be said about Ida and Hock-hoe was that whatever happiness they found in life was not within the boundaries of marriage. Right from the very beginning, Ida withdrew from the marital bed and slept in a separate room next to Hock-hoe's, and so began their years of loveless existence. The marriage was never consummated. A probable reason for the breakdown of their marriage was that their personalities could not be more different – one was an extrovert, the other an introvert. Ida was also a year older than Hock-hoe which might not mean much when you're in your early twenties but would have left an impression if they were in their early teens. Both knew each other when they were ten years old, possibly younger. Ida was also much more exposed after her education in Singapore. Hock-hoe revealed years later to his children that they were incompatible from the outset. Communication between them was like "hen and duck". Evidently missing in their marriage was the romance and awe at the beginning of every relationship – the thrill of the pursuit, the whisper of sweet words, the perfume of roses, the sweetness of chocolate and music that engages the heart. Lim Chong-eu, a school mate and later, Chief Minister of Penang, recounted how anxious Hock-hoe looked when he personally came to school one day to hand an invitation to his ex-teacher to attend his wedding. Well, he had a lot to be anxious about.

Even if their personalities were similar, there was a general view, more or less universal, that modern girls were "unmarriageable girls". In September 1931 an article appeared in the *China Weekly Review* highlighting what seemed to be two catastrophic issues facing China – the state of the economy resulting in high unemployment rate and China's "unmarriageable modern girls". The article suggested that because of Western influences, China had undergone considerable social and political changes, that moral decline was on the rise and concluded that the husband of a modern girl would not be the "master of the family". The marriage, according to the article, would eventually end in divorce. At the end, the author left his reader with a last thought – "who dares venture to marry a modern girl?" Concerned the article might discourage parents from sending their daughters to school, a reader sparked off a long series of debates that lasted for over a year by requesting newspapers to allow ongoing discussions of the subject in their correspondence column. Opinions subsequently poured in. What was notable was the number of people who agreed with the article's view. Not surprisingly, those who agreed were mostly men. The handful who disagreed signed off anonymously with names like "marriageable", "modernism" and *audi alterem partem* (listen to the other side).

Presumably, they were women. What the article and ensuing comments offered were insights into the thinking of the times.

Arranged marriages had worked for generations because a woman had to submit herself to a man, endure anguish with grace and often do without the affections from the husband. A wife was merely domestic and her only interest in life was to care for her family. Silence and obedience were her virtues. Ida, regrettably for Hock-hoe, was none of that. Growing up in Singapore would have exposed her to the popular culture that had consumed the imaginations of the younger generation – the flapper lifestyle.

Something else set Ida aside from many other young brides – her fabulous wealth. As settlement with the executors, both she and Noes came to inherit 400,000 guilders in cash each, which might not sound like a huge amount, but considering that the average adult Javanese male was only earning one hundred and sixty guilders a year in 1930, it was no meagre sum. In Straits Dollar equivalent, her inheritance amounted to over half a million dollars, making her twice as rich as Lee Choon-guan, who died the same year as Oei Tiong-ham and whose estate was valued at a quarter of a million dollars. Compared to her husband Hock-hoe, Ida was flush with cash. Hock-hoe, who earned a basic salary working as an assistant at his father's bank, was asset rich but not cash rich. Despite owning shares in his family bank, his father refused to declare any dividends, preferring to plough profits back into real estate rather than distribute out to shareholders. It was only when estate duties were raised to sixty percent in 1940 did Chor-ee relent and, for the first time in the bank's history, paid out a five percent dividend in 1941.

There is no doubt that Ida's inheritance allowed her many excesses, and the 1930s was a great age for such indulgences. It was also a great source of tension between wife and husband. Struck by the harsh austerity of the Great Depression, people were desperate for diversions and found ways to have fun. Inexpensive amusements like board games such as Scrabble and Monopoly came onto the scene. Night clubs and cabarets became popular venues to socialise, dance and show off one's fashion. The 1930s was also Hollywood's golden age. Movies offered an exhilarating form of escape, inspiring glamour not only in fashion but also in lifestyle. Two inventions that were exemplary objects of modernity and glitziness, constantly featured in movies were motorcars and airplanes. They captured the imagination of the masses and inevitably became high-end recreational toys for the rich and famous.

So, when the Penang Flying Club first opened its doors for membership in 1934, Ida and Noes were the first ladies to sign up for flying lessons in Penang. The club had three new De Havilland Gipsy Major Moth planes with a British instructor in charge of the training programme. Based at the Bayan Lepas aerodrome, the club had access to one of the best runways in the country. Airplanes first featured in that part of the world about twenty years earlier when a flying Dutchman by the name of Louis Bouwmeester Jr visited the Settlement and gave a series of flights on the *Antoinette*, a monoplane with outstretched wings and a slender elongated body that gave it the appearance of a dragonfly in 1911. Not long after that, aviation tragedies began appearing on newspapers, immediately drawing attention to the dangers of these flying machines and at the same time horrifying the world at large. The fact that they were dropping out of the skies like flies while safety and engineering concerns were still at large hardly seemed to matter to these two Oei girls. Ironically, it was this danger that gave flying an air of romance and allure. In any event, by the time Noes obtained her Class "A" licence in August 1935 as well as the distinction of being the first Chinese woman to fly solo in the colony, Ida had already switched interests and was on to another pursuit – globetrotting.

In July 1935, less than eighteen months after her wedding, Ida took off on a cruise to Europe, again without her estranged husband. Her partner in crime for this thrilling adventure was her childhood friend, Chi-chi. Chi-chi and Ida were close, not only because they were related

– Chi-chi was married to one of Tiong-ham's sons from wife number three – but it seemed they shared many interests. Both were famously high-spirited. One of Chi-chi's wilder feats was making headlines in 1924 when she gave a police officer an "exciting chase" in their motorcars on Stamford Road. The bewildered police officer managed only to get a fleeting glimpse of her car number plate before he lost sight of her. All that he could do was issue her a summon for "rash driving". Both ladies were attractive and highly fashionable. The most influential tastemaker in Singapore and the first woman to be awarded the Member of the British Empire, Mrs. Lee Choon-guan, often had them as her guests at social events and house parties at Mandalay Villa. Ida thrived in these social gatherings. Her liveliness, charm and magnetism often made her the centre of attraction in any company. As Vera Ardmore, female columnist for the *Morning Tribune* noted of Ida, "Here is another modern Chinese girl. She drives a car, she flies an aeroplane, swims, dives, plays a good game of tennis and rides and is yet as exotic and glamorous as a hot house flower in the evening. She and her friends all in the very simple Chinese gowns of the loveliest materials, made a most attractive group and many an admiring glance both from residents and tourists went their way."

So, in that summer of 1935, both Chi-chi and Ida boarded the *SS Conte Rosso*, a luxurious Italian transatlantic ocean liner known for its lavish Italian interiors and outdoor dining areas, a feature uncommon for ships of that era. The two ladies had planned to be away for two years, their first stop being the South of France where they intended to stay until the winter before going to Paris, London, and Holland. Their very act of touring as "two modern girls", without chaperones and without husbands, was given a whole section in a column in the *Sunday Tribune*. While their adventurous spirits might have impressed society at large, the mood back home in Penang was anything but. Protocol required wives to remain with their husbands and care for their family. In-laws expected unquestioning obedience from their daughters-in-law and control over their comings and goings. Single young girls were subjected to even stricter protocols which dictated them to remain confined to the four walls of their rooms. They were barred from looking out of their windows for fear neighbours might consider them frivolous. The only time they were allowed out was during Chinese New Year at *Chap Goh Meh*, an evening where single ladies, dressed in their best, are seen throwing oranges into the sea with the hope of finding good husbands. So, we can only imagine the angst back at Homestead. Old fashioned Chor-ee disapproved of many things. Noes driving a car to pick Kim-hoe at work from the bank for lunch was already regarded as absurd. Ida travelling on a luxurious liner and spending two years abroad in Europe without Hock-hoe would have sent his blood pressure reeling. For him, that would have been the ultimate height of nonsense.

Hock-hoe was certainly not a happy man either. For unknown reasons, both Ida and Chi-chi shortened their worldly adventures and returned just before the summer the following year. By then Hock-hoe had lost his patience with his high-spirited wife and attempted to put his foot down but to no avail. Bickering and outbursts became regular bouts in their relationship. Ida continued to do as she pleased, spending more time in Singapore where she was welcomed by her circle of high society friends. The times when she was back in Penang, she often went out on her own in the evenings and, when asked where she had been by Hock-hoe, her reply was blasé – "Ask no question and you will be told no lies". Finally, the inevitable happened. The antidote for an unfulfilled marriage was to take a lover, and that was precisely what Ida did.

He was widely rumored to be a married man with family and of high social standing. An articulate, well-spoken, and confident man, he was a friend of Hock-hoe and a member of the Penang Flying Club. Though never verified, Ida and he might have developed a relationship before her marriage to Hock-hoe. But she had other male friends who were close to her too and for a short while, rumours persisted that one of them might have been intimate with her. In any event, the identity of the lover was mostly a matter of conjecture for everyone in town except her inner circle. By early 1940, she fell pregnant. Unsuspecting initially until Ida's body began to show signs of change, Hock-hoe discovered aghast that his wife was pregnant. How much sadness, rage, jealousy, and humiliation he felt, no one knows. Suffice to say that he laid down his conditions – that if the baby was a girl, he would accept her as his own, but if it was a boy, Ida would have to agree to a divorce for her to continue to stay in Homestead. She would also have to make a commitment to disassociate the boy from him and the family. Hock-hoe's terms were empathetic on the one hand but unfair on the other. Like everything else to do with life, family matters were overwhelmingly biased in favour of boys. Accepting another man's son might have wounded his masculine pride whereas a girl was of less consequence.

Divorce was considered taboo in colonial society. It was uncommon for Chinese couples to air their grievances and wash their dirty linen in public so there was no effective legal machinery for dealing with marital disputes. But this did not mean that Chinese never left their spouses. Since it was not compulsory to register a marriage, an unhappy spouse could run away or agree for mutual separation and that would generally be recognised and constituted as a "divorce". In the early years of colonial rule, attempts were made to modify English law to consider local customs, but they were scanty in nature because the colonial courts found it difficult to incorporate customary laws into an essentially English legal system. Among the difficulties, particularly with regards to Chinese family law, was the lack of ability to define a woman's position. Chinese laws allowed for polygamy whereas English laws only recognised monogamy. However, when a man died intestate in the colony regardless of race, English laws would apply, entitling the widow to one-third of his estate – this then posed a grave problem for women whose husbands had more than one wife. The law treated the children of the various wives as having equal rights, but the women were not treated as such.

As Hock-hoe and Ida had chosen to enter a "Christian marriage" in the presence of a Marriage Registrar when they wedded in 1933, they had to go through the normal motions of a divorce to nullify the marriage, the details of which then became a topic of conversation around town. After the War, Ida moved out on her own with her mother and baby. Hock-hoe overcame his shyness with the ladies and went on a matrimonial spree by taking up five secondary wives who collectively bore him seventeen children. Cheng-kin and Chor-ee were intent on filling Homestead with as many children as possible and made it known to Hock-hoe's wives that whoever gave birth to a son would earn herself the cherished position of principal wife. Hock-hoe produced his first son in 1946, just before Chor-ee's 78th birthday.

Fig. 22: Two modern girls and their mothers. From left to right: Mrs. Lim Nee-soon, Ong Tjiang-tjoe, Chi-chi and Ida. Mrs. Lim Nee-soon had bound feet. Singapore. 1920s.
Source: Yeap Chin-joo.

As Equals: The Oei Women of Java

Fig. 23: Ida, a free-spirited modern girl, Penang. Late 1930s.
Source: Yeap Chin-joo

33

Forbidden Romances

In most societies, ethical and religious teachings have long portrayed recently divorced single mothers as women of liberal dispositions who have abandoned themselves to unscrupulous habits. Shunned and cruelly punished, they were regarded as society's pariahs along with homosexuals and other offenders who had committed a transgression deemed repulsive by others. Any woman, or for that matter, any person who destabilised values fundamental to matrimonial and social codes would have been vilified and incarcerated.

Just when it must have seemed that Ida was falling into a life of scorned obscurity, life became somewhat happier. From a restless figure who never seemed to fully commit or settle into a stable position, Ida took to motherhood well, finding joy in her role as a mother and invested her love in her son whom she named Francis. Her adultery and divorce had hardly caused a dent in her position within her family and society. Instead of withdrawing into a life of quiet domesticity, she bounced right back into the limelight when in 1947, she joined the Penang Chinese Amateur Players in a play titled "Lady Precious Stream". It was staged at New World Park, Penang's latest landmark for entertainment, in aid of the Women's Service League where Ida took the lead role as Precious Stream. Her fellow cast member included civic dignitary, Dr. Ong Chong Keng, who was a Federal Legislative Council member and the man who introduced the national identity card in the country. The performance was a great success, enthralling the audience. Even The Governor-General, Malcolm Macdonald, was so impressed that he went backstage to personally congratulate the players. Ida's period of glory continued.

Over the next decade, she devoted herself to horse racing, a sport with origins in the military and one which was highly dominated by men. If women took part, they were more visible as spectators. Within just a few years, she became owner of one of the biggest racing stables in the country, again challenging gender norms and the restrictive notion that public and leisure spaces were considered male territory while the private world of home was the prescribed setting for women. Her fellow racing associates soon realised her non-conformist nature when she did what most of them feared – renamed her horses. Renaming horses was a bad omen and a long-held superstition in the racing fraternity. But that didn't bother Ida. She boldly changed the names of four of her horses after characters from the Knights of the Round Table – King Arthur, Princess Guinevere, Lancelot and Merlin – and then trounced the myth when they won her $75,000 in winnings. The irony, of course, is that it took a woman to brush aside a superstition held by men in a male dominated sport.

It was around this time that she met Charles Parker, the ex-CID (Criminal Investigation Department) chief in Penang who came to Malaya shortly after British reoccupation. Charles left the Police Force, took up horse training and became trainer to Ida's string. In the meantime, they developed a relationship and he moved in with her. He was a tall, broad-shouldered handsome-looking man who doted on and idolised her. Charles was seven years older than Ida but very much the passive partner in the relationship. He basically did everything for her – made her coffee first thing in the morning, brought her breakfast, fed and bathed her dogs, looked after her guests, polished her shoes and kept her garden tidy. Ida paid the bills, dictated what they did, where they went and whom they met. Taking on a foreign lover was still considered risqué and a "sin against society" back then. Colonial etiquette required Europeans to avoid interracial romance. Failing to do so could jeopardise their own careers or even risk them being ostracised by their own community. In 1937, Sir Vandeleur Grayburn, Chief of the Hongkong & Shanghai Bank famously dropped a bombshell on his British executives, cautiously reminding them that taking on wives who are "foreign, native, half-caste is definitely taboo".

In passing, one interracial curiosity is worth noting. The preoccupation with "race" in the Straits Settlements did not exist before the late 19th century. Intermarriages and romance among ethnic communities were commonplace, especially in the early generations of settlers. And nowhere is this better illustrated than in Penang. Francis Light, founder of Penang, took a Eurasian wife by the name of Martina Rozelles, whose identity was recorded as Siamese but was also thought to have part French, Portuguese or Malay blood. David Brown, a lawyer turned pioneering nutmeg plantation owner of Scottish origin in the early 1800s had a relationship with a native woman by the name of Nonia Ennui, then a Eurasian woman of Portuguese descent named Barbara Lucy Melang and sired a number of children with his Malay housekeeper and another Malay woman. Meanwhile, Mohamed Merican Noordin, a well-known Indian Muslim merchant of the same era as Brown took several wives from different races including a European woman. Ku Hung-ming, the controversial late Qing scholar whose godfather was another Scotsman by the name of Forbes Scott Brown was born in Penang to a Chinese father and a Portuguese mother. In fact, there was already a distinct Eurasian community right at the beginning of Penang's history of the Straits Settlements even before the British arrived. What profoundly changed all that was when the British introduced the concept of "race" based on social Darwinism and other related race theories preoccupying Europe at that time. In 1871, the administration implemented a system of "racialising" to segregate communities in terms of religion, language, origin and so forth. The primary aim was to divide and rule, ensure their grip on power, and by so doing, they established a perceived superiority to justify their

As Equals: The Oei Women of Java

Fig. 24: Ida and her son, Francis
Source: Yeap Chin-joo.

political hegemony. By the time Ida took Charles as a lover, such a relationship would have been regarded as brazen almost to the point of scandalous.

As the years passed, Charles became one of the most successful post-War trainers in the country, but he also grew dependent and needy on Ida's attention. At least once in a heated argument, according to Ida's daughter-in-law, she told him to leave but would support him nonetheless. Charles died of a tragic car crash one day in 1966. It was also the end of Ida's racing days.

34

A Modern Woman

For all her personal shortcomings, Ida was a remarkable woman. In 1950, she gave an interview to the *Sunday Times* that ran under the headline "Malayan girls can equal men" in which she contended that women had shown that they could keep pace with men and deserved equal status. No one demonstrated this better than she. Ida lived in an age that rigidly delineated the spheres and responsibilities of men and women, confining women to the home with the sole duty of rearing children while male territory was strictly the public world of business, politics and leisure. Ida was compelled to enter a marriage out of duty and commitment with no romantic love. As a wife, she refused to be subsumed into the traditional role and broke free from the shackles of an unhappy marriage when she committed adultery. A fair question to ask, if not such a simple one to answer, is how and why Ida evaded the wrath of public shunning.

Being a migrant-centric community, the Straits Settlements was principally a male-dominated society. A population census taken in the colony in 1911 put the population at precisely 714,069 souls, of which sixty-five percent were male and thirty-five percent were female. Traditionally, women were not encouraged to migrate as they were required to remain home to tend to ancestral rites while men ventured abroad in search of money. Laws also prevented women from doing so. Before 1894, it was illegal for women to emigrate. And because Chinese formed more than half the colony's population, it is safe to say that the disparity was even greater, putting the Chinese male to female ratio closer to seventy males to thirty females. By the 1930s the ratio began to balance out, but that was partially due to a clamp-down on immigration on account of the Depression, which had led to high unemployment rates. But since women were not included in the clamp-down, the colony witnessed a surge in women migrants with close to two hundred thousand arriving on the shores by mid-1930s. Instead of men migrating to find work, Chinese women began leaving their homes to earn an income for their families. These women were mostly domestic helpers sourced from Kwantung in southern China. Locally known as *amah-chieh*, they were easily identified by their black and white *samfoo*. They were also mostly celibate which meant that they avoided marriage and therefore did not help in the plight of young men in search of brides.

What all this meant was that the readily available pool of marriageable women in the 1930s in the colony was extremely limited. In the end, several men looked to the ancient Chinese custom of buying servant girls called *mui tsai* (little sister) from impoverished homes, initially to serve primarily as helpers around the house. When they reached sexual maturity, and if they were attractive, *mui tsai* were often seduced by the master of the house, their positions elevated to that of a concubine or sometimes wife. Since only the poor sold their children, most of these girls were uneducated or had received very little education. Isolated from intelligent society and with a restricted knowledge of the world, they invariably had very little interest in what was going on in the world except for mythologies, spiritualism, superstitions, and other similar subjects which the average educated male was not conversant in.

Once married, a Chinese woman assumed the identity offered to her by her place in the marriage. She took her husband's name, and thereafter, her husband would represent her interests. In return, she had to serve and please every family member, especially the parents-in-law, in order to conform to the social norms of filial daughter-in-law, submissive wife, and nurturing mother. A Chinese wife was subjected not only to their husband's family but also to clan and family associations. If he died before her, she was entitled to a third of his estate and the balance would be divided between his children. If she died before him, on the other hand, he kept everything until his death, at which time, it went to the children. In a divorce or separation, the woman would be left without an identity and therefore without a place and a position in society. In any event, divorce was not really an option for many of them. They rather endured an unhappy marriage, often, out of economic necessity.

In a society short of women, even more so educated ones, Ida was a rarity. Larger than life, kind to her friends, provocative, educated, and sensual with a tendency to say exactly what she thought, Ida personified the independent modern woman. Right from an early age, she sought to define an identity, asserted herself as a human being and found her own social niche. Her affair and divorce were not perceived as scandalous because there was no public denunciation of it as such. People may have gossiped, expressed saucy remarks and/or rumourmongered but always in private or behind closed doors. Her wealth and who her father was might also have given her clout, shielding her from public rejection. Snubbing her would have deprived them of the company of a charming, educated, well-known and very well-connected woman. Ida was also greatly admired by both men and women. She paved the way for open discussions on how women's lives might be different and how their experiences could extend beyond the roles assigned to them, by moving out of the prescribed boundaries set by social norms. Ida also changed the rules for women by arguing that women needed to be independent so they could marry and remain married out of choice, not economic necessity. And for that to happen, what was required were equal rights, education, and fundamental changes in society's viewpoints about men and women and the nature of their relationship.

All this is of course a striking difference with how society viewed their own daughters, sisters, wives, and mothers. There is a certain irony that while they may have tolerated and accepted Ida's lifestyle, they may not have necessarily been so accepting if the same held true for their own family members.

Towards the end, the once-upon-a-time lightning rod for controversy faded into obscurity, living a quiet and modest life in Penang. Her son, Francis, grew up without knowing who his real father was. Ida and Hock-hoe remained cordial after the divorce. They greeted each other with respect but basically kept separate lives. Despite their ill-fated marriage, she held the belief that she remained Hock-hoe's one true love and that none of his other wives could ever match her standards. Indeed, she was right, for there was no one quite like her in Penang. Hock-hoe may have longed for a blissful life with her but fate, alas, was not on their side. Her relationship with Lucy was not especially close but in later years, Francis came to work for Lucy's family for a while. As for her half-sister Hui-lan, she had met Ida and Noes only once in Penang, en-route to Peking when she and Wellington stayed overnight to pick up freight. Ida and Noes came to meet them and explained that they were sisters, or "Mrs. Khiam's granddaughters". Hui-lan recognised the two ladies with the characteristic Oei "crooked finger" and that they had married well. Other than that, the older sister said nothing further. They were not close, but it would not be surprising if Ida had developed an admiration for her famous older sister. Ida kept a large photograph of Hui-lan sitting on a bench with her three Pekinese dogs at the back garden of her house, Twin Oaks in Washington taken some time in the 1950s before Wellington's retirement. The photo, placed prominently on the front page of her private album, suggests a hint of adoration, and might explain Ida's flying and acting stints. Ida's photo album was revealing in one other way too, that she was extremely photogenic. Ida smiled a good deal in all her photos – as a child, as a teenager, as a young woman, in middle age and old age – all throughout her life except the day that was meant to be her happiest, her wedding day.

Ida passed away in Penang in 1989, at age 76.

Fig. 25. An elegant portrait of Hui-lan.
Source: Mary Evans Picture Library
© Illustrated London News Ltd/Mary Evans

Oei Hui-lan

35
Accounts of Hui-lan's Life

During her lifetime, Hui-lan published two biographies. The first, in 1943, was written together with Mary Van Rensselaer Thayer, a society columnist for *The Washington Post* who was also Jacqueline Kennedy's biographer. Even before it hit the bookshelves of America, the book gained notoriety because Wellington, who was then Ambassador to Britain, was evidently unaware of his wife's book project. It seemed he found out about the book only after his arrival in New York days before its launch. Anxious the contents were too politically charged and insensitive to the plight of her fellow countrymen and women, Wellington immediately instructed his office to dispatch six thousand telegrams to all the bookstores in America the day before release. Together with State Department pressure, eight thousand bookstores abruptly cancelled their orders. The action, as you can imagine, caused quite a stir and the reading public immediately raised the question: why? Rumors ranged from "Is there too much romance in the biography of the wife of the Chinese Ambassador" to "Is she criticising China's policies?". Whatever the rumours were, Wellington's frantic episode proved to be great publicity for Hui-lan and her book. It was finally released a month later after her flustered husband vetted through the entire contents. Her second biography was published in 1975, written together with Isabella Taves, a relatively unknown writer. By then Hui-lan's life had paled by comparison to her heydays of the 1930s and 1940s.

In any event, her two biographies were incredibly unrevealing on some aspects of her private life – there was no mention of either her first marriage to Caulfield Stoker or their son Lionel, she had made herself ten years younger than she actually was, and said nothing of her father's opium past. But the two collaborators, Van Rensselaer Thayer in particular, did a masterful job of selling Hui-lan and her fabulous life to the reading public. Their accounts of her father's "concubines" were not all together heart-warming, particularly about Lucy. Hui-lan had accused Lucy of poisoning Tiong-ham. Her only evidence was the encounter with an Indian fortune-teller whom Hui-lan had personally arranged for Tiong-ham to meet. Prophesising that danger would come his way, the fortune teller produced a name for Tiong-ham which magically appeared on a blank sheet of paper when submerged in a glass of water. The paper was, of course, provided by Hui-lan, and the name was, of course, Lucy's. Hui-lan was close to her father and so was Lucy to her husband, so jealousy was possibly a motive for the baseless allegation. What makes all this even more puzzling was that Hui-lan only decided to disclose her assertions twenty years after Tiong-ham's death – not even during the lengthy legal battles over the deceased father's assets when the disinherited sons fought so hard to discredit Lucy. Surely, if there was any ounce of truth, it would have surfaced at court.

The first book enjoyed considerable success, perhaps thanks to the sensation it caused before release. The Washington-based *Evening Star* announced excitedly that it "has become the book thousands of people throughout the country would be willing to give their No 17 ration coupon to obtain". Another New York paper suggested that "Every woman ought to read it." John Selby's popular syndicated column for the Associated Press, *The Literary Guidepost*, describes Hui-lan's story as "a fabulous life in a tale whose glittering threads weave through the diplomatic circle of three continents against a background of wealth. A story as packed with color as an Oriental mosaic, as exhausting in detail as a circus."

In contrast, her second book, written thirty years later in 1974 when Hui-lan was in her mid-eighties and no longer a public figure, received mixed reviews. Regardless, Lewis Austin from the Foreign Affairs magazine had the following to say, "The author of this intriguing memoir is a remarkable woman, and her chronicle of a glittering pre-revolutionary lifestyle is well worth reading, for its glimpses of human character and of international politics." Hui-lan indeed played a role in her husband's extraordinary career, where her main task was to present modern China to an apprehensive West. More importantly, it was to persuade political allies to support China's future. And with that thought in mind, the next few chapters are devoted to how she did just that.

36

A *Difficile* Lady

In all their years serving China in the Foreign service, perhaps the most difficult guest the Koos had to deal with was Madame Chiang Kai-shek, the First Lady of the Republic of China. In Hannah Pakula's epic biography of the illustrious lady, President Roosevelt was quoted as calling her a "prima donna" and that "of all the notables who visited the Roosevelts during their twelve year tenure, Madame posed the most problems." At first, everyone including the President's wife, Eleanor, had great admiration for her – everyone, except the President who once told Lord Halifax, the British Ambassador that he was "scared stiff" of her. During her nine-day stay at the White House, Madame Chiang brought with her nephew and niece and a seemingly endless string of aides, all forty of them, including nurses, secretaries, reporters and servants. With such a demanding number, Eleanor enlisted the help of her former "Number One White House Maid", Maggie Rogers, to supervise the staff. Even with reinforcement, Madame Chiang's "imperious behaviour" caused a great deal of strain to the White House helpers. She would endlessly summon them by clapping her hands as if they were "coolies". She ate most of her meals in her room and when she felt like joining the Roosevelts for dinner, Madame casually gave late notice, often changing her mind even after she agreed. Because of her skin problem, her bed linens had to be changed daily. Not only was she brittle and demanding, her young Kung nephew and niece too expected royal treatment. It wasn't long before Eleanor's perception of China's First Lady changed. At a dinner party, Madame Chiang famously answered Roosevelt's question with one simple hand gesture. When asked how she would handle a problematic American labour leader like John Lewis, in China – Madame, without saying a word, raised her "beautiful, small hand" and "slid across her throat..."

So when Madame Chiang announced her last-minute intention to visit Washington for President Eisenhower's inauguration and stay at the embassy, Twin Oaks, Wellington and Hui-lan fretted. They had ten days to make arrangements. "The main difficulty was the need of doing much to get it (Twin Oaks) in shape for such a distinguished and *difficile* lady on such short notice", Wellington stressed. To make sure his concerns were fully understood, he emphasised the word *difficile*. It is also worth noting that he chose a French word, the language that is, in his own words, "so well suited to the intricacies and exigencies of diplomacy", to explain the situation.

A chock-full of preparations swung into action at once. Hui-lan ordered new curtains and a sofa for the drawing room and library. Wellington prepped his staff and together with Hui-lan planned out the various dinners and reception during her stay. But there was a hitch – no invitation for the inauguration had yet been sent to Madame Chiang. Evidently, the State Department objected to her attendance on the grounds that it would be difficult to seat her properly as there was no precedent set. By then, Mao Tse-tung's Communist party had defeated the KMT, leading to the latter's retreat to Formosa, or modern-day Taiwan, so the Chiangs were no longer holding the seat of power in China. Hui-lan's sources were even more explicit, revealing there were strong objections from the Republicans because of "their (Madame Chiang and the Kungs) lack of support during the Eisenhower campaign". In any event and after much deliberation, the invitation was delivered, by which time, Madame Chiang had decided not to attend due to a measly cold.

But that was not the end of it. Two months later, Madame Chiang again informed of her intention to visit Washington but on an even shorter notice. She had personally written to President Eisenhower requesting for a meeting. The President obliged and invited her for tea at the White House. In less than four days, the Koos had to coordinate her visit – a mammoth task made all the more difficult by the fact that they had to also organise three formal dinner parties, a reception and two lunches in her honour. On top of this gargantuan undertaking, Wellington was in the midst of negotiating for the withdrawal of KMT troops in Burma. After the defeat by Mao's Communist party, a splinter group from the KMT army fled to Burma in 1950. Frustrated with the violation of its sovereignty, Burma threatened to submit a formal complaint to the United Nations, and so, Wellington was pulled in to negotiate. Having to deal with two complicated undertakings and in total exasperation, Wellington sighed: "A situation like this could not even be imagined by people not in the service."

The customary lead time for extending invitations among the diplomatic circles is a three-week notice. The Koos only had a few days. With Wellington's social secretary away on honeymoon, Hui-lan, together with three others, was tasked to draw up the guest list, make calls and send invites. "The problem of entertaining for her (Madame Chiang) and making appointments with people she wanted to see entailed much time. I was frequently able to sleep only a few hours a night and my husband had to get along with even less", remarked Hui-lan. Madame Chiang apparently kept irregular hours. What complicated matters further was the social schedules of many congressmen and senators from this new administration had already been fixed weeks beforehand. Help came in the form of John Simmons, the Chief of Protocol at the State Department. Being a former Ambassador himself and accustomed to the Chinese practice of "giving face", Simmons empathetically did what he could to help. By some extraordinary luck, he successfully persuaded Vice-President Nixon and his wife to call off another function arranged some months before in their honour. And so, for the next few days, the Who's Who of American politics were kept engaged, rearranging their busy schedules to accommodate their Chinese friends.

As Equals: The Oei Women of Java

The Koos knew full well the expectations of their First Lady. Hui-lan first met her in Shanghai, sometime in mid-1920s, before her marriage to Chiang Kai-shek. They were introduced by a friend, Elsie Tang, Tang Shao-Yi's eldest daughter and sister to Wellington's second wife. Even then, Hui-lan noted how "serious minded" Ms Soong was and that she made no attempt to join the fun at parties. Nonetheless, both women shared a number of similarities: Both served in the Chinese Women's Association in London, Hui-lan as Chairwoman and Madame Chiang as its President in the 1940s. Both made the *qipao* an iconic national dress and a symbol of emancipation for Chinese women. More importantly, both revelled in publicity. Both knew the importance of Western media and used it to their advantage to promote a positive impression of China in their efforts to raise money from Americans for war relief in China. Together they introduced "an image of modern, charismatic femininity that distanced itself from not only the rigid imperial robes but also the artificial exoticism of the stars of the moment in Shanghai and Hollywood". To Americans, they both represented the progress China had made toward modernity. Madame Chiang charmed Americans with her perfect, Southern-accented English and oratorical skill while Hui-lan captivated them with her sense of style and her cosmopolitan lifestyle.

Even their temperaments were comparable. Both had a tendency for being tenacious. Both were well-known for getting their way and both were accustomed to having the very best. And so, it was only a matter of time before both brushed each other the wrong way. When General Chiang's army seized Peking in 1928, Hui-lan's beloved palace was confiscated, and for a while, occupied by General Chiang and Madame Chiang. Wellington tried to reason with his wife with what she described as "gloomy words": "Our way of living cannot last much longer. Why should we, out of four hundred million people, be so favoured by the gods and have wealth, glory and all we desire?" Hui-lan was obviously devastated but remained tactful when she noted that

A Difficile Lady

Madame Chiang kept the "home in good order". Then, in 1943, the same year as Madame Chiang's historic visit to America as a guest of the Roosevelts and five months after the release of two books by the Chinese First Couple, Hui-lan went ahead and published her own memoir. So infuriated was Madame Chiang that she demanded Wellington, who was in Britain, to cancel the orders and buy up all the copies that could be found (hence the frantic episode of sending out thousands of telegrams to bookstores). Deemed insensitive to the sufferings of her fellow countrymen, the irony was that the very same thing for which Hui-lan was criticised for in her book was the very same thing that helped her portray a modern China. Perhaps it was a case of being upstaged that irked the First Lady.

In any case, when Madame Chiang arrived at Twin Oaks, the Koos had everything laid out perfectly. She was warmly greeted by a welcoming committee of about twenty-five people from the embassy and government agencies. Wellington, out of respect, gave up his suite for her, while Hui-lan cancelled all her personal social engagements. Furthermore, as Hui-lan delicately explained, "The embassy was Chinese territory and, as the First Lady of China, I ceded my place in the receiving line to her and my usual seat opposite my husband at the dinner table." Hui-lan also noted that Madam Chiang "preferred simple food and thoughtfully brought her own silk sheets". Every possible little detail was taken care of during her stay, even to the extent of ensuring Madame Chiang's delicate hands were given soothing reprieve with cologne-soaked hot towels from "clammy" greetings during the endless rounds of handshakes.

Hui-lan and Wellington's teamwork was immaculate and polished. The Presidential tea at the White House holds a clear example of how well they read each other's cue. Madame Chiang was determined to discuss a few pressing matters, particularly military aid and America's Free China policies with the President. But realising it was to be a social affair with the President's wife and another couple present, she requested

Wellington to "pitch in" to aid the discussion whenever he could. As it turned out, the President was "careful" in seating his Chinese guest, placing Madame Chiang on his right with Wellington some distance away next to Mrs Eisenhower and Hui-lan next to General Bedell Smith. This made conversation a little strained with the topic skirting around rather trivial matters – Chop suey, the President's love of painting, and the life story of the President's butler. To break out from the pointless chatter, Wellington skilfully diverted attention towards Mrs Eisenhower, whose sister was a great admirer of Hui-lan. With Hui-lan holding court at her end of the room, it gave a break for Madame Chiang to have a *tête-à-tête* with the President. Shortly, Wellington made another elegant maneuver by drawing attention to the President's painting, which got everyone out from their seats, giving a chance for them to change the seating arrangement. When they were done admiring the painting, Wellington took Mrs Bedell Smith's seat to the left of the President while Hui-lan filled his seat next to Mrs Eisenhower. That way, Wellington was able to speak directly to the President and pitch in to assist Madame Chiang, without leaving Mrs Eisenhower neglected.

It was the same seemingly effortless affair during the formal dinner parties at the embassy. On the one hand, considerations of decorum such as seating arrangements had to be properly thought through. One tiny slip of making the wrong table placement, either through ignorance or carelessness, could "hurt your country", observed Hui-lan. Another painstaking responsibility was the invitation list, because who you invite in the diplomatic world is often perceived as a reflection of your government's stance. Hui-lan had to spend two onerous hours to appease Mrs Malone, a friend and a steadfast supporter of China, who was greatly disappointed when she and her husband were accidentally left out from the dinner invite. On the other hand, as hostess, Hui-lan was also required to create a relaxed atmosphere for guests to mingle and talk freely. She was well-acquainted with many in the political world and had the natural ability to make people feel comfortable, often

A Difficile Lady

breaking the ice with her sharp wit and amusing exchanges. At the formal dinner in the embassy on the first evening, a number of bigwigs including the Speaker of the House, Secretary of Defense and Attorney-General were present. Before Wellington and the most senior member of the guests – in this case, the Speaker – could propose their toasts, a *faux pas* occurred when two American guests rose without any warning to make their speeches. The Speaker was apparently annoyed by all this. Madame Chiang, sitting next to him, was engaged in deep conversation with the Secretary of Defense who sat on her other side. She tried to appease him, but it was evidently Hui-lan who managed to defuse the awkward situation by incisively requesting another guest to do his impersonation of Winston Churchill – and to the amusement of everyone, got the whole room roaring with laughter.

Madame Chiang's five-day visit brought the embassy a week of intense dialogue, feasting, and stately splendour, on a scale not often seen before. They had well over three hundred guests to greet, meet and feed, and, not to mention, interviews and speeches that had to be delivered. Included in the rollcall were members of Congress, the State Department, the armed forces, influential members of society, embassy staff, other Chinese government agencies, representatives from the press and radio broadcast stations. Madame Chiang was delighted to meet so many people and acknowledged the success to both Wellington and Hui-lan. It was "due to our experience and personal popularity that we could assemble together such parties of important people on such short notice," noted Wellington. The following day, a grateful General Chiang sent a personal cable to Wellington thanking him for their efforts. When the whole affair ended, in a moment of reflection Wellington remarked: "the sudden calm and quietness of Friday made a great contrast, conveying the impression of having a dream that had entirely evaporated, the normal world having returned."

37
Wealth & Style

Wellington Koo was arguably the most notable diplomat of modern China. For the most part of his career, Hui-lan remained his wife. They divorced shortly after he resigned in 1956. She had been his wife almost as long as his diplomatic career, her life completely entwined with his work. As a couple, they made a formidable team, even if their marriage appeared to have been formed out of patriotic duty than a twinning of hearts. In Hui-lan's own words, it was a team that "functioned for years" even after the "marriage was breaking up behind the façade we presented to the world".

One of the difficulties faced by Chinese diplomats back then was the perception the West had of China. When Wellington and Hui-lan arrived in London after his appointment as Chinese Minister to Britain in 1921, *Punch*, in bad taste, published a patronising ballad about him – deriding his name, his education and where he came from. In another instance, Hui-lan retold Wellington's legendary story in her biography where he attended a large social function. Seated next to an American, his neighbour turned to him and foolishly asked Wellington, "You like soupee-soupee?". Wellington smiled and nodded without uttering a word. After dinner, he rose to deliver his speech in impeccable English to much applause. When Wellington sat down again, he turned to the American and smugly replied, "You like speechee-speechee?" Hui-lan recounted the story merely to illustrate an example of the difficulties they faced in representing China to Western eyes.

The West viewed China as one of the oldest civilisations in the world but not a modern one. She was ancient but impossibly backward. The old Manchu regime was seen as corrupt and regressive. Her citizens abroad were subjected to harsh stereotypes, unkind condescension and often treated with great suspicion. They found themselves excluded from most employment, neighbourhoods, and social circles, partially because of their poor command of English. Their shapeless hand-sewn clothing, curious eating habits and even more curious rituals turned many suspicious minds away from them. The fact that they tended to dominate a particular trade earned them the deprecating name of "washee-washee". Those that came to the West lived within but quite separately from the rest of the country. The sensational press, too, did much to feed xenophobic images of them to the Western world – "they wallow like pigs and burrow like rats" while at night they lie "packed... liked sardines".

Professor Molly Wood, in her article about the role American women played in early 20th century foreign service, observed one important criterion for the success of a diplomat – the ability to display wealth as it mirrored prestige and prosperity. Another crucial advantage was having a "beautiful, charming, well-dressed and socially talented wife". Diplomatic service was a game played by princes and nobility in the West. There was no money in the profession back then. For those hoping to make a career of it would require their own independent income or access to family wealth to subsidise the low wages and high out-of-pocket expenses associated with overseas travel and social activities. In fact, one of the major requirements for joining the American diplomatic service at the turn of the 20th century was that the appointments were all qualified by reason of the candidates possessing sufficient wealth. For purposes of comparison, a British ambassador in the early 1920s drew a basic salary of USD12,000. To maintain and pay for the upkeep of the embassy, the British ambassador received a rather generous allowance of USD85,000, thus making his total package of around USD100,000 per annum – a handsome sum by any means. An American ambassador on the other hand, drew a flat salary of USD17,500 with no extra allowances. The American representatives had to pay the running expenses of the embassy from his own salary.

Foreign service in China before the turn of the 20th century was almost at the very opposite end of the scale. Diplomatic appointments overseas were regarded as hardship postings for the simple reason that life abroad was not easy for the appointed minister. To encourage them to join, they would, with almost certainty, receive some form of special promotion after serving their terms abroad. Chinese ministers would also be given the funds needed to cover every conceivable expense. And since they were not required to produce budgets, they had the discretion to take as many or as few secretaries and attachés to the country, which all but invited much abuse and temptations. After the Boxer Rebellion, reforms were introduced to put the foreign service on a more modern footing. Head of the mission and staff members were subjected to appointments by the foreign ministry. Each mission was required to submit periodic reports and produce an annual budget so that by the time Wellington joined, the Chinese foreign service was kept on a tight leash. Noting two specific occasions, once towards the end of Yuan Shikai's rule in 1916 and another during the brief restoration of Emperor Puyi back on the throne in 1917, Wellington had to use his own share of his family inheritance to supplement expenses of his missions abroad. Even under the KMT government, when he became Ambassador to France, Wellington's basic salary was USD600 a month or USD7,200 a year – a fraction, compared to what it had been for his American and British peers ten years earlier. We might reasonably deduce that his earnings would not have been sufficient to support his wife's lavish lifestyle, let alone maintain embassies in cities with a costly standard of living such as London, Paris and Washington.

What Hui-lan brought to the marriage, as she later avowed, was financial. Growing up in the Dutch East Indies, she had learnt from her father what money can do. It was "Papa's fortune" that enabled them to move so easily in the social circles of Europe. The Koos lived in a style far beyond that of other Chinese in government – a Rolls Royce as opposed to second-hand cars, luxury hotels instead of boarding houses, an army of servants, including a chauffeur, footman, nannies, governess, chef and butler instead of the standard government issue of two household staff. When they moved to a new legation such as Portland Place in London, it was Papa's money that paid for the renovation and sumptuous trimmings. Hui-lan had the entire building refurbished and kitted out, all except a small room on the floor where Dr Sun Yat-sen was briefly kept prisoner. Even though the Koos knew they could not claim the expenses back from government or take any of its furnishings when they left, Hui-lan spared no expense. It was also Papa's money which paid for the two hundred-room Peking palace. Hui-lan then spent one and a half times more the cost of the residence on renovations. The property was bought for Hui-lan but registered in Wellington's name because, in Hui-lan's own words, "the arrangement was necessary in those days because if it had been in my name he as a Chinese man would have looked ridiculous". Such was the decorum required of a woman no matter how progressive her outlook was. It was also her money which paid for a house in Neuilly on Boulevard Maillot facing the Bois de Boulogne in which they lived when Wellington was appointed the Chinese Minister to Paris in 1932 shortly after his reappointment following the Mukden Incident.

Hui-lan knew that appearances mattered – "If Papa had not owned the showplace of Java, he would never have won special privileges or entertained Java's most impressive visitors". But to her credit, it was her sophisticated eye for detail that made her stand out. She was a genius at it and always took a combination of time and money to find the perfect balance between creating a breath-taking and functional interior. Chinese legations, even in the major cities, were dreary to say the least. When Wellington officially took charge of the Paris office, he was alarmed by the state of the legation. Upon arrival at the main gates along Rue de Babylone on his first day of work, he was surprised to see the grim entrance, draped in black. His staff who accompanied him in the car explained that apart from the Chinese legation, which occupied the first and second floors, the building was also leased to several tenants. As it happened, someone just died, and a funeral was taking place on the top floor of the building. Adding to the folly was that just as he was about to settle into his new desk, the phone rang – he picked up the call and the person on the other end asked to book cinema seats for the evening. Apparently, next door was the local cinema. All that can be said is that the office had been there for the past thirty years and no one had bothered to have the place upgraded.

In Wellington's mind, Paris had gained importance over the years because of political developments in Europe with the rise of Nazi power in Germany. Paris was also the traditional centre of European politics and was a convenient location to look after China's interest at the League of Nations. It was therefore important for China to be strongly represented in the city. Upon his recommendation, the Chinese government gave the approval for a new legation, and Hui-lan was tasked to look for a new place. It wasn't until 1935 when France agreed to raise the legation to an embassy did things gather momentum.

They found an old rundown building on the Avenues Georges V and got the funding from the Ministry of Finance to purchase the entire building as well refurbish the interiors. Over the next year or so, Hui-lan and her team completely transformed the old building into a glorious showpiece of Chinese beauty. She was resourceful and painstakingly detailed in her search of *objets d'art* and fine Chinese furnishings for the embassy, personally undertaking dangerous voyages by air from Paris all the way to Shanghai. Such trips earned her the honour of the first woman to ever make that hazardous passage. In the end, it was all worth the effort. The finished interior was a scintillating display of a modern China intended for "European statesmen whose goodwill means loans and political support for Chiang Kai-shek's young, stable and enlightened government". Never in history had Chinese legations been more tastefully decorated in a style "where the East and West met on easy footing, where Europe's great and near-great could get to know, if not understand, their Asiatic counterpart".

Besides her discerning taste for interiors, there was also style, and no one wore it as strikingly as Hui-lan. Fashion was a lens through which elite Western society visualised their links with the rest of the world. Because the West associated fashion with modernity, they used dress to gauge the stages of development in other societies. Wellington recalled the amusing confusions among even the most senior of Chinese officials when it came to foreign dressing when he was a young minister. At one formal function, he was completely amazed when a senior official appeared in a morning coat with striped trousers but without a collar for the photo shoot. Wellington tried to correct the dressing anomaly by gently suggesting that the gentleman tie a handkerchief around his neck. Looking puzzled, the gentleman responded by telling Wellington that in China during summertime, when officials put on their robes, they were never required to wear a collar – which was certainly correct. Another, a young Chinese law student, dressed in a frock coat, striped pants and a top hat was naively mistaken when he paid a courtesy call to a provincial Governor who thought him a foreigner. Even ladies from the elite class had trouble figuring out the specific rules when it came to Western clothing. Princess Gongsang Norbu, head of the Tibetan bureau, appeared one evening in a half Mongolian, half Chinese loose dress, but wearing a hat adorned with fruits and flowers which Wellington thought was more fitting at an Easter parade. Such were the fashion conundrums of the age.

Hui-lan was a different league altogether. From the moment she arrived in London in the late 1910s, she was a sensation. Not only did she contribute to the cosmopolitan vibe of post-war London and Shanghai, she also re-gendered cosmopolitanism, a traditionally male domain, by presenting Chinese fashion as a cultural style and making it available to Western women. She was a major client of the couture and inspired leading houses in Paris, including Callot Soeurs, to incorporate Chinese styles and motifs into their designs. Mass circulated magazines about high society such as *Sketch* and *Tatler* showcased her in chic Western and Oriental costumes. Across the Atlantic, the *Washington Herald* described her as "Western to the finger-tips" while *Vogue* saluted her as a "citizen of the world" for her progressive approach of fostering amity between East and West. In the diplomatic circles, she was known as the "glamour lady of China".

Hui-lan has been chronicled and immortalised by over a dozen renowned artists and photographers, among them Emil Otto Hoppe, the hugely celebrated turn of the century photographer whom Cecil Beaton referred to as "the master". Already famous in London magazines for his portraits of figures in politics, literature and the arts, Emil spent twenty years compiling his list of the world's prized beauties across the globe for his highly-publicised book *The Book of Fair Women* – Hui-lan was the only Chinese woman on his list. A decade later, and just when Madame Chiang Kai-shek was beginning to get noticed on the world stage, Hui-lan was voted among the top ten best-dressed women in the world. Even in Paris, the style capital of the world, she was singled out as one of the smartest-dressed women in society. Her portraits, photographs and dresses today are part of the collections of the National Portrait Gallery in London, the Metropolitan Museum of Art in New York, and the Peranakan Museum in Singapore.

Wealth & Style

Fig. 26: A group photo of Wellington Koo, Hui-lan and members of staff at the Chinese Embassy in Paris. Hui-lan had the building completely refurbished, turning it into a glorious display of Chinese beauty.
Source: Yao-hua Tan.

Fig. 27: A group photo of Hui-lan with her aunt, Maud, sitting on her left. Photo taken outside the beautifully refurbished Chinese Embassy on Avenues Georges V, Paris.
Source: Yao-hua Tan.

38

Madame Ambassadress

There is no doubt the residences and embassies Hui-lan created became symbols of Chinese beauty. They were also the foremost residence for social liaisons during an uneasy age and Hui-lan became its leading hostess. As Professor Molly Wood explains, women who "organised lavish dinner parties, worried about her clothes, and 'cultivated' influential friendships" have been dismissed as "superficial", when in fact they were only doing their job by "initiating social contacts necessary for the conduct of diplomacy". Social events and entertaining were ways for diplomats to build cordial relations with people of influence. It was fairly common for formal diplomatic negotiations to be supplemented by "friendly informed negotiations" which often took place at the homes of the diplomats. These informal gatherings provided unrivalled opportunities for networking, personal contact, and conversation, but on the other hand they were incredibly taxing. American Ambassador, Earl Packer, noted that "the wives carry a terrific burden". They had not only to feed, house and entertain privileged guests but also ensure the staff were available to their beck and call. Hui-lan took on that role magnificently.

From a young age, she had been bred to be the perfect career hostess, looking after, in the most captivating and attentive manner, royal guests and foreign dignitaries who called on her father. She had learnt to conduct herself among powerful personalities, engage in charming conversation, snuff out awkward situations and be hypersensitive to their indulgences and likings. By the time she married Wellington, hosting became second nature and so began a productive partnership.

While Hui-lan complained about her husband's lack of appreciation towards her, Wellington was aware of his wife's social graces and charming disposition. After China's failure at the Paris Peace Conference, Wellington was urgently required in London to represent China in setting up the League of Nations – a diplomatic group mooted by US President Woodrow Wilson after the bloodshed of WWI, to resolve conflicts before they end up in warfare. A representation in the group would give China the prestige and a voice in world affairs and security that it so badly needed. But in October 1919, three months before its first Council meeting, President Wilson, a close ally of Wellington's, suffered a stroke and was left debilitated for the remainder of his presidency. All this meant that there was a great deal of tension in the air when Wellington began negotiations in London in January 1920. He would need Hui-lan's feminine charms to help mediate the informal diplomacy crucial to his work. In her own words, "Wellington could not manage the intricacies of life in London without my familiarity with English ways and customs, my knowledge of how to behave with royalty and nobility".

Hui-lan had performed her duty with such grace and distinction that the following year in 1921, Washington's *Sunday Star* dubbed her "one of the most successful political hostesses that London has known for many a year and by her grace, tact and astute knowledge of the public has accomplished wonders in making the European world understand the aspirations of the orientals". Six years later, when she was living in Peking, *Time* magazine ran an article titled "Wise Wives", observing the chaotic mess in the Republic. While the "strong men of China welter in anarchy and her great diplomats flounder bewildered... only two wise wives loom from China today", noted the magazine. It further added, "Today, in Peking at the semi barbaric court of the great Manchurian Warlord Chang Tso-lin, Mrs Wellington Koo is par excellence the cosmopolitan aristocrat of feminine China". The recognition put her well ahead of Madame Chiang Kai-shek who had not yet appeared in the political scene. (The other wife mentioned in the article was Soong Ching-ling, widow of Dr Sun Yat-sen and sister of Madame Chiang).

What made Hui-lan uniquely exceptional was also her flawless command of the European languages – English, French, Dutch and German – as well as Asian languages including Chinese, Malay and a smidgeon of Burmese. Most of the spouses married to Chinese officialdom only spoke Mandarin which meant that the language barrier made it difficult for them to entertain at home and socialise elsewhere. But it was not only the spouses who had trouble with languages not patently their own. The ministers too found it daunting. Recounting the difficulties of being confronted by language barriers, Wellington noted the anxiety of a colleague when the latter learnt of his new assignment as minster to Paris. Out of courtesy, Wellington arranged a luncheon for his colleague to meet his French counterpart in China. Over the course of lunch, both men found it a great challenge to strike up conversation. Feeling apprehensive and realising he might not be able to do much in Paris, his colleague appealed to Wellington for them to exchange posts – Wellington ended up taking the Paris legation while his colleague took London. Wellington's command of French, it had to be said, was only partial. A great admirer of the language, Wellington admitted he "had always cherished an ambition to speak it well", and in all probability, relied on his wife as translator. Even the formidable Madame Chiang Kai-shek, the mouthpiece of the Nationalist government, could only manage English and her native mother tongue.

Hui-lan also took on nuanced roles serving as an intermediary between Wellington and key personnel, setting up meetings and often laying the groundwork before the appointments. Her personal contact with people of influence often helped Wellington in his own work. She was enchanting and had a magnetism that made her the centre of attraction in any company. Influential men and women, the likes of Winston Churchill; Edda Ciano; Young Marshal, the Manchurian warlord; the dashing and charming Joseph Kennedy Jr; media magnate

Henry Luce; Madame Chiang Kai-shek and even Queen Mary warmed up to her and welcomed this charismatic Chinese ambassadress. But it would appear that the trait that drew others to her was also the one that pushed her away from her husband. In a contemplative frame of mind, she once observed, "He (Wellington) resented my being welcomed among Europeans, treated as one of them, even among the titled or very rich. He really would have preferred a sweet, modest little wife. Yet he used me."

Hui-lan was also strikingly outspoken and often shared her opinions bluntly. And it was that celebrated trait of hers which became quite a powerful instrument, even in the world of diplomacy. When WWII broke out, the Koos made a decision to send Hui-Lan and the children to New York while Wellington remained behind at the Paris legation. During her time in New York, she became become a well-oiled publicity machine for China. She had access to the media which saw her speaking frankly to the press, at public lectures and radio talk shows about China's war efforts against Japan and the need for China relief. A journalist from the Midland journal suggested she was "more a meteor than orchid" when she spoke openly on US aid to China. China together with Britain and the allied nations were recipients of Roosevelt's lend-lease programme. But what China received was a fraction of what Britain was accorded. Hui-lan boldly pleaded to America declaring that China was on the verge of an economic collapse that would imperil the entire United Nations' war efforts. The same journalist went further and made a rather interesting observation – "unlike the three Soong sisters whom she admires, Mme. Koo works alone. Maybe this is why she throws aside finesse" – this, in reference to Hui-lan's straight-talking tendencies. The British viewed her activities in New York as "anti-British". But Wellington defended her actions stating that they were "quite in line with the general tone of Madame Chiang's speeches in the United States." He further added the position she took "was not at all unnatural to Chinese spokesmen, in view of the obscure and often unfriendly attitude of the British in their dealings with the Japanese over China."

So, it is of course no surprise then that when Wellington was selected to be Ambassador to London in 1941, the British took their time in giving him a formal approval. Evidently, the British government preferred another Chinese candidate who was English rather than American-educated, for the position. On discovering the cause of delay, the Chinese government made known their displeasure to the candidate who was instructed to inform his British supporters of how his superiors felt. Wellington was immediately given approval and Hui-Lan was brought to London to help him in the mission. A master mediator and publicist, the power couple by no means deviated from the objective, which was to win British support for China's cause against Japanese aggression. Britain soon began to change her views from one of reservation and restraint, towards one which was more sympathetic and friendlier towards China. "China had become a popular hero in the eyes of the British people.", he noted.

That isn't to say that Hui-lan had softened her approach. She continued to speak her mind, quite often, and sometimes with the backing of her husband. When Britain accorded diplomatic recognition to the Communist regime as the legitimate government of China in 1950, not only did Britain abandon support for her ally, the KMT government, but also went against her own anti-Communist stance. Britain's controversial decision sparked outcry from various Chinese quarters among whom was Madame Chiang. In flat-out rage, the First Lady made an emotive speech in New York: "It is with heavy heart that a former ally, Britain, which sacrificed millions of lives on the altar of freedom, has now been taken by its leaders into the wilderness of political intrigue. Britain has bartered the soul of a nation for a few pieces of silver." Sensing he may be pushed into an awkward corner, Wellington sent his outspoken wife on his behalf to attend a press party organised by Martha Rountree, creator of NBC's Meet the Press program. The guest of honour was British Attorney-General, Sir Hartley

Shawcross who held strong views in favour of Britain's acknowledgment of the Communist regime. At the party just before the press programme, Shawcross asserted that Britain's decision was solely based on one crucial motive – trade – even though as a nation, they did not approve of the ideology, to which Hui-lan retorted: "the United Kingdom was apparently willing then to prostitute herself for a few dollars". Hui-lan's response was so scorching that even Wellington approvingly noted 'it as "well-nigh unanswerable".

At the height of Wellington and Hui-lan's service, Sino-American relationship reached its strongest point. America viewed China as a friend. Both countries came together as allies to fight for a common cause and as part of the Big Four victors of WWII, China was accorded great power status. In recognition of her protracted war efforts, she was given the honour of being the first to sign the United Nation charter – quite a feat considering as only two decades ago, China had been a pawn to the great powers. It was, as Wellington noted, a "great achievement" of one of China's national objectives – the ending of the unequal treaties and the conclusion of new treaties with Western powers on equal terms. Hui-lan came into this realm without knowing much about diplomatic protocols nor about establishing China's influence around the world. She had to learn. Following her father's philosophy in life, being "adequate" was simply not enough – she had to "excel". No doubt many historians attributed the positive relations and the significant political strides among nations to Madame Chiang's immense influence. But even China's formidable Dragon Lady acknowledged Hui-lan's notable contributions to the country. When a group of Chinese officials praised Wellington for his unflinching efforts in the recognition of China abroad, Madame Chiang astutely responded, "Don't forget the ambassador's wife played a great role too," which of course was the greatest compliment Hui-lan could possibly receive. And indeed, it was. She was, in her own words, "half a team".

After her divorce with Wellington, her life scaled down considerably,

As Equals: The Oei Women of Java

Fig. 28: Madame Wellington Koo posing with her two Pekingese at home in Twin Oaks, the official residence of the Chinese Ambassador in Washington, D.C. 1950s. Twin Oaks today is listed as a historic building and placed on the National Register for Historic Sites.
Source: Yeap Chin-joo.

eventually fading from the news. She moved to New York and lived alone in a one-bedroom apartment overlooking the river on the East side with her two dogs, a Lhasa Apso and a Shih-Tsu, until her death in 1992. She was one hundred and three. By then, she went by her given name at birth – Oei Hui-lan.

POSTFACE

Written almost one thousand and eight hundred years ago, the Chinese poem *Woman* by Fu Xuan in the Prologue portrays a vivid picture of how women were regarded – sons were cherished, daughters were of no consequence. How this view came about is a question not easily answered. But what can be said is that the Chinese have had a gendered view of the world for as long as anyone can remember, thanks to a black and white swirly symbol called *Yin Yang*. No one can confidently say who created the *Yin Yang*, but oracle bones from the Shang Dynasty four thousand years ago tell us they were used by shamans for divination. For these ancient people, *Yin Yang* divided the world into two – into "dark and light", "hard and soft", "female and male". The belief became so widespread and well-established that when China had its first philosophic boom during the time of the Hundred Schools of Thought (600–221BC), major thinkers heavily borrowed the symbolic swirl to shape Chinese thinking.

Its concept was reflected most particularly in the efforts of one man, Kong Qiu, better known to us today as Confucius. During the time he lived, China was made up of a patchwork of competing kingdoms troubled by conflicts and bloodsheds with warlords at loggerheads over territorial rights. Philosophers like Confucius came up with competing ideas to build better societies, so from that era came many great writings. Rather unfortunately for Confucius, he was not popular as a strategist on methods of government, but as a teacher, he was exceptional.

The wise sage was engaging and inclusive, and he promised solutions for peace and prosperity for the worried youth. Oddly enough, Confucius remained one of the most ill-fated philosophers in world history. For a man who came to personify Chinese thinking, he never received the recognition he deserved during his lifetime. The only people who acknowledged him were his loyal group of students. At around his death, he was certain his teachings had not made any impact on society. Confucius died in 479 BC at the age of seventy-two of natural causes. What he didn't know was that his philosophy continued to spread among his devotees. After almost three centuries later, during the Han dynasty (206BC–220AD), Confucius' teachings would go on to become the official imperial philosophy of China. "Confucianism" became the source of foundational thoughts for Chinese politics and society and would remain so for the next two thousand years.

Following his death, all that he said and all that he taught during his lifetime was faithfully inked on bamboo and wooden strips by his pupils. These written texts, known to us as the *Analects*, is by far the most important from the Confucian collection of works. Divided into twenty chapters, Confucius seemed to have touched on numerous aspects of life, teaching his followers how to behave in society and in politics. But when it came to the subject of women, the man of many words and many thoughts evidently had not much to say. Some scholars believe that Confucius' vague language neglected to fully define women's roles, therefore giving ample room for others to come up with their own interpretations. Over time, these versions – like the binding cloths of the farmer girl's mangled feet – became a little tighter, a little blemished, further fortifying patrilineal traditions, adding more pain and anguish to women. The most severe phase of tightening was during the time of Song Dynasty, or about the time when Yao-niang performed her arousing dance for her foot fetishist Emperor.

Indeed, there were periods in Chinese history when women enjoyed a relatively liberal life – rare though it may have been. The earliest, as far as can be told, was before Confucianism came about during the Shang Dynasty (1600–040BC). We know this thanks to the discovery of a royal tomb in Anyang in 1976 belonging to a powerful Queen named Fu Hao. From the inscriptions on her tomb, records spoke of her many valiant achievements as a warrior then, rising through the ranks to become China's first female warrior and the kingdom's most successful military general of her time. She was also an active politician, a high priestess and oracle caster. Her success paved way and produced a line for other females to follow. But their freedom didn't last long. When Zhou overthrew the last Shang ruler, the new Zhou King established laws, regulations and moral values which came to serve as models for generations to come. Zhou rulers removed Fu Hao and other women generals from their records, so that they appear to not have existed.

Then came the Tang Dynasty (618–907AD), two thousand years after Fu Hao. Women again were able to enjoy a relatively liberal life. The era was lauded as the golden age for women. It boasted one other achievement which no other dynasty could – the creation of the only female Emperor in China – Wu Ze-tian. In the eyes of early Chinese historians, Wu was viewed as ruthless, cruel and scheming. Rumours of monstrous crimes circulated throughout the centuries of how she smothered her own one-week-old daughter, ordered the suicide of her grandchildren, poisoned her husband and killed her own siblings. The formidable Wu was believed to have also cold-bloodedly dealt with her enemies and ministers who did not live up to her expectations; and in her old age, shockingly maintained a harem of young men. Yet, none of these exploits would have drawn any criticisms if she had been born a man. Just how true these stories were remain a matter of debate because there was just so much resentment against her – because she was anti-Confucianism and, most of all, because she was a woman.

As a ruler, however, a number of things accounted for Wu's achievements. Foremost, she elevated the status of women. Under her rule, women could become prime ministers and hold senior positions in the administration. Buddhism was allowed to flourish and became the official religion of the state. In endorsing Buddhism, Wu basically sidelined the long-held Confucian belief against female rule. She made other significant improvements including expanding China's empire deep into Central Asia. Her diplomacy opened up trade and saw goods from foreign countries entering China. Though the significance of her policies and reforms wasn't much recognised by imperial historians, the impact it had was immense. China experienced great prosperity and stability during her time, laying the foundation for her legendary grandson, Xuanzong of Tang, under whose reign China became the most prosperous country in the world.

In any event, Confucianism left a lasting imprint on society in China for centuries. For two thousand and five hundred years, it stood the test of time by enriching and adapting to shape itself but at a terrible price for women. For hundreds of millions of women, it was undoubtedly one of the most systematic deep-rooted sexist philosophies in history. Under its doctrine, they suffered in absolute silence, ingrained in their collective psyches that they were inferior to men for what felt like eternity. It wasn't until after the May Fourth Movement in 1919 when their painful journey began to change, thanks to the New Culture youths. Taking cues from the West, reformists adopted the New Woman trope as the embodiment of modernity, leading to a series of events that would change the course of Chinese history and one that propelled China towards modernity. The paradoxical conclusion of all this was that it took a "woman" to change China, even though she was, at that time, only a representational character.

No doubt it took several more decades, beginning with the establishment of the People's Republic of China (PRC) in 1949 when real changes began to unravel for women and profoundly transform millions of lives. Marriage laws were reformed. Prostitution, concubinage, arranged marriages and child betrothal were abolished. Women were educated and provided opportunities in the workforce.

For the first time, during the Great Leap Movement (1958–1992) and Cultural Revolution (1966–1976), China saw women welders, female machinists, tractor drivers and oil-field workers – showing that they, too, can take on responsibilities of men. Rather than being seen as a distinct entity to men, women were treated the same as the other half of the population – Mao puts it best – "Women hold up half the sky".

Indeed, the consequences of the Great Leap Forward Movement and Cultural Revolution were disastrous to say the least, with millions of lives ruined, but if there was one positive outcome, it would be that reforms implemented to close the gender gap proved rather effective. From just over six hundred thousand in 1949, the number of Chinese women working today has gone past four hundred and sixty-five million, translating to a female participation rate of sixty-eight percent, or among one of the highest in the world. Life expectancy of Chinese women too has improved remarkably. At thirty-six years in 1949, the average life span of Chinese women has more than doubled to 76.7 years today. Even more extraordinary is that for the first time in China's history, girls have outnumbered boys in education. In 2019, World Bank data noted female enrolment at tertiary institutions at almost sixty percent compared to forty-eight percent for boys in the same year. More women (50.6 percent) in China are continuing their post-graduate studies than men. Getting better-educated means better job prospects, therefore better salaries, and thus, better status within society. Alongside men, women have helped transform China from a poverty-stricken rural society to one of the fastest growing economies in the world. Not only have they brought about higher productivity but also greater diversity and complementarity of thought, resulting in better decision-making in the workplace and at home. They have also shown that healthy, educated women are more likely to have healthier and more educated children, creating a virtuous and sustainable cycle of development.

If history is anything to go by, then one thing is certain: the gender gap not only hurts women, but everyone else too. By closing the gap, China has lifted itself out from its century of humiliation, and transformed into a global powerhouse, all within a comparatively short period of time – surely that is a progression which Confucius would endorse too.

Yet for all their influence, we don't know much about these modern women, the trail blazers who paved the way for others, for the simple reason that their lives went mostly unrecorded. Sidelined from historical accounts and public memories, their existences forgotten owing to their primary roles as wives and mothers – their lives so ordinary and inconsequential that it would seem inconceivable to talk about them. If they were indeed crafted into the narrative, like Fu Hao or the Great Wu Ze-tian, they were portrayed as crude stereotypes with extreme personas – the submissive "China doll", the sinister "Dragon Lady", or simply, the troublesome wife who caused problems for men. In *As Equals*, I want to share an alternate perspective, that even the ordinary and seemingly inconsequential can be as important as the history of power and of the great men. I want to draw readers into a position to understand to what degree Chinese women participated in history, how they featured and influenced major events and just how big a role they played in the scheme of things. I want to offer a more representational interpretation of history and in so doing, level out the inequalities of the past.

The book covers a span of roughly ten decades – from the late 1880s right through the 1990s. In as much as it tells a story, it provides a platform for discussion. For that reason, the book follows a thematic narrative, but chapters are broadly organised in a chronological sequence. Despite some overlapping periods, the paths of the three women hardly crossed, but what connects them are two parallel narratives: the glamourous and dark sides of modernity. Their stories intertwine and their collective experiences reveal how they embodied the entire modernity era.

Born at a time when the great majority of Chinese women continued to live under the Confucian veil and when Sinophobic fears were heightened, Hui-lan, Lucy and Ida deserve to be remembered. Compared to their bound-foot, servile, subservient, and antiquated predecessors, they punctured through cultural stereotypes and brushed aside the double burden of being born Chinese and female. What they did, and did rather spectacularly, was step out of the mould and challenge long-held assumptions that women could only play supportive and nurturing roles within the family and community. Not only were they daughters, sisters, wives, and mothers, but also father, husband, and head of family.

Their identities were weaved on many looms, shaped at different points of their lives – from being born female to a society that had always given priority to men, as Foreign Orientals in their own birth country, through Tiong-ham's quest for modernity, and as marginalised Chinese in an era where aversion towards Orientals was a staple of cultural politics in the West. They lived through two world wars, rapid industrialisation and fundamental shifts in cultural thinking, both in the East and West. At the same time, their private lives were inescapably scrutinised and exposed by the tabloids and public. Yet, they asserted themselves as both a woman as well as a human being, surpassing the limitations expected of women while at the same time, dispelling the notion that women must emulate men in order to be treated as equals. Unless we understand the social context and realities of the times in which they lived – how ingrained foot binding had become, how hypnotic it was to see a human fly a plane and how modern eyes viewed the rest of the world – we cannot begin to appreciate the complexities, the contradictions, the conflicts and the courageous lives they led.

Their privileged education, etiquette, manners, household environments, social preferences, dress sense, all of which were considered necessary to adapt to the new age, were seen by modern eyes as civilised. They were exceedingly intelligent and perceptive. Having the advantage of speaking several languages also allowed them to bridge the communication barrier, putting them at ease amongst Europeans. No doubt Tiong-ham's wealth immeasurably enriched their lives, granted them economic independence and partially shielded them from life's travails. But it is perhaps more accurate to say that a large part of what shaped them and made them who they were was their strong sense of individualism. Much like Tiong-ham, their confidence and courage were boundless. They sought to define their own identity and seemed unperturbed by what others thought of them. Nor were they easily coerced to conform to societal norms despite knowing full well the price of being different – being isolated, ridiculed and rejected. Ultimately, the three Oei ladies chose an independent life, establishing their own self other than being a mother or a wife, and choosing to live their lives not through their family but as their own person. They were free to make their own choices, free to form their own identities, but most of all, they offered a sense of what is possible to millions of other women.

Daryl Yeap

ACKNOWLEDGEMENTS

The idea for this book came about from a casual conversation about Oei Tiong-ham but over the course of my research, the story evolved into that of the three women. For that, I have to thank Nunthinee Tanner for setting into motion that initial discussion and for her generous hospitality during my time writing in Bangkok. While research work can sometimes be solitary, the subject has led me to rely on the knowledge and support of others. I am thankful to Kwee Hong Sien who provided me with an enormous amount of old family photographs, introduced a constant stream of people and tracked down sources during the research process. I would also like to thank Dr Peter Post who shared deep knowledge of his work on Oei Tiong-ham and Kian Gwan. A special thanks to Dr Loh Wei-leng for her kind support, guidance and patience taking late night calls from me. There is also a long list of family members and friends who have contributed pieces of information, suggestions and photographs: my parents, Stephen and Irene Yeap, my aunts, Jennifer, Natalie and Janette Yeap, Amy Heah, Pamela Ong, Suzie Saw, The Hon. Tuan Leong Wai-hong, Goei Bien-tik, Yeap Chin-joo, Yao-hua Tan, Eric Oei, Audrey Oei, Poppy Kwee and Kenneth Bé – thank you to all of you. A word of appreciation to Lily Chan for her introductions to publishers, as well as my sister, Peta Yeap on her design directions. To the people at World Scientific Publishing – Chua Hong-koon and his wife Mary Ann, thank you for seeing the value of this book and spending many hours reading through and guiding the manuscript to the form it is today – As Equals is considerably better as a result. To the editors who worked on the many versions of the script, Triena Ong, Nicole Ong, Adeline Woon and Claire Lum. I am particularly appreciative of Claire whose fresh eyes and sense of enthusiasm helped polished up the script. To Loo Chuan-ming, who painstakingly worked on the design and layout of the book and Nic Liem for the illustration on the front cover. And finally, Dr Ying-ying T. Yuan, for devoting her time to read the book at its final stages, sharing her thoughts and encouraging comments. I am also deeply appreciative of the connections she made for me in New York.

ABOUT THE AUTHOR

Daryl Yeap is the author of *The King's Chinese: From Barber to Banker, the story of Yeap Chor-ee and the Straits Chinese.* She has spent most of her career in the finance industry, working as a banking analyst for various financial institutions before joining her family company. Her first book, The King's Chinese, tells the story of the Straits British Chinese immigrants, told through the life of her great-grandfather, Yeap Chor-ee. *As Equals* is her second book.

BIBLIOGRAPHY

Abbenhuis, M. M., 2006. The Art of Staying Neutral. The Netherlands in the First World War, 1914-1918. s.l.:Amsterdam University Press.

Abraham, A., 2002. THE TRANSFER OF THE STRAITS SETTLEMENTS: A REVISIONIST APPROACH TO THE STUDY OF COLONIAL LAW AND ADMINISTRATION. Journal of the Hong Kong Branch of the Royal Asiatic Society, Volume 42.

Adams, S., 2009. Chinese Sexuality and the Bound Foot. In: Peakman J. (eds) Sexual Perversions, 1670–1890. s.l.:Palgrave Macmillan, London.

Akio, T., 2010. China's "Public Diplomacy" toward the United States before Pearl Harbor. The Journal of American-East Asian Relations, 17(1).

Algemeen Handelsblad, 1889. Nederlandsche Kolonien. 15 Oct.

Anon., 1887. Crown Colonies. 7 March, p. 11.

Anon., 1979. PHASES OF CHANGE IN CONFUCIANISM. Cina, Issue 2.

Anthony, R. J., 1993. ASPECTS OF THE SOCIO-POLITICAL CULTURE OF SOUTH CHINA'S WATER WORLD, 1740-1840. The Great Circle, 15(2).

Auerbach, S., 2013. Margaret Tart, Lao She, and the Opium-Master's Wife: Race and Class among Chinese Commercial Immigrants in London and Australia, 1866—1929. Comparative Studies in Society and History, 55(1).

Barr, A. E., 1893. Flirting Wives. The North American Review, 156(434).

Bataviaasch Nieuwsblad, 1888. Wat een Chinees In Indie vermag. 25 June.

Bataviaasch Nieuwsblad, 1889. Uit Andere Bladen. 9 Sept.

Birkle, C., 2006. Orientalisms in "Fin-de-Siècle" America. Amerikastudien / American Studies, 51(3).

Birmingham Daily Gazette, 1907. Yellow Peril. Undesirable Chinese Flocking Into England. Government Warned. Striking Statement by an Expert. 2 Jan.

Birmingham Gazette, 1920. His Chinese Wife. Love Laughs at Wealth and Devotion. Ideas Far Apart. 20 Apr.

Blusse, L., 2000. Retour Amoy: Anny Tan - Een vrouwenleven in Ondonesie, Nederland. s.l.:Balans.

Booth, A., 1980. The Burden of Taxation in Colonial Indonesia in the Twentieth Century. Journal of Southeast Asian Studies, 11(1).

Booth, A., 2013. Colonial Revenue Policies and the Impact of the Transition to Independence in Southeast Asia. Bijdragen tot de Taal-, Land- en Volkenkunde, 169(1).

Bosma, U. & Curry-Machado, J., 2012. Two islands, one commodity: Cuba, Java and the global sugar trade (1790-1930). New West Indian Guide, 86(3/4).

Bibliography

Bosma, U., 2012. Post-colonial Immigrants and Identity Formations in the Netherlands. s.l.:Amsterdam University Press.

Brandtzæg, S. G., Goring, P. & Watson, C., 2018. Travelling Chronicles: News and Newspapers from the Early Modern Period to the Eighteenth Century. s.l.:Library of the Written Word- The Handpress World.

Brooks, E. M., 2009. The Enlightenment European Perception of China: Sinophilia, Sinophobia, and Modernity, s.l.: s.n.

Brown, M. J., Bossen, L., Gates, H. & Satterthwaite-Phillips, D., 2012. Marriage Mobility and Footbinding in Pre-1949 Rural China: A Reconsideration of Gender, Economics, and Meaning in Social Causation. The Journal of Asian Studies, 71(4).

Bryce, J., 1907. Some Difficulties in Colonial Government Encountered by Great Britain and How They Have Been Met. The Annals of the American Academy of Political and Social Science, Jul.Volume 30.

Buck, P. S., 1931. Chinese Women: Their Predicament in the China of Today. Pacific Affairs, 4(10).

Buckingham Express, 1895. The Ducal Wedding. A Brilliant Ceremony. 9 Nov.

Bud, R. & Shiach, M., 2018. Being Modern. s.l.:UCL Press.

Burt, S., 2012. The Ambassador, the General, and the President: FDR's Mismanagement of Interdepartmental Relations in Wartime China. The Journal of American-East Asian Relations, 19(3/4).

Campion, A., 2005. The Changing Role of Women During the Rise of Neo-Confucianism, s.l.: s.n.

Carroll, J. M., 2009. A National Custom: Debating Female Servitude in Late Nineteenth-Century Hong Kong. Modern Asian Studies, 43(6).

Ch'en, J., 1979. China and the West: Society and Culture 1815-1937. s.l.:Harper Collins Publishers.

Chakrabarty, D., 2011. The Muddle of Modernity. The American Historical Review, 116(3).

Chan, H., 2017. FROM COSTUME TO FASHION Visions of Chinese Modernity in Vogue Magazine, 1892–1943. Volume 47.

Chan, L. M. V., 1970. FOOT BINDING IN CHINESE WOMEN AND ITS PSYCHO-SOCIAL IMPLICATIONS. CANADIAN PSYCHIATRIC ASSOCIATION JOURNAL, 15(2).

Chan, S., 2015. The Case for Diaspora: A Temporal Approach to the Chinese Experience. The Journal of Asian Studies, 74(1).

Chen, C. & Bo, Q., 2012. The Ancient Origins of Chinese Traditional Female Gender Role: A Historical Review from Pre-Qin Dynasty to Han Dynasty, s.l.: s.n.

Chen, J. T., 1970. The May Fourth Movement Redefined. Modern Asian Studies, 4(1).

Chen, S. Z., 1929. The Chinese Woman in a Modern World. Pacific Affairs, 2(1).

Chervin, R., 2013. Wellington Koo's Dream of National Identity: Transitioning to a Modern China (1946-1956). Undergraduate Honors Theses. 330., Issue Spring.

Chia, J. L., 2012. Piercing the Confucian Veil: Lenagan's Implications for East Asia and Human Rights. Journal of Gender, Social Policy & the Law, 21(2).

Clark, K. J. & Wang, R., 2004. A Confucian Defense of Gender Equity. Journal of the American Academy of Religion, 72(2).

Claver, A., 2009. A colonial debt crisis: Surabaya in the late1890s. In credit and debt in Indonesia, 860-1930: From peonage to pawnshop, from kongsi to cooperative. pp. 143-159.

Claver, A., 2014. Dutch commerce and Chinese merchants in Java. Brill, p. 105.

Clements, J., 2008. Wellington Koo: China (Makers of the Modern World). London: Haus Publishing.

Clifford, N. R., 1992. Spoilt Children of Empire: Westerners in Shanghai and the Chinese Revolution of the 1920s. s.l.:Middlebury.

Clulow, A. & Mostert, T., 2018. The Dutch and English East India Companies. s.l.:Amsterdam University Press.

Collins, T. J., 2010. Athletic Fashion, "Punch", and the Creation of the New Woman. The Johns Hopkins University Press, 43(3).

Conroy, H., 2014. Female Body Modification through Physical Manipulation: A Comparison of Foot-Binding and Corsetry. History Undergraduate Theses, Issue Spring.

Coomber, N., 2011. The Performative Construction of Identity in the Shang and Zhou Dynasties, s.l.: University of Oxford.

Coppel, C. A., 1989. Liem Thian Joe's unpublished history of Kian Gwan. Southeast Asian Studies, September.27(2).

Craft, G. S., 2015. V.K. Wellington Koo and the Emergence of Modern China. The University Press of Kentuky, p. 17.

Craig, G. A., 1952. The Professional Diplomat and his Problems, 1919-1939. World Politics, 4(2).

Curtis, T., 1850. Female Education. The Massachusetts Teacher (1848-1855), 3(6).

Davenport, H. J., 1919. The War-Tax Paradox. The American Economic Review, 9(1).

Day, C., 1900. The Dutch Colonial Fiscal System. Publications of the American Economic Association, 1(3).

De Indische Courant, 1924. Oei Tiong-ham Japansch Onderdaan?. 17 July.

De Locomotief, 1907. Ingezonden Stukken. 5 Apr.

De Locomotief, 1907. Prince Waldemar. 25 Jan.

De Nieuwe Vorstenlanden, 1889. Nederlandsch-Indie. De Nieuwe Vorstenlanden, 19 June.

De Sumatra Post, 1924. Oei Tiong-ham. 4 Nov.

De Telegraaf, 1907. Chineesch Concert. 20 Apr.

De-Preanger-bode, 1917. Japanners in de suiker. 14 Sept.

Bibliography

Dennis, A. L. P., 1924. The Foreign Service of the United States. The North American Review, 219(819).

Derks, H., 2012. History of the opium problem: The assault on the East, Ca. 1600-1950. Brill, Volume 105.

Dick, H., 1993. The rise and fall of revenue farming: Business elites and the emergence of the modern state in Southeast Asia. s.l.:Palgrave Macmillian.

Dieleman, M., Koning, J. & Post, P., 2010. Chinese Indonesians and Regime Change. Chinese Overseas, Volume 4.

Doran, C., 1997. The Chinese Cultural Reform Movement in Singapore: Singaporean Chinese Identities and Reconstructions of Gender. Sojourn: Journal of Social Issues in Southeast Asia, 12(1).

Eastern Daily Mail and Straits Morning Advertiser, 1905. Madame Bassett's Recital. 7 Dec.

Eindhovenschdagblad, 1924. De Voortvluchtige Millionaer. 25 Mar.

Entract, J., 1972. LOOTY, A SMALL CHINESE DOG, BELONGING TO HER MAJESTY. Journal of the Society for Army Historical Research, 50(204).

Fang, X., 2014. China's Foundational Thought and Ancient Philosophers. International Journal of Liberal Arts and Social Science, 2(2).

Fitzgerald, L. J., 1968. COLONIAL INFLUENCE ON THE ASSIMILATION OF THE INDONESIAN CHINESE. Naval War College Review, 20(10).

Flaksman, A. M., 1973. Education in Switzerland. American Secondary Education, 4(1).

Fowler, J. A., 1923. Netherlands East Indies and British Malaya, A Commercial and Industrial Handbook. Washington: United States Department of Commerce Bureau of Foreign and Domestic Commerce.

Freedman, M., 1950. Colonial Law and Chinese Society. The Journal of the Royal Anthropological Institute of Great Britain and Ireland, 80(1/2).

Fritschy, W., 1997. A history of the income tax in Netherlands. Revue belge de Philologie et d'Histoire, 75(4), pp. 1045-1061.

Fritschy, W., 1997. A History of the Income Tax in the Netherlands. Revue belge de philologie et d'histoire, 75(4).

Frost, M. R., 2005. Emporium in Imperio: Nanyang Networks and the Straits Chinese in Singapore, 1819-1914. Journal of Southeast Asian Studies, 36(1).

Galloway, J., 2005. The Modernization of Sugar Production in Southeast Asia, 1880-1940. Geographical Review, 95(1).

Gambe, A., 1996. Overseas Entrepreneurship in Southeast Asia, s.l.: s.n.

Gao, X., 2003. Women Existing for Men: Confucianism and Social Injustice against Women in China. Race, Gender & Class, 10(3).

Gelfand, E. L., 1988. Towards a Merit System for the American Diplomatic Service 1900-1930. Irish Studies in International Affairs, 2(4).

Goh & Goh, D. P., 2010. Unofficial contentions: The postcoloniality of Straits Chinese political discourse in the Straits Settlements Legislative Council. Journal of Southeast Asian Studies, 41(3).

Gordon, A., 2014. Rising Profits and Fears of Forfeiture in Neutral Netherlands East Indies during World War One. Social Scientist, 42(7).

Gorman, B. W., 1958. What Can We Learn from the Swiss Schools? The Phi Delta Kappan, 39(8).

Gould, M., 2004. Flirting with Disaster: Sexual Play in the Victorian Periodical: Van Arsdel Winner 2003. Victorian Periodicals Review, 37(3).

Grand, S., 1894. The Modern Girl. The North American Review, 158(451).

Habakkuk, J., 1979. Presidential Address: The Rise and Fall of English Landed Families, 1600-1800. Transactions of the Royal Historical Society, Volume 29.

Harper, T. N., 1997. Globalism and the Pursuit of Authenticity: The Making of a Diasporic Public Sphere in Singapore. SOJOURN, 12(2).

Hauser, B. R., 1999. DEATH DUTIES AND IMMORTALITY: WHY CIVILIZATION NEEDS INHERITANCES. Real Property, Probate and Trust Journal, 34(2).

Heidhues, M. F. S., 1972. Dutch colonial and Indonesian nationalist policies toward the Chinese minority in Indonesia. Law and Politics in Africa, Asia and Latin America, 5(3), pp. 251-261.

Heijns, A., 2016. Translating China: Henri Borel (1869–1933).

Heilmann, A., 2011. Sex, Religion, and the New Woman in China: A Comparative Reading of Sarah Grand and Alicia Little. Victorian Review, 37(2).

Helle, H. J., 2017. China: Promise or Threat? A Comparison of Cultures. Studies in Critical Social Science, Volume 96.

Hershatter, G., 2004. State of the Field: Women in China's Long Twentieth Century. The Journal of Asian Studies, 63(4).

Het nieuws van den dag voor Nederlandsch-Indië, 1904. Gelijkstelling met Europeanen. 11 Apr.

Het nieuws van den dag voor Nederlandsch-Indië, 1905. Naam Verandering. 8 Feb.

Hirschman, C. & Teerawichitchainan, B., 2003. Cultural and Socioeconomic Influences on Divorce during Modernization: Southeast Asia, 1940s to 1960s. Population and Development Review, 29(2).

Hodgkiss, J. & Brook, D., 2002. Rooted in Time. Historic Gardens Review, 11(Winter).

Hoogervorst, T., 2017. Urban Middle Classes in Colonial Java (1900–1942) Images and Language. Bijdragen tot de Taal-, Land- en Volkenkunde, Volume 173.

Hooker, M. B., 1969. The Relationship between Chinese Law and Common Law in Malaysia, Singapore, and Hong Kong. The Journal of Asian Studies, 28(4).

Hooper, B., 1975. Women in China: Mao "v." Confucius. Labour History, Issue 29.

Horesh, N., 2020. "One country, two histories": how PRC and western narratives of Chinese modernity diverge. Journal of Global Faultlines, 7(1).

Hu, A., 2016. Half the Sky, But Not Yet Equal: China's Feminist Movement. Harvard International Review, 37(3).

Hu, S., 1951. How to Understand a Decade of Rapidly Deteriorated Sino-American Relations. Proceedings of the American Philosophical Society, 95(4).

Hubbard, J. A., 2012. Troubling the "New Woman:" Femininity and Feminism in The Ladies' Journal (Funü zazhi), s.l.: Thesis submission. The Ohio State University.

Hughes, L., 2007. A Club of Their Own: The "Literary Ladies," New Women Writers, and "Fin-de-Siècle" Authorship. Victorian Literature and Culture, 35(1).

Hunter, M., 1921. The Inheritance Tax. The Annals of the American Academy of Political and Social Science, Volume 95.

Ibrahim, A., 1970. DEVELOPMENTS IN THE MARRIAGE LAWS IN MALAYSIA AND SINGAPORE. Malaya Law Review, 12(2).

Jacobsen, R. B., 1976. Changes in the Chinese Family. Social Science, 51(1).

Java-bode, 1889. Een pachtersgeschiedenis. Java-bode Handels-En Advertentieblad Voor Nederlandsch-Indie, 1889 Oct.

Java-bode, 1889. Nieuws, handels-en advertentieblad voor Nederlandsch-Indie. Java-bode, 9 Sept.

Jay, J. W., 1996. Imagining Matriarchy: "Kingdoms of Women" in Tang China. Journal of the American Oriental Society, 116(2).

Jay, J. W., 1996. Imagining matriarchy" Kingdoms of women in Tang China. Journal of the American Oriental Society, 116(2), pp. 220-229.

Jin, F., 2011. With this Lingo, I Thee Wed: Language and Marriage in Autobiography of A Chinese Woman. Journal of American-East Asian Relations, 18(3-4).

Johansson, P., 2016. Fantasy Memories and the Lost Honor of Madame Chiang Kai-shek. Journal of American-East Asian Relations, 23(2).

Kalas, R. J., 1993. The Noble Widow's Place in the Patriarchal Household: The Life and Career of Jeanne de Gontault. The Sixteenth Century Journal, 24(3).

Keevak, M., 2016. The "Chineseness" of English Styles in the Long Eighteenth Century. The Eighteenth Century, 57(4).

Kemasang, A., 1985. How Dutch Colonialism Foreclosed a Domestic Bourgeoisie in Java: The 1740 Chinese Massacres Reappraised. Review (Fernand Braudel Center), 9(1).

King, F. H., 1983. The History of the Hongkong Shanghai Banking Corporation. London: Athlone Press.

Knight, C. R., 2010. Exogenous Colonialism: Java Sugar between Nippon and Taikoo before and during the Interwar Depression, c. 1920-1940. Modern Asian Studies, 44(3), pp. 477-515.

Knight, R. G., 2014. Sugar, Steam and Steel. s.l.:University of Adelaide Press.

Ko, D., Winter 1997. The body as attire: The shifting meanings of footbinding in seventeenth-century China. Journal of Women's History, 8(4), pp. 8-27.

Koda, H., 2001. Extreme beauty: The body transformed. New Haven and London: The Metropolitan Museum of Art: Yale University Press.

Koo, H.-L. & Van Rensselaer Thayer, M., 1943. Hui-lan Koo. An autobiography. New York: Dial Press.

Koo, V. W., 1936. V.K. Wellington Koo Papers. 28 Dec.

Koo, W. M. & Taves, I., 1975. No Feast Last Forever. New York: The New York Times Book Co.

Koo, W. V., 1917. The New China and Her Relation to the World. New York, The Academy of Political Science.

Koo, W. V., 2023. Reminiscences of Vi Kyuin Wellington Koo 1975. 1975. Oral history. Chinese oral history project, Columbia Center for Oral History, Columbia University. [Interview] (14 December 2023).

Kunio, Y., 1989. Interview: Oei Tjong Ie. Journal Southeast Asian Studies, 27(2).

Kunio, Y., 1989. Interview: Oei Tjong Tjay. Southeast Asian Studies, Sept.27(2).

Kwartanada, D., 2017. Bangsawan prampoewan. Enlightened Peranakan Chinese women from early twentieth century Java. Wacana, 18(2).

Laarman, C., 2012. Representations of post-colonial migrants in discussions on intermarriage in the Netherlands, 1945-2005. In: Post-colonial Immigrants and Identity Formations in the Netherlands. s.l.:Amsterdam University Press.

Lai, D., 2011. THE UNITED STATES AND CHINA IN POWER TRANSITION, s.l.: Strategic Studies Institute, US Army War College.

Landroche, T. M., 1991. Chinese women as cultural participants and symbols in nineteenth century America, s.l.: Dissertations and Theses. Paper 4291.

Leader, S. G., 1973. The Emancipation of Chinese Women. World Politics, 26(1).

Leath, R. A., 1999. "After the Chinese Taste": Chinese Export Porcelain and Chinoiserie Design in Eighteen-Century Charleston. Historical Archaeology, 33(3).

Lees, L. H., 2009. Being British in Malaya, 1890-1940. Journal of British Studies, Jan. Volume 48.

Leow, R., 2012. 'Do you own non-Chinese mui tsai?' Re-examining Race and Female Servitude in Malaya and Hong Kong, 1919-1939. Modern Asian Studies, 46(6).

Leow, R., 2012. Age as a Category of Gender Analysis: Servant Girls, Modern Girls, and Gender in Southeast Asia. The Journal of Asian Studies, 71(4).

Lewis, S. L., 2009. Cosmopolitanism and the Modern Girl: A Cross-Cultural Discourse in 1930s Penang. Modern Asian Studies, 43(6).

Li, L., 1977. Brief reviews of books. Journal of the American Oriental Society, 97(3).

Li, M., 1999. We Need Two Worlds. Chinese Immigrant Associations in a Western Society. s.l.:Amsterdam University Press..

Li, T.-C. (., 2011. Women of New China. Pakistan Horizon, 64(4).

Li, Y., 2000. Women's Movement and Change of Women's Status in China. Journal of International Women's Studies, 1(1).

Bibliography

Liang, H., 1998. Fighting for a New Life: Social and Patriotic Activism of Chinese American Women in New York City, 1900 to 1945. Journal of American Ethnic History, 17(2).

Lim, J. S. H., 2015. The Penang House and the Straits Architect 1887-1941. s.l.:Areca Books.

Lim, S., 2018. Widowed Household Heads and the New Boundary of the Family. In: Rules of the House. Family Law and Domestic Disputes in Colonial Korea. s.l.:University of California Press.

Ling, H., 2000. Family and Marriage of Late-Nineteenth and Early-Twentieth Century Chinese Immigrant Women. Journal of American Ethnic History, 19(2).

Liu, J.-q., 1998. Education of Females in China: Trends and Issues. The Journal of Educational Thought (JET) / Revue de la Pensée Éducative, 32(1).

Locher-Scholten, E., 2000. By Way of a Prologue and Epilogue: Gender, Modernity and the Colonial State. In: Women and the Colonial State. s.l.:Amsterdam University Press.

Locher-Scholten, E., 2000. Marriage, Morality and Modernity: The 1937 Debate on Monogamy. In: Women and the Colonial State. s.l.:Amsterdam University Press.

Locher-Scholten, E., 2000. Summer Dresses and Canned Food: European Women and Western Lifestyles. In: Women and the Colonial State. s.l.:Amsterdam University Press.

Lopez, H., 2016. Daughters of the May Fourth, Orphans of Revolution. History in the Making, 9(6).

Lusk, H. H., 1907. The Real Yellow Peril. The North American Review, 186(624).

Ma, X., 2000. The Sino-American Alliance During World War II and the Lifting of the Chinese Exclusion Acts. American Studies International, 38(2).

Mackie, G., 1996. Ending footbinding and infibulation: A convention Account. American Sociological Review, 61(6), pp. 999-1017.

Mackie, J., 1991. Towkays and Tycoons: The Chinese in Indonesian Economic Life in the 1920s and 1980s. Indonesia.

MacNair, H. F., 2013. The Chinese abroad their position and protection: A study in international law and relations. s.l.:Gale, Making of Modern Law.

Mahy, P., 2013. The Evolution of Company Law in Indonesia: An Exploration of Legal Innovation and Stagnation. The American Journal of Comparative Law, 61(2).

Malay Tribune, 1927. Supreme Court. Million-Dollar-Legacy Applications. 14 Dec, p. 10.

Malay Tribune, 1931. "Unmarriageable" Chinese Girls. 20 Nov, p. 5.

Malaya Tribune, 1934. Colony's Finance. 9 Aug.

Maloni, R., 2010. DISSONANCE BETWEEN NORMS AND BEHAVIOUR: EARLY 20 TH CENTURY AMERICA'S 'NEW WOMAN'. Proceedings of the Indian History Congress.

McKinley, A. E., 1901. The Transition From Dutch to English Rule in New York: A Study in Political Imitation. The American Historical Review, 6(4).

McMahan, A. L., 2012. Why Chinese Neo-Confucian Women Made a Fetish of Small Feet. Grand Valley Journal of History, 2(1).

McMahon, K., 2013. Women Rulers in Imperial China. NAN NU 15, 179(218).

Midland Journal, Rising Sun MD, 1943. Who's News This Week. 26 Feb.

Milton, G., 1999. Nathaniel's nutmeg. New York: Penguin Books.

Morris, D., 2000. The language of the sexes: Episode of the Human Sexes. s.l.: Discovery Channel.

Nelson, E. S. & Liu, Y., 2016. The Yijing, Gender, and the Ethics of Nature. In: The Bloomsbury Research Handbook of Chinese Philosophy and Gender. s.l.:Bloomsbury Press.

New York Tribune, 1920. France Declared Regaining Grip on Economic Life. 10 June.

Ng, C. K., 2017. Boundaries and Beyond: China's Maritime Southeast in Late Imperial Times. s.l.:NUS Press.

Oei, J., 1995. Letter to Hervey. s.l.:s.n.

Offerhaus, J., 1921. The Private International Law of the Netherlands. The Yale Law Journal, 30(3).

Onghokham, 1989. Chinese Capitalism in Dutch Java. Southeast Asian Studies, 27(2).

Ouida, 1894. The New Woman. The North American Review, 158(450).

Pakula, H., 2009. The last empress: Madame Chiang Kai-Shek and the birth of modern China. New York: Simon & Schuster.

Panglaykim, J. & Palmer, I., n.d. Study of Entrepreneurialship in Developing Countries: The Development of One Chinese Concern in Indonesia. Journal of Southeast Asian Studies, 1(1).

Park, N. E., 1997. Corruption in Eighteenth-Century China. The Journal of Asian Studies, 56(4).

Park, R. E., 1923. The Natural History of the Newspaper. American Journal of Sociology, 29(3).

Patten, S. N., 1914. The Evolution of a New Woman. The Annals of the American Academy of Political and Social Science, Volume 56.

Peterson-Withorn, C., 2017. From Rockefeller to Ford Forbes 1918 ranking of the richest people in America. Forbes Magazine, Sept.

Pleck, E. H., 2014. Seeking Female Sexual Emancipation and the Writing of Women's History. Social Science History, 38(1-2).

Png, P. S., 1969. The Straits Chinese in Singapore: A Case of Local Identity and Socio-Cultural Accommodation. Journal of Southeast Asian History, 10(1).

Post, P., 1996. The formation of the pribumi business élite in Indonesia, 1930s-1940s. Bijdragen tot de Taal-, Land- en Volkenkunde, 152(4).

Post, P., 2002. The Kwik Hoo Tong Trading Society of Semarang, Java: A Chinese business network in Late colonial Asia. Journal of Southeast Asian Studies, Jun, 33(2), pp. 279-296.

Post, P., 2009. Java's Capitan Cina and Javanese Royal Families: Status, modernity and Power Major-titular Be Kwat Koen and Mangkunegoro VII Some Observations. Journal of Asia-Pacific Studies, Issue 13.

Post, P., 2011. A Business Career Not Wanted. The Life of Jack Oei Tjong Ie Chairman of the Board of the Oei Tiong-ham Concern, 1950-1963. Yogyakarta, NIOD Institute for War, Genocide and Holocaust Studies, Amsterdam.

Post, P., 2019. Bringing China to Java The Oei Tiong-ham Concern and Chen Kung-po during the Nanjing Decade. NIOD Institute for War, Holocaust and Genocide Studies.

Post, P., 2019. Founding an ethnic Chinese business empire in colonial Asia: The strategic alliances of Major Oei Tiong-ham, 1895-190. JMBRAS, Dec.

Post, P., n.d. Profitable partnerships: The Chinese business elite and Dutch lawyers in the making of Semarang. Major-titular Oei Tiong-ham and Mr C.W. Baron Van Heeckeren.

Raub, P., 1994. A New Woman or an Old-Fashioned Girl? the Portrayal of the Heroine in Popular Women's Novels of the Twenties. American Studies, 35(1).

Reardon-Anderson, J., 1986. Chemical Industry in China, 1860-1949. The University of Chicago Press, Volume 2.

Rejali, S., 2014. From Tradition to Modernity: Footbinding and Its End (1839- 1911) – the History of the Anti-Footbinding Movement and the Histories of Bound-feet Women in China. The Journal of Historical Studies, 3(1).

Rierson, S. L., 1994. Race and Gender Discrimination: A Historical Case for Equal Treatment Under the Fourteenth Amendment. Duke Journal of Gender Law & Policy, 89(118).

Rothstein-Safra, R., 2017. The Rhetoric of Transgression: Reconstructing Female Authority through Wu Zetian's Legacy. Honors Undergraduate Theses, Issue 253.

Rouse Jorae, W., 2010. The Limits of Dress: Chinese American Childhood, Fashion, and Race in the Exclusion Era. Western Historical Quarterly, 41(4).

Rush, J. R., 1983. Social Control and Influence in Nineteenth Century Indonesia: Opium Farms and the Chinese of Java. Indonesia, Issue 35.

Rush, J., 1991. Placing the Chinese in Java on the eve of the twentieth century: The role of the Indonesian Chinese in shaping modern Indonesian life. Southeast Asia Program Publications, pp. 13-24.

Russo, A., 2013. How Did the Cultural Revolution End? The Last Dispute between Mao Zedong and Deng Xiaoping, 1975. Modern China, 39(3).

Salmon, C., 1991. A critical view of the opium farmers as reflected in a syair by Boen Sing Hoon (Semarang 1889). Indonesia, July, Volume Special Issue, pp. 25-51.

Savage, G., 1998. Erotic stories and public decency: Newspaper reporting of divorce proceedings in England. The Historical Journal, 41(2), pp. 511-528.

Scharff, D. E., 2019. Changing Family and Marital Structure in China, s.l.: American Enterprise Institute.

Scheltema, J. F., 1907. The opium trade in the Dutch East Indies. American Journal of Sociology, September, 13(2), p. 104.

Schiebinger, L., 2000. Feminism and the Body: Oxford Readings in Feminism. New York: USA:Oxford University Press Inc..

Schluessel, E., 2016. The Law and the "Law": Two Kinds of Legal Space in Late-Qing China. Extrême-Orient Extrême-Occident, Volume 40.

Science, 1886. England's Colonies. 7(173).

Sears, L. J., 2010. Modernity and Decadence in Fin-de-Siècle Fiction of the Dutch Empire. Indonesia, Trans-Regional Indonesia over One Thousand Years, Volume 90.

Seed, P., 2002. Early Modernity: The History of a Word. The New Centennial Review, 2(1).

Selby, J., 1943. The Literary Guidepost. Wilmington Morning Star, 29 Apr.

Seshagiri, U., 2006. Modernity's (Yellow) Perils: Dr. Fu-Manchu and English Race Paranoia. Cultural Critique, 62(Winter).

Seshagiri, U., 2010. Race and The Modernist Imagination. Ithaca and London: Cornell University Press.

Seth, S., 2013. Nationalism, Modernity, and the "Woman Question" in India and China. The Journal of Asian Studies, 72(2).

Shih, S.-M., 1996. Gender, Race, and Semi colonialism: Liu Na'ou's Urban Shanghai Landscape. The Journal of Asian Studies, 55(4).

Shih, S.-m., 2001. The Lure of the Modern: Writing Modernism in Semicolonial China, 1917-1937. Berkeley Series in Interdisciplinary Studies of China.

Shu, X. C., 2014. The Creation of Female Origin Myth: A Critical Analysis of Gender in the Archaeology of Neolithic China. otem: The University of Western Ontario Journal of Anthropology, 22(1).

Simal-Gonzalez, B., 2020. Ecocriticism and Asian American Literature: Gold Mountains, Weed flower and Murky Globes. Springer Nature, p. 54.

Soerabaijasch Handelsblad, 1890. Uit de Indische Bladen. Soerabaijasch Handelsblad, 26 Nov.

Soerabaijasch Handelsblad, 1907. Brieven Uit Semarang. 30 Jan.

Stevens, S. E., 2003. Figuring Modernity: The New Woman and the Modern Girl in Republican China. NWSA Journal, 15(3).

Stoler, A. L., 1989. Making Empire Respectable: The Politics of Race and Sexual Morality in 20th-Century Colonial Cultures. American Ethnologist, 16(4).

Stoler, A., 1992. Sexual Affronts and Racial Frontiers: European Identities and the Cultural Politics of Exclusion in Colonial Southeast Asia. Comparative Studies in Society and History, pp. 514-551.

Bibliography

Stone, N., 2017. The Yellow Peril in Britain. 30th International Academic Conference, 24 April.

Stone, N., 2017. The Yellow Peril In Britain. Venice, IISES.

Stuart, G. H., 1936. American Diplomatic and Consular Practice. s.l.:D. Appleton-century; First Edition.

Sumatra-bode, 1917. Handel in gele slavinnen. 20 April.

Sun, X., 2018. The Tragedy of Widows in Traditional China. Liberated Arts: A Journal for Undergraduate Research, 4(1).

Sunday Mirror, 1918. The Oriental Vogue. 1 Sept.

Sunday Tribune, 1937. A Woman Peeps At Singapore. 28 Mar, p. 10.

Supartono, A., 2010. Faces and Places: Group Portraits and Topographical Photographs in the Photo Albums of the Sugar Industry in Colonial Java in the Early Twentieth Century, s.l.: Ohio University.

Suratminto, L., 2013. EDUCATIONAL POLICY IN THE COLONIAL ERA. International Journal of History Education, XIV(1).

Symes, C., 2011. When We Talk about Modernity. The American Historical Review, 116(3).

Tai, P. H. & Kuo, T.-c., 2010. Chiang Kai-Shek Revisited. American Journal of Chinese Studies, 17(1).

Tang, E., 1970. British Policy Towards the Chinese in the Straits Settlements: Protection and Control 1877-1900). Oct.

Tang, E., 1970. British Policy Towards the Chinese in the Straits Settlements: Protection and Control 1988-1900.

The Evening Star, Washington, 1943. Collaborator Tells How Madame Koo Worked on Book. 23 Apr.

The Evening Telegraph and Star, 1888. John Chinaman in London. 2 Aug.

The Herald, 1895. She has landed her Duke. The Herald Los Angeles, 21 Sept.

The Mercury Leeds, 1920. The Mercury Leeds. 26 Apr.

The Singapore Free Press and Mercantile Advertiser, 1920. Chinese Woman's Suit For Divorce. 19 May.

The Singapore Free Press and Mercantile Advertiser, 1924. Late Mr Oei Tiong-ham. 3 July, p. 6.

The Singapore Free Press and Mercantile Advertiser, 1925. Matters Chinese: A Public Benefactor. 22 July, p. 54.

The Singapore Free Press and Mercantile Advertiser, 1927. Sugar King's Estate. Supreme Court Litigation Continued. The Singapore Free Press and Mercantile Advertiser, 30 Oct, p. 7.

The Singapore Free Press and Mercantile Advertiser, 1934. Anna May Wong Explains Her Sophistication. 26 Nov.

The Sketch, 1918. An Oriental Countess. 13 Nov.

The Straits Times, 1910. Danger for British Girls. 18 May.

The Straits Times, 1917. The Census. An Interesting Compilation of Statistics. 15 Jan, p. 7.

The Straits Times, 1921. Dutch Indies Taxes. The Straits Times, 2 Sept, p. 9.

The Straits Times, 1936. Why Chinese Prefer Malaya. Dutch Taxes, Laws and Policy. 3 Oct.

The Straits Times, 1950. Malayan Girls Can Equal Men. 2 July, p. 5.

The Sunday Star, Washington DC, 1921. Tales of Well-Known Folk in Social and Official Life. 13 Nov.

The Washington Herald, 1920. Name of Chinese Diplomat linked to British Countess. 31 Oct.

The Washington Herald, 1920. Society. 13 Oct.

Therrien, M. S., 2013. From Liberation to Sexual Objectification and Violence: Chinese Women and the PRC. HOHONU, 12(Spring).

Thomas, J., n.d. Merchants and maritime marauders: the East India Company and the problem of piracy in the eighteenth century. The Great Circle, 36(1).

Trocki, C., 2002. Opium and the beginnings of Chinese capitalism in Southeast Asia. Journal of Southeast Asian Studies, June. Issue 33.

Tsai, S. K., 1996. Women and the State in Post-1949 Rural China. Journal of International Affairs: Contemporary China: The Consequences of Change, 49(2).

Tsao, L. Y., 1912. The Life of a Girl in China. The Annals of the American Academy of Political and Social Science, Volume 39.

Turnbull, C. M., 1972. The Straits Settlements 1826-67 Presidency to Crown Colony. London: Athlone Press.

Tusan, M. E., 1998. Inventing the New Woman: Print Culture and Identity Politics during the Fin-de-Siecle: 1997 VanArsdel Prize. Victorian Periodicals Review, 31(2).

Tyson Li, L., 2007. Madame Chiang Kai-shek: China's Eternal First Lady. New. York: Atlantic Monthly Press.

Umekawa, S., 梅川純代 & Dear, D., 2018. The Relationship between Chinese Erotic Art and the Art of the Bedchamber: A Preliminary Survey. Imagining Chinese Medicine.

Underwood, J. H., 1907. The Taxation of Inheritances. s.l., National Tax Association.

Van Der Kroef, J. M., 1951. Indonesia and the Origins of Dutch Colonial Sovereignty. The Far Eastern Quarterly, 10(2).

Van der Meer, A. H. C., 2014. Ambivalent Hegemony: Culture and Power in Colonial Java, 1808-1927. s.l.:Rutgers University.

Van der Meer, A. H., 2017. Performing Colonial Modernity Fairs, Consumerism, and the Emergence of the Indonesian Middle Classes. Bijdragen tot de Taal-, Land- en Volkenkunde, Volume 173.

Van der Putten, J., 2010. Negotiating the Great Depression: The Rise of Popular Culture and Consumerism in Early-1930s Malaya. Journal of Southeast Asian Studies, 41(1).

Van Dijk, K., 2007. The Netherlands Indies and the Great War, 1914-1918. s.l.:Brill.

Van Rensselaer Thayer, M., 1943. Mme. Wellington Koo. Vogue, 1 Jan, p. 30.

Vandenbosch, A., 1930. A Problem in Java: The Chinese in the Dutch East Indies. Pacific Affairs, 3(11).

Vandenbosch, A., 1943. The Effect of Dutch Rule on the Civilization of the East Indies. American Journal of Sociology, 48(4).

Vliet, L. v., 2014. The Netherlands - New Developments in Dutch Company Law: The "Flexible" Close Corporation. Journal of Civil Law Studies, 7(1).

Vogue Italia, 2015. Soong Mei-Ling, Oei Hui-lan. Once upon a time. June, p. 246.

Waciega, L. W., 1987. A "Man of Business": The Widow of Means in Southeastern Pennsylvania, 1750-1850. The William and Mary Quarterly, 44(1).

Walton, F., 1913. Divorce in England, the United States and Canada. The Yale Law Journal, 22(7).

Walujono, A., 2014. The Discrimination of the Ethnic Chinese in Indonesia and Perceptions of Nationality. Scripps Senior Theses. Paper 508.

Wang, H., 2012. Portrayals of Chinese Women's Images in Hollywood Mainstream Films — An Analysis of Four Representative Films of Different Periods. Intercultural Communication Studies, XXI(2).

Warren, J. F., 2019. Capitalism and addiction-the Chinese, revenue farming, and opium in colonial Singapore and Java, 1800–1910. Bulletin of Concerned Asian Scholars, 27(1).

Wasserstrom, J. & Liu, X., 1989. Student protest and student life: Shanghai, 1919–49. Social History, 14(1).

Webster, A., 2011. The Development of British Commercial and Political Networks in the Straits Settlements 1800 to 1868: The Rise of a Colonial and Regional Economic Identity? Modern Asian Studies, 45(4).

Wee, K. K. S., 1973. Chinese Law and Malayan Society: A Comment on Mary Ng v. Ooi Kim Teong. Malaya Law Review, 15(1).

Wee, K. K., 1974. ENGLISH LAW AND CHINESE FAMILY CUSTOM IN SINGAPORE: THE PROBLEM OF FAIRNESS IN ADJUDICATION. Malaya Law Review, 16(1).

Wilson, H. R., 1938. The education of a diplomat. s.l.:Longmans, Green and Co; 1st edition.

Wiseman, R., 2001. THREE CRISES: MANAGEMENT IN THE COLONIAL JAVA SUGAR INDUSTRY 1880s - 1930s, s.l.: University of Adelaide, Department of History.

Wood, M. M., 2005. Diplomatic Wives: The Politics of Domesticity and the "Social Game" in the U.S. Foreign Service, 1905-1941. Journal of Women's History, 17(Number 2).

Wood, M. M., 2007. Commanding Beauty and Gentle Charm: American Women and Gender in the Early Twentieth-Century Foreign Service. Diplomatic History, June.

Wright, A., 1909. Twentieth century impressions of Netherlands India. s.l.:London, Lloyd's Greater Britain Pub. Co..

Xiaoqun, X., 2007. The Rule of Law without Due Process: Punishing Robbers and Bandits in Early-Twentieth Century China. Modern China, 33(2).

Xie, X., Yan, X. & Zhi, Z., 2004. STRENGTHS AND CHALLENGES IN CHINESE IMMIGRANT FAMILIES. Great Plains Research, 14(2).

Xu, G., 2001. The Issue of US Air Support for China during the Second World War, 1942-45. Journal of Contemporary History, 36(3).

Xu, L., 2015. Rethinking woman's place in Chinese society from 1919 to 1937: a brief study inspired by the film New woman. MA (Master of Arts) thesis.

Yamamoto, N., 2011. PRINT POWER AND CENSORSHIP IN COLONIAL INDONESIA, 1914-1942, s.l.: Faculty of the Graduate School of Cornell University.

Ye, W., 1994. "Nü Liuxuesheng": The Story of American-Educated Chinese Women, 1880s-1920s. Modern China, 20(3).

Young, L., 1982. The Shang of Ancient China. Current Anthropology, 23(3).

Yu, Y.-s., Chiu-Duke, J. & Duke, M. S., 2016. Chinese History and Culture: Seventeenth Century Through Twentieth Century. s.l.:Columbia University Press.

Yuen, W. T., 2014. The Chinese Community in Dutch Indonesia Population and Socio-Economic characteristics. Malaysian Journal of Chinese Studies, 3(2).

Yung, J., 1997. "It Is Hard to Be Born a Woman but Hopeless to Be Born a Chinese": The Life and Times of Flora Belle Jan. Frontiers: A Journal of Women Studies, 18(3).

Zhang, B., 2018. On the Change of the Female Status in the Tang Dynasty from the Horse-riding Tomb Figurine. Advances in Social Science, Education and Humanities Research, Volume 300.

Zhang, C., 2008. From Sinophilia to Sinophobia: China, History, and Recognition. Colloquia Germanica, 41(2).

Zhu, Q.-h., 2018. Women in Chinese Philosophy: Yin-Yang Theory in Feminism Constructing. Cultural and Religious Studies, 6(7).